DIVERSITY MATTERS

Constitutionalism and Democracy

GREGG IVERS AND
KEVIN T. MCGUIRE,
EDITORS

Diversity Matters

JUDICIAL POLICY MAKING IN THE U.S. COURTS OF APPEALS

Susan B. Haire and
Laura P. Moyer

UNIVERSITY OF VIRGINIA PRESS
CHARLOTTESVILLE AND LONDON

University of Virginia Press

Printed in the United States of America on acid-free paper

First published 2015

9 8 7 6 5 4 3 2 1

Library of Congress Cataloging-in-Publication Data

Haire, Susan B., author.
Diversity matters : judicial policy making in the U.S. courts of appeals / Susan B. Haire and Laura P. Moyer.
pages cm. — (Constitutionalism and democracy)
Includes bibliographical references and index.
ISBN 978-0-8139-3718-2 (cloth : alk. paper) — ISBN 978-0-8139-3719-9 (e-book)
1. Judges—United States. 2. Minority judges—United States. 3. Women judges—United States. 4. Judicial process—United States. 5. Appellate courts—United States. 6. Sex discrimination against women—Law and legislation—United States. 7. Race discrimination—Law and legislation—United States. I. Moyer, Laura P., 1978– author. II. Title.
KF8775.H35 2015
347.73'2403408—dc23

2014038396

In memory of
Susette, Sheryl, and Wanda —S.B.H.

To Aiden —L.P.M.

CONTENTS

ACKNOWLEDGMENTS

Many people helped to bring this project to fruition. At the outset, Barry Edwards provided invaluable coding assistance, cleaned existing data sets, and enhanced the efficiency and accuracy of data collection by writing a computer program that automated data collection for the expanded dataset. Excellent research assistance was also contributed by Allie Ackermann, Sara Haire, Rosalie Haug, Kerry Jones, David Hughes, Phil Marcin, and Kimberly Miller.

We appreciate the support for this project from Dick Holway of the University of Virginia Press and the series coeditors, Kevin McGuire and Gregg Ivers. In particular, we are indebted to Kevin for his helpful advice and persistence in shepherding this manuscript through the publication process.

We acknowledge those who were instrumental in generating sources of data used in this book. We thank Lee Epstein, William Landes, and Richard Posner for making available their data. Established with the support from the National Science Foundation, the Multi-User Database of the Decisions of the U.S. Courts of Appeals was also an important data source for this project. Biographical information was provided from the Federal Judicial Center, and we thank the Administrative Office of the U.S. Courts for use of a map from their web site. Librarians in the Fifth Circuit libraries in New Orleans and Baton Rouge provided generous assistance in helping us access Reynaldo Garza's oral history transcripts. Many oral histories used for this volume are from the Women Trailblazers in the Law Project, a public service program of the American Bar Association's Senior Lawyers Division and Commission on Women in the Profession. The transcripts of these interviews are available at the Manuscript Division of the Library of Congress.

Although this volume represents original research, some of our earlier scholarship inspired this project. In particular, chapter 4 expands on a version of "Diversity, Deliberation, and Judicial Opinion Writing" (Haire, Moyer, and Treier 2013) that appeared in the *Journal of Law and Courts*. Chapter 5 draws insights from "Rethinking Critical Mass on the Federal Appellate Courts" (Moyer 2013), which appeared in the *Journal of Women, Politics, and Policy*.

The comments and input of many individuals helped to strengthen our work along the way. In particular, we wish to recognize the anonymous reviewers, Shawn Treier, Donald Songer, Stefanie Lindquist, David Klein, Wendy Martinek, Todd Collins, Kevin Scott, Margaret Williams, and Susan Johnson for their constructive advice and suggestions at many stages in the project. Whatever errors remain are our own.

Haire acknowledges the support of the Department of Political Science at the University of Georgia for providing research leave, graduate research assistance, and generous colleagues, particularly John Maltese. She is also thankful to the department for providing the opportunity to meet and collaborate with many graduate students, including a remarkable scholar and person who is now her coauthor on this book. Haire is grateful for her previous service as the Law and Social Sciences Program Officer at the National Science Foundation—an experience that gave her interdisciplinary insights on the subjects investigated in this book. Finally, Haire acknowledges that this project would not have been completed without the unwavering support of her parents, Mary and Chuck Brodie; inspiration provided by her daughters, Alison and Sara; and the love and (daily) encouragement from her husband, Rob.

Moyer is grateful for all those individuals who helped her to cultivate and deepen her interest in the study of identity politics, particularly Amy Lang, Vicky Wilkins, Arnold Fleischmann, Susan Haire, and Wayne Parent. She is especially grateful for the training she received from the Political Science Department at the University of Georgia, where many of the ideas for this project first emerged. Funding from the Dean's Award for Social Science Research and the University of Georgia Graduate School supported dissertation research related to this project, including interviews with judges that were used in this book; Stephen Wasby was instrumental in helping to identify judges for these interviews as well sharing many resources related to circuit practices and norms. Moyer also wishes to express her deep gratitude for the institutional support she received from both Louisiana State University and the University of Louisville, including research assistance, travel funds, and summer funding through the LSU ASPIRE program. She would like to thank her colleagues from both institutions who shared their candid insights about the process of writing a book and hopes that she can one day pass this excellent advice on to others. Likewise, she is grateful for her students' many perceptive observations about race and gender over the years and especially the insights of Jerel Williams. Lastly, Moyer wishes to express her indebtedness to her family for their enthusiastic support throughout her entire academic career and in this undertaking. Her parents, Sally and Charlie Moyer, have been a constant source of encouragement and generously helped make the transition to a new city a smooth one so she could continue her work without interruption. Most of all, she is grateful for her husband, Ray, who has been tireless in his commitment to her success, and for their son, Aiden, who is a daily source of joy.

DIVERSITY MATTERS

INTRODUCTION: A JUDICIARY IN TRANSITION

> *I would hope that a wise Latina woman with the richness of her experiences would more often than not reach a better conclusion than a white male who hasn't lived that life.*
> —Justice Sonia Sotomayor

An argument frequently advanced by advocates for an inclusive judiciary is that the representation of women and minorities ensures that the federal courts fairly reflect the experiences of a diverse population. According to this view, a diverse judiciary allows historically excluded groups an opportunity to advance perspectives, issues, and interests that had been previously ignored (Kenney 2013). Underlying this normative argument is a series of empirical questions: Do women judges bring a "different voice" to the bench? Are minority judges responsive to the concerns of minority groups? Does the presence of minorities and women on a collegial court affect the policies advanced by that court? How have white male judges responded to increasing diversity within their ranks? Does the number of women and minorities seated on the bench affect judicial behavior? This book addresses these questions, and, in doing so, informs current debates about affirmative efforts to identify qualified women and minorities to fill vacant judicial positions.

The U.S. Courts of Appeals: A Judiciary in Transition

Within the federal judicial system, the federal courts of appeals are the intermediate appellate courts that serve, for most litigants, as their court of last resort because of the Supreme Court's comparatively smaller caseload (Hettinger, Lindquist, and Martinek 2006, 11–14). Tens of thousands of appeals come through the courts of appeals each year and are typically decided by three-judge panels from each circuit. Each circuit varies in geographic size and in the number of judicial seats assigned to it; for instance, the First Circuit (Maine, Massachusetts, New Hampshire, Puerto Rico, and Rhode Island) has only six authorized seats, while the Ninth Circuit (Alaska, Arizona, California, Hawaii, Idaho, Montana, Nevada, Oregon, Washington, Guam, and the Northern Mariana Islands) currently has twenty-nine authorized seats. Figure 1 shows the geographic boundaries of each circuit in the federal courts of appeals.

Over the past thirty years, there has been a great deal of change in the composition of the federal courts of appeals, as evidenced by the increasing numbers of white women, minority men, and minority women (Hurwitz and Lanier 2008). The bar graph in fig-

FIGURE 1 Circuit boundaries

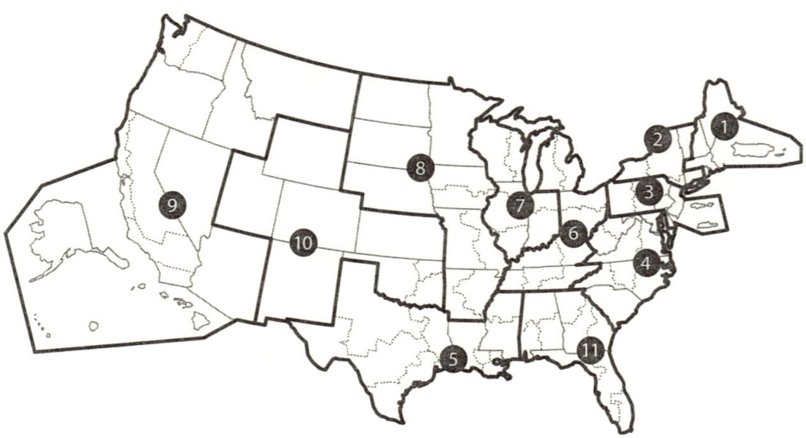

Source: Administrative Office of the U.S. Courts, http://www.uscourts.gov/uscourts/images/CircuitMap.pdf.

ure 2 shows several snapshots of the composition of the courts of appeals, marking the end of the Carter administration, the Reagan administration, the George H. W. Bush administration, the Clinton administration, and the George W. Bush administration. Each one of these periods indicates a growth in the number of women, minorities, or both. Of these appointment cohorts, President Reagan appointed the highest percentage of white males to the appellate bench (92.3 percent), while President Clinton appointed the lowest (49.2 percent)—though Clinton's record on diversity has since been overtaken by President Obama.[1]

Scholars generally point to the Carter administration as a turning point for diversity on the lower federal bench (Goldman 1997; Slotnick 1982-83). When President Carter assumed office, the normative argument for a diverse judiciary was particularly compelling given the near absence of women and minorities on the federal bench. At the start of the Carter administration, only four African American judges had ever served on the federal courts of appeals: William Hastie, a Truman appointee; Thurgood Marshall, a Kennedy appointee; and Wade McCree and Spottswood Robinson, Johnson appointees. Likewise, only two women, Florence Allen (Sixth Circuit)

FIGURE 2 Snapshots of diversity on the federal courts of appeals

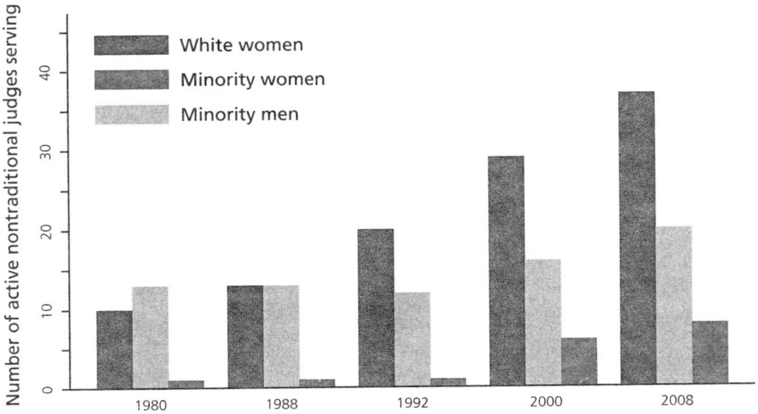

Note: Numbers represent all active service appeals court judges who served at any point during the year indicated. Minority men include African Americans, Latinos, and Asian Americans. Minority women are African Americans and Latinas.

and Shirley Hufstedler (Ninth Circuit), had served as circuit judges. Through policy guidance and executive order, Carter directed circuit court nominating commissions to make a special effort to identify qualified women and minorities (Goldman 1997).

However, the first half of the Carter administration did not yield many minority and female appointees (Goldman 1997). When tensions surfaced between officials at the Justice Department and the White House counsel's office, which was frustrated over the slow pace of affirmative action, the president became more personally involved. After the midterm elections, the number of nontraditional appointees increased substantially, particularly with the passage of the Omnibus Judges Act of 1978. By the end of his administration, Carter had appointed a historic nine African Americans, including the first African American woman, Amalya Kearse, to sit on the circuit bench. His efforts were not limited to increasing the ranks of black judges. The first Latino to sit on the courts of appeals, Reynaldo Garza, was appointed by Carter.[2] Additionally, Carter filled nearly one-fifth of the vacancies on the appeals court bench with women.

Although opposed to affirmative action as a public policy matter, Reagan was openly supportive of appointing women and minorities to the federal bench. His campaign promise and appointment of Sandra Day O'Connor was clearly a testament to this belief. Yet when selecting nominees to the lower federal appellate courts, Reagan's appointees were overwhelmingly male (95 percent). In his first term, he appointed one African American and one Hispanic to the circuit bench. He did not appoint any minority judges to the appeals courts in his second term. Over two terms, Reagan appointed four women to the appeals courts. As the bar graph in figure 2 shows, white women made gains relative to minority men during this time period and served in equal numbers by the time Reagan left office.

Reagan's successor, George H. W. Bush, set a Republican record for the most women appointed to the lower federal courts at that time, seven of which were to the courts of appeals (Goldman et al. 2003). Bush also added two African American men (Clarence Thomas and Timothy Lewis) and two Latinos (Ferdinand Fernandez and Emilio Garza). As figure 2 shows, at the end of Bush's presidency white women pulled ahead of minority men as the most common nontraditional demographic group.

Despite the fact that Clinton faced unprecedented resistance from Senate Republicans in getting his judicial nominees confirmed (Goldman 2002, 257), he had the largest impact on diversifying the federal appellate bench in terms of race, ethnicity, and gender up to that point in time (Goldman et al. 2001). His administration made it a priority to obtain a judiciary that "looks like America" and was less concerned with the ideological positions of nominees (Carp, Stidham, and Manning 2014, 159–60). Clinton also distinguished himself by going beyond just appointing white women and minority men: he added five minority women (three African Americans and two Latinas) to the appeals courts. As figure 2 shows, during his presidency, all nontraditional demographic groups experienced gains in representation.

The progress made by Clinton in adding nontraditional judges continued during the two terms of George W. Bush, who more than doubled his father's record on the appointment of women and minorities. George W. Bush appointed fourteen white women (compared to fifteen by Clinton) as well as two African American women and a Latina; among his male appointees, four were black and two were Latino. Many of these judges had strong conservative bona fides, such as membership in the Federalist Society (Scherer and Miller 2009). Analyses of Bush's judges have generally supported the contention that he was successful in obtaining a judiciary consistent with his conservative political values (Goldman et al. 2005). Unlike previous Republican presidents, Bush was able to draw from a large pool of qualified women and minorities in the legal profession, a result of growth in the legal pipeline. The trend toward diversification has only accelerated under the Obama administration, which has exceeded even Clinton's record on judicial diversity. The face of the federal judiciary has truly undergone a dramatic change over the past three decades.

Studying Judicial Diversity and Its Effects

With this backdrop, we now turn to the central question motivating this book: how have changes in the composition of the appellate bench affected judicial policy making? We recognize that judicial diversity likely "matters" in a broader context; for instance, it may affect perceptions of the legitimacy of the federal judiciary (Scherer and Curry 2010; Kenney 2013, 17). However, here we are most interested in exploring how diversity has affected the behavior of judges as individuals and as groups, and whether it has had a measurable impact on legal outputs and the content of the law. Thus far, the scholarship on the federal courts of appeals has tended to emphasize a lack of differences (at least in the voting behavior) between traditional and nontraditional appointees to the bench—perhaps an unsurprising finding given the shared professional socialization and elite status of most federal judges. There are some exceptions to this overall pattern, however. For instance, in civil rights cases, scholars have found that women and minority judges on the appeals courts are more likely to find for alleged victims of discrimination and can affect the behavior of their white male colleagues (Boyd, Epstein, and Martin 2010; Kastellec 2013; Morin 2014). Earlier work also showed that women judges of color are more likely than either white women or minority male judges to side with the criminal defendant in criminal appeals (Collins and Moyer 2008).

To gain leverage on these questions, we draw upon theoretical frameworks from political science, social psychology, and sociology about the relationship between identity and behavior. Our approach is empirical in nature, drawing on both original and existing datasets on the federal courts of appeals, but also on a wealth of untapped oral histories and revealing interviews with former and current circuit judges. Moreover, because this study extends through 2008, we are able to consider the decisions of nontraditional appointees from both political parties, allowing us to make stronger, more generalizable claims about race and gender than previous research that only examined Democratic appointees. From these sources, we believe we have assembled, to date, the most comprehensive examination of the question: does judicial diversity matter?

Outline of the Book

Subsequent chapters of the book examine the basic contention that socializing experiences associated with gender, race, and ethnicity affect the formation of opinions and political behavior. One major stream of literature on identity politics emphasizes the degree to which individual political behavior is shaped by perceptions of one's group interests, while another theoretical perspective argues that the changing demographic composition of an organization can affect the behavior of both majority and minority members within that group or organization. In addition to approaches that consider race and gender separately, intersectionality scholars argue that women of color face unique challenges that are distinct from those affecting white women and minority men (Crenshaw 1989, 1991).

Chapter 1 focuses on racial and ethnic diversity within the appellate courts, tracing the paths to the bench of African American and Hispanic judges and connecting these experiences with scholarship about group consciousness and political behavior. Analyzing the voting behavior of these minority judges, we test whether black and Latino judges each exhibit distinctive decision making and vote in ways that reflect documented racial differences in public opinion and legislative behavior on salient issues.

Chapter 2 shifts to focus on the addition of women to the federal appellate bench. We begin by examining gendered experiences in law school and the legal profession and how these experiences may have colored women's views on sex discrimination. Drawing from experimental research in social psychology, as well as comments from female judges, we also investigate whether female judges emphasize norms of cooperation and consensus with colleagues on the panel. Finally, we evaluate how gender shapes women's behavior in different ways, specifically related to the era in which women and men were socialized.

Chapter 3 builds on the two previous chapters and introduces the concepts of intersectionality (Hancock 2007) and race-gendering (Hawkesworth 2003) to our exploration of judicial behavior. These concepts refer to the multidimensional nature of identity, and how women of color can experience discrimination that is a result of their position as a "double minority"—not just racism plus sexism, but something more. We trace how women of color have figured in different presidential administrations' attempts to diversify the federal judiciary, relative to white women and minority men. Our analyses in this chapter test whether minority women have experienced marginalization and invisibility (Hammonds 1997) from their interactions with colleagues, and whether, as legislative research has found, they engage in substantive representation for both their race and their sex.

Chapters 4 and 5 shift the unit of analysis away from the individual to group dynamics. Chapter 4 focuses on the small-group interactions of the panel and how differing levels of diversity may affect the deliberative process. We initially investigate how heterogeneity in panel composition affects unanimity in decision making. Then, we turn our attention to evaluating a premise shared by many: "the broader the range of experiences found in an appellate panel, the less likely it is that relevant considerations will be overlooked. Conversely, the more homogeneous the judiciary, the more likely it is that the judges' intuitions will coincide" (Posner 2008, 116). We evaluate this expectation by studying the relationship between panel heterogeneity and attention to issues in unanimous majority opinions. Finally, we investigate whether the different perspectives brought by nontraditional judges affect the voting behavior of white male judges. Then, in chapter 5 we expand the scope of our inquiry beyond panel dynamics to consider diversity at the circuit level. We examine court-level norms and practices and elaborate on specific ways that different circuits responded to diversification within their ranks. Two theoretical frameworks about organizational diversity, critical mass theory and critical actor theory, guide our discussion and analyses in this chapter (Kanter 1977; Dahlerup 2006). Specifically, we evaluate how different levels (and measures) of diversity are related to circuit consensual norms as well as how they impact substantive representation by nontraditional judges.

In the conclusion, we summarize the major findings of the book and what they mean for the question: does judicial diversity matter? From these conclusions, we consider how recent shifts in the demographic composition of the federal judiciary under the Obama administration may affect policy making in these courts.

Before proceeding further, we provide an overview of the observation strategy for the empirical analyses that follow in the remaining chapters. As a general matter, readers will find that each chapter displays short summaries with the results of statistical models, but that more detailed tables of results are included in the appendix.

Drawing on New Data Sources

To investigate how diversity affects judicial policy making, we utilize a combination of new and existing datasets on courts of appeals' decisions and judges, as well as interviews, oral histories, and writings of circuit judges. We believe that this allows us to engage in a comprehensive examination of our subject, while recognizing that subjective perceptions (as documented by judges' comments) are an important piece of the puzzle.

In all chapters we rely on data from the Federal Judicial Center's biographical database, which provides information on each judge's demographic traits, previous career experiences, legal education, appointment year, and the identity of the appointing president.[3] We supplement these observations with information gathered from archived oral histories of courts of appeals judges and interviews conducted with one of the authors. Oral histories came from a number of sources, including the American Bar Association's Women Trailblazers Project, the Federal Judicial Center, the California Appellate Court Legacy Project, the Library of Congress, the U.S. Court of Appeals for the Fifth Circuit Library, and the University of Pennsylvania Law Library Archives.

Two decision-making databases were used for analyses in this book: the Multi-User Database of the Decisions of the U.S. Courts of Appeals and data on decision making originally collected by Cass Sunstein and updated by Epstein, Landes, and Posner in 2013.[4] We collected original data to update the Multi-User Database of the Decisions of the U.S. Courts of Appeals (Songer 1997; Kuersten and Haire 2007) so that the data extend through the end of 2008.[5] Following the same procedure as the original database, the universe of decisions with published opinions was stratified by circuit-year, and a random sample of thirty cases was generated from each stratum and coded.[6] Variables in the new Multi-User Database were coded to be consistent with those in the original database.[7] After merging the updated Multi-User Database with judicial background data from the Federal Judicial Center described above, we also include a measure of individual policy preferences, the Epstein et al. (2007) Judicial Common Space scores, in those analyses that require controls for individual judge ideology.[8] A listing of these indicators, and other variables, is provided in the appendix to this chapter.

We use various statistical techniques that build on the logic of a linear regression model, allowing us to estimate the effects of individual and group-level diversity while controlling for other influences on decision making. The choice of statistical model for each analysis depends on the outcome of interest. For example, we rely on estimates generated from logit models when our dependent variable is dichotomous, such as when we model the likelihood that an outcome is liberal or conservative.[9] When we are interested in other decision-making outputs that are not dichotomous, we utilize statistical models that take into account the measurement properties and distribution of the dependent variable.

The theoretical frameworks advanced in this book suggest that the effects of judge race and gender will vary with the type of case. As a result, in the individual level analyses presented in chapters 1 and 2, we initially specify and test a model for all contested cases in the Multi-User Database: those in which a lower court was reversed or a member of the appellate panel disagreed with the majority opinion. Then, we estimate separate models that focus on criminal cases and appeals dealing with economic issues that center on questions of distributive politics.[10] Previous research and our theoretical framework emphasize that civil rights cases may be particularly salient issue areas for women and minority judges. In those analyses, we draw on the Epstein, Landes, and Posner (2013) database that includes observations from 1995 through 2008 and identifies appeals that are classified as raising Title VII race discrimination claims or sex discrimination claims.

In the analyses presented in chapter 4, we develop measures of demographic composition for each panel and use the Multi-User Database to analyze the frequency with which separate opinions occur and the attention to issues in unanimous majority opinions.[11] To evaluate the reactions of white males to minority and female judges on the panel, we use the Multi-User Database to examine separate opinion writing and voting by this racial cohort.

For our examination of court-level diversity, other measures on circuit characteristics, such as dissent rates, merits terminations, and circuit size, are obtained from Epstein, Landes, and Posner (2013) and the Administrative Office of the U.S. Courts.

In sum, we believe that the data we have assembled give us the leverage to assess trends in diversification over time; give attention to groups often overlooked in discussions of diversity, such as minority women; observe how nontraditional judges appointed early in our time period matured into leaders in their courts; and study both individual and group aspects of diversity. We begin, in the following chapter, by assessing the impact of efforts to diversify the race and ethnicity of judges appointed to the federal appellate bench.

1

RACE, ETHNICITY, AND JUDGING

These determinations require a judge to draw upon something that is not found in the case reports that line the walls of our chambers. Rather judges draw upon the breadth and depth of their own life experience, upon the knowledge and understanding of people, and of human nature. And inevitably, one's ethnic and racial background contributes to those life experiences.
—Judge Edward M. Chen

In the introduction, we highlighted the varying efforts of Democratic and Republican administration officials to identify qualified minority nominees to fill vacancies on the federal appellate bench. Although presidents garner electoral support among African Americans and Latinos when selecting judges of color (see Scherer 2005b), officials also advance policy arguments for increasing the presence of minorities in the judiciary. One rationale underlying the push for descriptive representation in the judiciary is a substantive one: minority judges bring important and traditionally excluded perspectives to the bench (Ifill 2000). As noted by Judge A. Leon Higginbotham, "having minorities on the court . . . proffers an enrichment of experiences that one can use to examine issues" (Washington 1994, 12).

Underlying Judge Higginbotham's observation is the premise that socializing experiences associated with race and ethnicity affect the formation of opinions, and those opinions and experiences continue to be reinforced by a judge's identification with a racial or ethnic group. In this chapter, we draw on existing research to develop this theoretical perspective and empirically evaluate the claim that minority judges' decisions are distinct from those made by their white colleagues. In doing so, we recognize that this effort is not new; however, the increased number of racial minorities appointed to the bench over the past decade provides a new opportunity for empirical researchers. Many previous studies on the role of race in federal appeals court decision making were centered on Democratic appointees, particularly those appointed by Carter (Gottschall 1983). During the 1980s, only three African Americans were appointed by Presidents Reagan and George H. W. Bush. During the Clinton administration, the number of minorities on the appeals court bench increased substantially, with nine African American and seven Latino appointees. George W. Bush was more successful than his Republican predecessors in identifying minority candidates for the circuit bench; he appointed six African Americans and three Latinos to the federal appeals courts.

Given this increased diversity in appeals court appointments under both Democratic and Republican administrations, we examine decision making from 1982 to 2008. As a result, we are well positioned to revisit the contention raised by supporters of diversity in judicial selection that minority appointees bring a "representative voice" to the bench.

Racial Identity and Politics

Understanding the role of race and ethnicity in judicial decision making necessarily begins with an inquiry centered on racial identity. Situated at the intersection of sociology and psychology, social identity theory has directed scholars to examine the relevance of group closeness, including those associated with racial and ethnic groups. This theory suggests that an individual's identity can be conceptualized in terms of group identification—that is, the degree to which the individual is aware of belonging to a group and having a psychological attachment based on his or her perception of shared beliefs, feelings, interests, and ideas with others in the group (Matthews and Prothro 1966; McClain et al. 2009).

Consistent with this approach, scholarship on black racial identity and its effects on political behavior identifies multiple physical, psychological, sociopolitical, and cultural dimensions with a particular emphasis on the role of in-group "closeness" (McClain et al. 2009). Distinct from the concept of racial identification, race consciousness suggests that beliefs about the standing of one's racial group may be tied to the view that collective action provides an avenue through which the group can advance its interests. From this perspective, race consciousness will be held by those in minority groups who feel "close" to their own race as a result of being oppressed (Miller et al. 1981). An individual's perception of linked fate is an important cognitive component of racial group consciousness (McClain et al. 2009). In the context of black political behavior, scholars have found that the history of slavery in the United States and African Americans' shared struggle with discrimination in the twentieth century have promoted a sense of shared destiny (McClain et al. 2009). In a 1984 survey of African Americans, when asked if they believe what happens generally to black people in this country will have something to do with what happens in their own lives, 64 percent responded affirmatively (Dawson 1994, 79). Research also finds that these perceptions of linked fate are strongly related to support for racial policies (Dawson 1994). When little information is available to make political decisions, African Americans may be expected to rely on the status of their racial group as a cognitive cue (Miller et al. 1981). As one scholar suggests, "as long as African American life chances are powerfully shaped by race, it is efficient for individual African Americans to use the perceptions of the interests of African Americans as a group as a proxy for their own interests" (Dawson 1994, 61).

Research on the relationship between race and public opinion provides support for this perspective. When evaluating policy proposals where race is salient (such as affirmative action), African Americans are dramatically more supportive than whites of proposals to expand the role of government in addressing problems of racial inequality (Kinder and Winter 2001). The racial divide in public opinion is not limited to explicitly race-based policy issues. When evaluating economic policy matters, scholars have found a similarly large gap in respondents' views about inequality, suggesting that blacks view the economic system as biased whereas whites believe the system is fair (Kinder and Winter 2001; Sigelman and Welch 1991). A similar cleavage has been documented when comparing respondents' views of the criminal justice system. In one study, scholars scrutinized the causal mechanism underlying the racial divide and found that blacks' unfavorable views of law enforcement are related to their beliefs that the criminal justice system is unfair, whereas white respondents tended to see the system as fair and tended to overlook differences between black and white civilians in police encounters (Hurwitz and Peffley 2005). In explaining these connections, the study's authors concluded: "African Americans, far more often than whites, are the subject of unfair and discriminatory treatment from law enforcement officers. Because so much of one's general sense of whether the criminal justice system is fair is experientially determined, these encounters (whether experienced personally or vicariously) contribute heavily in creating in much of the African American community a profound understanding that the justice system is inherently biased against them" (Hurwitz and Peffley 2005, 781).

Most studies that have examined the link between racial identity and political behavior have focused on African Americans. While many scholars emphasize the shared interests of minorities as a rationale for finding similarities in values and behavior, it is less clear whether the relationship between race consciousness and behavior operates similarly for other racial groups, like Latinos, who lack a shared past that includes enslavement and the often-contentious race relations of the civil rights era (McClain et al. 2009). Studies that have examined whether Latinos have a sense of linked fate report mixed findings, in part because substantial diversity exists among Latinos in terms of geographical origins (Lopez and Espiritu 1990; Leal 2007). Latinos in the United States share a common language and religion, but otherwise, they are varied in terms of their ethnic origins, with Mexican Americans representing the largest demographic group, followed by Puerto Ricans, Cubans, and Salvadorans. In a recent survey, when asked whether they identify with an ethnic group, survey respondents reported their country of origin rather than using the "Latino" or "Hispanic" label.[1] Indeed, many Latinos in the United States view themselves as white (Darity,

Dietrich, and Hamilton 2005), and a large proportion report that they have never experienced discrimination in the same manner as African Americans (McClain and Stewart 2006).

Given pan-ethnic variation, efforts to promote a Latino identity in the United States have placed an emphasis on common values shared by various groups that center on populist democracy, immigration, and language (Leal 2007). As a group, Latinos are more likely to trust and support an active role for government, including higher levels of spending, when compared to the views of white Americans (Leal 2007). On specific issues related to morality and religion (for example, divorce, suicide, abortion on demand), Latinos tend to be more conservative than whites (Leal 2007). Similar to the findings on black-white differences reported above, Latino-white cleavages emerged on policy issues where Latinos may perceive a "shared fate": immigration and bilingual education (Leal 2007). With respect to criminal justice, less than half of Latinos surveyed in 2007 reported that they have confidence that police officers will not use excessive force, compared with 73 percent of whites and 38 percent of blacks. Overall, other studies also report that Latinos tend to fall in the middle between whites and African Americans; for instance, they are more approving of law enforcement than African Americans, but less supportive than whites (Cheurprakobkit 2000; Weitzer 2002).

Collectively, research on racial and ethnic identities suggests that closeness to one's group varies, with black racial identities being strong and relatively stable, particularly when compared to Latinos (Huddy 2001; McClain and Stewart 2006). Although fragmentation among Latinos is fueled by variation in country of origin, the relative absence of national leaders and the low rate of Latino political participation are also contributing factors (Kaufmann 2003). However, even among African Americans, the influence of racial identity on political behavior varies with the salience of racial and ethnic categories (Huddy 2001). To the extent that Latinos and African Americans perceive a shared outsider status, then one would expect to see opinions and behavior consistent with this notion of commonality between these two groups. In the section below, we consider the backgrounds and experiences of African American and Latino judges on the courts of appeals to further evaluate the argument that these experiences are relevant in understanding a judge's racial and ethnic identity.

Racial Identity and Judging on the U.S. Courts of Appeals

AFRICAN AMERICANS: A SHARED STRUGGLE WITH DISCRIMINATION

With his appointment to the Third Circuit in 1950, William Hastie became the first African American to be named to the federal courts of appeals. It would be over a decade before another African American, Thurgood Marshall, would be appointed to the federal appellate bench in 1961. Five years later, Spottswood Robinson joined the D.C. Circuit. Although separated by a few years in age, these three judges had much in common, with overlapping paths to the bench that focused on legal efforts to desegregate. After graduating from Harvard Law School, Hastie joined in private practice his friend Charles Houston—who later became known as the man who "killed Jim Crow laws."[2] Several years later, Hastie would again work with Houston at Howard University where, as dean of the law school, he became acquainted with then-student Thurgood Marshall. Deeply influenced by Houston, Marshall committed himself to developing the litigation strategy for dismantling segregation. He worked for many years on behalf of the National Association for the Advancement of Colored People (NAACP) Legal Defense Fund, ultimately arguing *Brown v. Board of Education* before the U.S. Supreme Court, on which he would later serve. Robinson, like Marshall, graduated from Howard University Law School and, like Hastie, served as dean. He also followed the career path taken by Thurgood Marshall and worked for the NAACP for twelve years. These three judges shared experiences with segregation in their personal and professional lives that profoundly shaped their perspectives on the legal system (Hastie 1973; Kluger 1976; Brennan 1991; Wermiel 2003).

Firsthand experience with race discrimination also shaped the career choices made by Carter appointee A. Leon Higginbotham, who first enrolled at Purdue University in 1944 seeking a degree in engineering. Placed in unheated off-campus housing, Higginbotham requested from the university president that he and other black students be permitted to live in heated on-campus housing.

After the president responded that "the law doesn't require us to let colored students in the dorm, we will never do it, and you either accept things as they are or leave the university immediately," Higginbotham transferred and decided to pursue a legal career. He graduated from Yale Law School and served in the public and private sector prior to being appointed to the federal district court bench in 1964. Elevated to the Third Circuit by President Carter in 1977, Higginbotham served for sixteen years before stepping down in 1993. He did not leave the bench to retire; instead, he left federal judicial service so that he could teach and provide counsel on pressing civil rights issues, including those associated with redistricting in the United States and efforts in South Africa to dismantle apartheid (Washington 1994).

Although the first two black judges on the appeals court bench were named to seats in northeastern circuits, the Sixth Circuit would be the home court for five African Americans appointed through 2008. The first black judge appointed to this circuit, Wade McCree, was selected by President Johnson in 1966. Although McCree, like William Hastie, graduated from Harvard Law School, his career path was geographically centered in the Midwest. He had been the first African American to serve as a judge in the state trial court in Wayne County, Michigan, and became only the second African American judge to sit as a federal district court judge. Like Thurgood Marshall, McCree served as solicitor general (although the order of experience was reversed): McCree resigned from the Sixth Circuit to take on the Department of Justice post during the Carter administration.[3]

In the year following Wade McCree's appointment to the Sixth Circuit, President Johnson named another African American, Damon Keith, to the same federal district court position that had been held by McCree. A decade later, Keith was elevated to the Sixth Circuit after McCree stepped down. Two years following Keith's elevation, President Carter appointed Nathaniel Jones to join him on the bench, marking the first time that two African American judges would be seated on the same circuit. Influenced by Thurgood Marshall and Charles Houston, Jones had served as general counsel for the NAACP and directed the organization's litigation strategy against northern school segregation during the 1970s. Like

Carter, President Clinton appointed two African American judges to the Sixth Circuit: R. Guy Cole and Eric Lee Clay. Both graduates of Yale Law School, these two judges shared personal experiences similar to many African Americans born in the segregated South in the years following World War II.

African Americans would not be named to the federal appellate bench in the West or the South until the Carter administration. Carter named two African American judges, both Alabama natives and World War II veterans, to seats on the Ninth Circuit: Jerome Farris and Cecil Poole. Similar to other African American judges appointed by Carter, Farris had a mix of career experiences in the private and public sector, sitting as a state court of appeals judge at the time of the appointment. Poole had been appointed by President Ford to the federal district court in 1976, serving as a federal trial judge for over a decade before being elevated to the Ninth Circuit.

As the first African American to be elected in the South to a statewide office, Joseph Hatchett was a logical choice for Carter when deciding who would fill a vacancy on the Fifth Circuit (soon to be split from the Eleventh Circuit). Like many other African American judges, Hatchett had earned his law degree from Howard University. Although he was just a teenager during the civil rights movement, Hatchett recalled how he was deeply affected by the murder of a state civil rights leader.[4] On the Eleventh Circuit, he was eventually succeeded by another African American, Charles Wilson, who was appointed by President Clinton. Clinton also named an African American, Carl Stewart, to the Fifth Circuit and began the process of selecting the first African American to sit on the bench in the Fourth Circuit, Roger Gregory. Renominated by George W. Bush, Gregory would be joined by African American and Bush appointee Allyson Duncan.[5]

Over three terms, Reagan and George H. W. Bush appointed just three African Americans to the federal appellate bench. Lawrence Pierce, the first, was selected by Reagan for a seat on the Second Circuit. Like many of his African American brethren appointed by Democratic presidents, Pierce had experienced firsthand segregation while serving in the army during World War II. Close to an uncle who was an attorney and a role model, Pierce was inspired to pursue a legal career. With substantial experience as a prosecutor and police commissioner, Pierce was selected by the Nixon administration for a seat on the federal district court in 1971. Other African Americans appointed by Republican presidents also tended to have prosecutorial experience. George H. W. Bush's two black appointees (Clarence Thomas and Timothy Lewis) had prosecutorial experience; both also voluntarily departed, without retiring, from the appeals court bench. Thomas was elevated to the U.S. Supreme Court, and Lewis, who had assumed federal judicial service in his late thirties, resigned to pursue a career in private practice.

Nearly a decade later, George W. Bush appointed six African Americans to the circuit bench, including the first to sit on the Tenth Circuit. In many ways, the paths to the bench for the George W. Bush cohort of African American appointees represented a wider range of experiences and backgrounds. For example, Lavenski Smith was born, raised, and educated in Arkansas, having served on the state supreme court. His Arkansas-based background stood in contrast to the career experiences of Jerome Holmes, the most recent African American appointed to the circuit bench by a Republican. With a degree from Georgetown Law, Holmes clerked for a federal district court judge in Oklahoma and then subsequently for a Tenth Circuit judge. He returned to D.C. and joined a firm in private practice. A few years later, Holmes circled back to Oklahoma to serve as an assistant U.S. attorney. Although relatively few in number, black circuit judges appointed by Republican presidents were younger than other appointees, and they frequently had prosecutorial experience.

The shared experiences associated with growing up in the South (or having parents from the South) contributed to group closeness for African Americans who came of age during the civil rights era. Although less than one-fifth were appointed to seats in southern circuits, almost half of black judges (47 percent) appointed through 2008 were born in a southern state. Legal education also played a prominent role in socializing this group of black lawyers. Participating on a panel convened to discuss litigation during the civil rights era, Judge Damon Keith commented, "People ask me now, 'What shaped your life in terms of your interpretation of the law?' I always say, 'Howard'" (Wermiel 2003, 1413). Of the thirteen African

Americans who were appointed to the circuit courts prior to 1981, four were graduates of Howard University's school of law, three from Harvard, and two from Michigan. Over time, the list of law schools represented by African American judges has grown. Of the thirty African Americans appointed to the circuit bench by 2008, only six were graduates of public law schools: Michigan, Washington, Arkansas, and the University of California, Los Angeles (UCLA). Five graduated from Yale Law School, exceeding the tally of four for Howard University.

Although the eight black judges appointed by Republican presidents differed with their twenty-two black colleagues appointed by Democratic presidents on many issues, they shared a commitment that was tied to their racial identity. In a 1994 interview, former judge Timothy Lewis, appointed by George H. W. Bush to the Third Circuit, described his responsibility to be mindful of the legacy of the first black judges on the bench:

> The legacy of Hastie and Higginbotham is a legacy of striving for excellence in all phases of one's life. . . . This legacy involves recognition of one's work as a black judge and its importance to the black community and every litigant who appears before you. This legacy, I think, also involves a strong commitment to civil rights. . . . It is always important to understand that racism is alive and well in this country, and it is the responsibility of black leaders to do all they can to make sure that situation of racism in the country changes. Black judges fall into the category of black leaders. (Washington 1994, 244–45)

LATINOS AND IMMIGRATION: EMBRACING OPPORTUNITIES

As the first self-identified Latino to be appointed to the federal appeals court bench,[6] Reynaldo Garza followed a path similar to that taken by Anglos who had been appointed during this time period. In 1937, he had become acquainted with a rising young politician, Lyndon B. Johnson, who was running in a special election for a seat in the U.S. House of Representatives. Garza worked for Johnson's candidacy in the Mexican American community and later campaigned for the Kennedy-Johnson ticket. In 1961, President Kennedy named Garza to the federal district court bench, and eighteen years later, President Carter nominated Garza to a seat on the Fifth Circuit. Like most judges appointed during this time period, Garza had served in the military during World War II and enjoyed a lucrative career in private practice before taking a seat on the bench.

In contrast to his Anglo colleagues, Garza experienced a different childhood, growing up in a Texas border town as the child of middle-class Mexicans who immigrated to the United States. He understood well the powerful influence of economic opportunity on immigrants. When asked why Mexicans came to the United States without intending to becoming citizens, Garza responded: "To get a job people would do anything. They're not criminals. They're just coming down here to make a living for themselves and their families."[7]

Enrolled in college during the Depression, Garza coached high school sports to support himself in college and later enrolled at the University of Texas. When his father died during his first semester of law school, Garza took on additional work to support his mother. Despite the hardship, he was able to complete a B.A. and law degree within six years. Like other Hispanics, Garza was sensitive to the problems of social and economic inequality and recognized his own responsibility in working to address these problems. When asked why he wanted to become a lawyer, Garza responded:

> I remember reading one time in one of the gospels where Mary Magdalene was being stoned and Jesus was writing "he who is without sin throw the first stone" and everybody left. That made a terrible impression on me. People need help sometimes. They were ready to stone her and kill her and everything else. I remember that that was the first time I ever thought about being a lawyer was that gospel. I don't know but that made an impression on me that people need help, like Jesus helped that woman, I could help other people.[8]

Shortly after nominating Garza to a seat on the Fifth Circuit, President Carter named another Mexican American, Arthur Alarcon, to a seat on the Ninth Circuit. During the Mexican Revolution, Alarcon's family had fled to Southern California as a result of potential threats made against his grandfather, a law enforcement official.[9] Alarcon grew up in the Los Angeles area, and like others during this time period, served with distinction in World War II. By the age of twenty-one, Alarcon was the acting first sergeant of his company, responsible for approximately 200 soldiers. After returning from the war, Alarcon attended UCLA but transferred to the University of Southern California (USC) after being recruited to participate in a fast-track B.A./law degree program. Following a judicial clerkship, Alarcon decided to pursue employment as a prosecutor, in part because he believed that his options were limited:

> Well, at that time it was very difficult for people who belonged to minorities to get into the big law firms. There weren't any Hispanics, there weren't any blacks in the big firms or the middle firms. And so I decided that if I went to the DA's office and stayed there about three years, I could then bring into the field a lot of experience and perhaps overcome the reluctance to hire Hispanics and blacks. So that's why I chose the DA's office.[10]

Alarcon would serve as deputy district attorney for almost ten years before being recruited by Governor Pat Brown to serve as a legal adviser and chief of staff. His experience in the Democratic governor's office was particularly unusual because Alarcon was a Republican. In 1964, Governor Brown named him to the superior court for Los Angeles. Fourteen years later, in 1978, Governor Jerry Brown elevated Alarcon to the state court of appeals. Although Alarcon was interested in a seat on the California Supreme Court, he agreed to be considered for a position on the Ninth Circuit and was confirmed to a seat on that court in 1979.[11]

Although Garza and Alarcon both had judicial trial court experience, military service, and strong ties to Democratic Party leaders, their early career choices were different. Garza's legal career had focused on private practice whereas Alarcon's career had been centered on the district attorney's office. Both, however, had been quick to pursue opportunities that they believed held promise, a belief pursued by many immigrant families during this time period.

Over the next three decades, by the end of the George W. Bush administration, fifteen Latinos would be appointed to the circuit bench. In the Fifth Circuit, Reynaldo Garza was followed by three Mexican Americans. In the Ninth Circuit, Alarcon was joined by three Mexican Americans and two appointees of Spanish descent.

Although two-thirds of all Latino appointees to the federal appeals courts, primarily Mexican Americans, have been named to seats in these two circuits, other courts of appeals in the Northeast witnessed the appointment of those of Puerto Rican descent. Juan Torruella, the first Latino appointed by a Republican, was a federal district court judge in Puerto Rico when elevated to the First Circuit by Ronald Reagan. Clinton would name three judges of Puerto Rican descent (including Sonia Sotomayor) to the Second and Third Circuits.

In many ways, the career experiences of all Latino appointees to the circuit bench have been similar to those of Reynaldo Garza and Arthur Alarcon. Fourteen (of fifteen) appointees had experience as a trial court judge; eleven were sitting federal district court judges at the time of their appointment. Nine of the fifteen Latinos had established careers in private practice prior to judicial service, similar to the path followed by Reynaldo Garza. Four Latino judges, including Alarcon, pursued careers in public law as a district attorney, as a public defender, or with legal aid.

In addition to shared language and religion, a majority of Latino judges during this time period were the children of immigrants. Nevertheless, in contrast to the cohort of African American judges profiled above, a sense of linked fate may be missing among Latino judges as a result of differences in country of origin. To the extent that the paths to the bench taken by this cohort reflect common values, these values are centered on the promise of economic opportunity for themselves or their immigrant parents.

Our analysis of the socializing experiences of African American and Latino judges provides some insights on the centrality of race and ethnicity in developing these judges' identities. The profile of African American judges underscores the direct, and indirect, experiences with segregation and discrimination. In contrast, the analysis of Latino judges does not suggest widespread experience with race discrimination among early appointees and emphasizes instead the shared view of opportunities that life in the United States presented to their immigrant families.

Empirical research evaluating the connections between identity politics and judging report mixed findings. Early studies on judicial decision making largely centered on African American state trial court judges. In one study, Uhlman (1978) found that the decision making of African American judges was somewhat distinguishable from white judges, but for reasons other than their minority status. In another study, African American judges were more lenient in sentencing defendants of the same race (Welch, Combs, and Gruhl 1988). Although recent scholarship has found that African American trial judges are more evenhanded in their treatment of African American and white defendants when compared to the sentencing decisions made by white colleagues (Steffensmeier and Britt 2001), an analysis of decision making on state courts of last resort concluded that African American judges were more supportive of criminal defendants in sentencing cases when compared to their white colleagues in states that lacked an intermediate appellate court (Bonneau and Rice 2009).

Research on race effects in federal courts is similarly mixed. Early research on federal district courts did not find evidence that a judge's race was related to decision making (Walker and Barrow 1985). With increasing diversification of the bench, however, more recent scholarship suggests otherwise, with race playing a role in issue areas where minority status is salient (Chew and Kelley 2008). In one analysis, scholars found dramatic differences in decisions dealing with racial harassment: plaintiffs before African American judges are 3.3 times more likely to prevail than before white judges (Chew and Kelley 2008). Another study reported significant differences in approaches to employment discrimination claims, with white judges more likely to dismiss plaintiffs' claims at the summary judgment stage when compared to decisions made by minority judges (Weinberg and Nielsen 2011).

Similar to research findings on federal district courts, studies on the role of judge race in the courts of appeals suggests relationships will vary with the case context, specifically in areas that are racially salient. For example, given the black-white divide in public support for the criminal justice system, it is not surprising that one study reported a similar difference in judicial decision making: African American judges were more likely than white judges to support the position of the criminal defendant in cases before the federal courts of appeals (Gottschall 1983).

Cases involving discrimination may be particularly salient for African American judges on the courts of appeals. In an unpublished study, Crowe (1999) found that the race of the judge affected decision making in sex and race discrimination cases: African Americans were much more likely to vote in favor of the plaintiff when compared to voting by whites.[12] In more recent research, Kastellec (2013) found that black judges are more likely to support affirmative action in cases heard in the federal courts of appeals. Relatedly, Cox and Miles (2008) found that African American judges are more than twice as likely to vote for Section Two liability in voting rights cases.

Given the relative absence of Latino judges on the bench through the 1980s, early scholarship either placed all minority judges (including Latinos) into a single analytical category, or, if focused on the decision making of African Americans, pooled the votes of "non-black" judges into a single category. With sufficient diversity on the bench, we can assess whether Latino judges' decisions are similar to, or different from, those made by their African American and white colleagues. According to Johnson and Fuentes-Rohwer (2004), Latinos experience, to some degree, the social and legal consequences of being a minority in ways that are comparable to discrimination experienced by African Americans. However, research on identity politics reviewed earlier emphasizes the absence of a shared pan-ethnic identity among Latinos in the mass public. Moreover, when asked about their perceptions of race discrimination in society, Latinos fall somewhere between the views of African Americans and whites.

Recent research attempting to disentangle the effects of legislator race from those associated with the racial and ethnic characteristics of the electoral constituency provides some guidance (Juenke and Preuhs 2012). One study concludes that state legislators are responsive to the interests of the minority population in their district; nevertheless, legislative voting behavior demonstrates additional ideological variation that is unique to the representative's racial and ethnic background (Juenke and Preuhs 2012). A recent study of federal appeals court decisions documents differences between African American and Latino judges (Morin 2014). Likewise, we expect that, as racial minorities, Latinos and African Americans on the bench will decide cases in ways that are distinct from their white colleagues; moreover, we expect that, despite their minority status, Latino and African American judges' decisions will be distinct from one another. To the extent that differences in decision making emerge between these racial groups, they are more likely to be in those areas that are particularly salient to their group.

In summary, our theoretical framework predicts an overall pattern in judicial decision making that parallels findings reported in research on state legislators and the mass public. This framework emphasizes that the effect of racial identity will be greater in those issue areas where group consciousness is triggered. The similar paths to the bench for African American judges and their shared experiences with discrimination lead us to expect African American judges will be more likely to support liberal policy outcomes in issue areas where black Americans perceive patterns of race discrimination (for example, civil rights, criminal justice). We do not have similar expectations for Latino judges' voting behavior, given that Latinos in the mass public do not perceive race discrimination and bias in the criminal justice system in the same manner as African Americans. Because of their recent experiences with economic opportunity and immigration shared by the initial wave of Latino judges appointed to the circuit bench, we expect their votes to be more likely to support the positions taken by the "have-nots" in distributive politics cases, similar to the positions taken by Latino legislators on matters of economic policy (Casellas 2011).

Race, Ethnicity, and Judicial Decision Making

As described in the introduction, we draw on the Multi-User Database of the Decisions of the U.S. Courts of Appeals and the Epstein, Landes, and Posner (2013) update of the Sunstein database to yield observations for our analysis that examines votes in cases that span three decades, beginning in 1982 and ending in 2008. The Epstein, Landes, and Posner database includes variables for judicial backgrounds, including race. For the Multi-User Database, we merge case data with judicial background information and exclude cases with "mixed" policy outcomes as well as those that did not have an ideological direction with respect to the case outcome.[13] The dependent variable for our analysis in this chapter is the policy outcome supported by the judge's vote.[14]

As an initial assessment, we cross-tabulated 22,188 votes from the

Multi-User Database and find a modest, statistically significant relationship between policy outcome and judge race. Forty-three percent of African American judges' votes support the liberal position compared to 35.7 percent of white judges' votes. Votes by Latino judges were slightly more conservative, with 34.5 percent supporting the liberal position. We then shifted the unit of analysis from votes to judges, constructing voting records for each judge to reflect the degree to which that judge supported the liberal position across all cases in which she or he participated. Restricting the analysis to only those records with at least ten votes, we used box plots to examine voting behavior by race and include a control for party of the appointing president.

In figure 3, boxes represent first and third quartiles of the range, and the band within the box represents the median. "Whiskers" depict dispersion beyond the median, and points beyond these are considered outliers. While larger differences characterize voting by judges appointed by Democratic and Republican presidents, race and ethnicity also account for variation in judicial voting. Among

FIGURE 3 Box plots of voting records by judge race and party of appointing president, 1982–2008

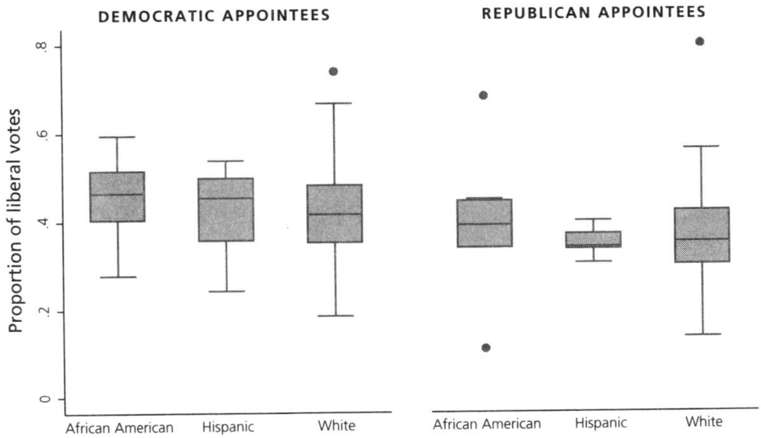

Note: N = 346. Compiled using data from the Multi-User Database on Decisions of the U.S. Courts of Appeals. Includes only appellate judges who cast at least ten votes during the time period of study (1982–2008). Weighted by number of votes cast. All issue areas included.

judges appointed by Democratic presidents, voting by African Americans tended to be more liberal than voting by white judges. As indicated by the "whiskers," the voting behavior of African American judges appointed by Democratic presidents also tended to be more cohesive than voting by white Democratic judges. Next, in a regression model, we estimated the effect of race on liberalism in judicial voting records. The results of the regression model indicate that a modest but statistically significant difference between African American and white judges' voting records remained after controlling for ideology.[15] The difference between voting records compiled by Latinos and whites was not statistically significant.

Because our framework posits that the effect of race and ethnicity will be greater in case types that are salient to the racial or ethnic group, we returned to our observations of individual votes and estimated four models that allow us to test that expectation. In the first model, we used all votes in cases where there was disagreement among panel judges or with the trial court below. The second and third models examine these effects in two subsets of cases: criminal appeals and distributive politics. All three of these models draw on observations from the Multi-User Database. The fourth model utilizes data from the Epstein, Landes, and Posner (2013) database and includes only race discrimination (Title VII) cases. As advanced earlier in this chapter, we expect that African American judges will be more liberal than other racial cohorts in their decision making, particularly in those models that estimate these effects in criminal and civil rights cases. We also expect Latino judges to be more likely to support the "have-nots" in distributive politics cases that raise issues of economic inequality.

Each model uses a set of dummy variables to measure race/ethnicity, coded "1" if the judge was African American or Latino and zero if not (the excluded reference category is white). The models include controls for the judge's ideology as well as the policy predisposition of the panel and the circuit. We also account for idiosyncratic differences associated with the circuit, the tendency of lower appellate courts to affirm the lower court, and change over time. A summary of the results for our variables of interest is displayed in table 1.[16]

In our model of votes in all contested cases, we did not find race

TABLE 1 Logit model estimates for effects of judge race on likelihood of a liberal vote

	MODEL 1: ALL CASE TYPES (CONTESTED)	MODEL 2: CRIMINAL APPEALS	MODEL 3: DISTRIBUTIVE POLITICS	MODEL 4: RACE DISCRIMINATION
African American	0.066 (.093)	0.156⁺ (.106)	0.092 (.149)	0.674* (.204)
Latino	–0.129 (.173)	–0.249 (.224)	0.258⁺ (.163)	–0.187 (.289)
N	9,566	7,460	3,258	1,589

Note: ⁺p < .10; *p < .05. Robust standard errors in parentheses. Excluded reference category is white. Models 1–3 use the Multi-User Database, 1982-2008 votes. Model 4 uses the Epstein, Landes, and Posner (2013) database, 1995–2008 votes. The differences between African Americans and Latinos are significant at the .05 level in models 1, 2, and 4. For additional information on estimates for other variables, see table A4.

to be related to the likelihood of voting for a liberal outcome.[17] Once we controlled for ideology, panel effects, circuit policy predisposition, and other factors, the modest differences observed in the bivariate analyses are no longer statistically significant. Statistically significant effects associated with race and ethnicity emerge, however, when we focus on more narrowly defined issue areas that are expected to be salient to African Americans and Latinos. In criminal cases, African American judges' votes are more likely to support the position of the defendant when compared to their white and Latino colleagues; however, only the difference between African American and Latino judges is statistically significant. Holding the values for other independent variables at their means, the predicted probability of a vote in favor of the criminal defendant is .19 for African American judges and .16 for Latino judges.[18] In distributive politics cases, Latino judges are slightly more likely to support the economically disadvantaged litigant when compared to votes by white and African American judges. The predicted probability of a liberal vote by Latino judges is .43, all else equal. By comparison, the predicted probability of an African American judge supporting a disadvantaged litigant in an economic case is .39 and, for white judges, .37.

In cases that raise issues of employment discrimination on the basis of race, African American judges are more likely to support the position of the plaintiff when compared to the votes of white and Latino judges. All else equal, the predicted probability of an African American judge supporting a liberal policy outcome in a race discrimination case was .47. In contrast, the predicted probability was .31 if the judge was white and .27 if the judge was Latino.

Conclusion

Earlier in this chapter, we theorized that judges who feel a closeness to their own race will be more likely to support policy outcomes consistent with their sense of shared fate. This theory predicts that, for African American judges who experienced directly, or indirectly, segregation in the South and elsewhere, their decisions are more likely to reflect a pro–civil rights policy position consistent with the views voiced by African Americans in the mass public. To evaluate this premise, we examined votes in civil rights cases, specifically appeals that raised a Title VII claim. African American judges were substantially more likely than their Latino or white colleagues to support the position of a plaintiff alleging race discrimination in the workplace.[19]

In criminal cases, we found a similar, albeit weak, relationship, with African American judges more likely to vote in favor of the defendant. The observations of two African American judges, Theodore McKee (a Clinton appointee) and Timothy Lewis (a George H. W. Bush appointee), illustrate how racial identity may be related to judicial perceptions in these issue areas. Prior to assuming his position on the circuit court, McKee had served as a state trial court judge. While in that position, McKee commented that there is not "equal justice under the law in this country . . . if a lower-class Black commits the same crime as an upper-middle-class white, there is going to be an incredible discrepancy of treatment . . . there are just so many stereotypes out there" (Washington 1994, 71). McKee then noted how these stereotypes can influence judging. "It is very easy for that very subtle, subliminal racism to creep in, and when the defendant comes into court you just disregard him and dehumanize him . . . as part of the stereotype of this dangerous mass out there waiting to take over our schools and our streets and break into our homes. I would hope that this doesn't happen to the same degree with Black judges as white judges. I think it still happens with Black judges but I hope it doesn't happen to the same degree" (Washington 1994, 72).

Sensitivity to a history of race discrimination is also apparent in comments made by Judge Timothy Lewis. When explaining why he pursued a career as an attorney, Lewis recounted that his father, a dentist, told him that blacks could use the law to overcome racism and contribute to their community and country (Washington 1994, 231). Lewis went on to describe his father's experiences:

> My father was beaten by army MPs when he was stationed at Fort Tucker in Alabama during World War II. He had the temerity to object when a store clerk in town refused to fix the stem on his watch because "niggers weren't allowed" into this particular shop. . . . When two passing MPs were called into the shop, they listened . . . and then they grabbed my father, took him outside, beat him up, threw him in a jeep, and took him back to base, where he was thrown in jail. (Washington 1994, 231)

We found no evidence that Latino and African American judges on the bench took positions in ways that suggest racial minority-majority blocs in decision making. In fact, differences in decision making between Latino and African American judges were observed in two of three issue areas. Latino judges were more conservative in their voting than African American judges in cases involving criminal defendants and claims of employment discrimination. Consistent with research on Latino political behavior, we find that economic policy issues associated with inequality yielded a different pattern in decision making. Latino judges are more likely than white and African American judges to support individuals in civil cases that raise issues of distributive politics.[20]

Although they share an identity as a jurist and member of the legal profession, courts of appeals judges possess multiple social identities. The specific case context can influence which identity is most salient at a given time as highlighted in our findings. Our theoretical framework in this chapter emphasized group identity and the role of socializing experiences in determining closeness to one's racial group. In the next chapter, we shift our attention to gender role theory as a framework for understanding differences in approaches taken by men and women on the bench.

2

GENDER AND JUDGING

Do women on the bench really make any difference in the development of the law? The maxim that a wise man and a wise woman come to the same conclusions is endlessly repeated, but I think only simplistic. . . . Nearer the truth, I think, is that being a woman and being treated by society as a woman can be a vital element of a judge's experience. That experience in turn can subtly affect the lens through which she views issues and solutions.

—Judge Patricia Wald

In this chapter, we explore potential differences in the approaches to judging taken by women and men on the appellate bench. Earlier, we focused on the role of social identity theory and the relevance of group closeness in understanding how race and ethnicity affect judicial decision making. Here, our theoretical framework centers on research by social psychologists and sociologists that emphasizes lifelong processes of socialization and allocation associated with gender roles that contribute to differences in attitudes and behavior.

After examining the personal backgrounds and legal careers of the first cohort of women appeals court judges and the socializing processes associated with their paths to the bench, we consider how female judges may be expected to bring a "different voice" to their decision making. From this perspective, the votes of women judges will vary from the decisions of their male colleagues; however, these differences are more likely to emerge in issue areas where gender is salient. Our framework tests this expectation and updates prior research by utilizing the dataset described in earlier chapters that includes votes by judges on the bench through 2008. Using interviews from oral histories, we explore the contention that the personal experiences of this cohort of women judges are relevant to understanding gender-related differences in voting behavior in sex discrimination cases. In the remainder of the chapter, we consider how a feminine approach to judging would manifest itself in procedural dimensions of decision making and test whether women judges, as opinion authors, are more likely to emphasize consensus building and compromise when compared to their male colleagues.

Women Judges: Navigating the Gendered Path to the Bench

As the first woman to serve on an Article III federal appeals court, Florence Allen had a great deal of experience breaking down gender barriers. She was the only woman in her class at the University of Chicago School of law in 1909, and she graduated second among males, who complimented her for her ability to think like a man (Ginsburg and Brill 1995). After the ratification of the Nineteenth Amendment, Allen, a former prosecutor, became the first woman in the nation elected to sit on a court of general jurisdiction. In 1922, she was elected to the Ohio Supreme Court and became the first woman to serve on any state's highest court. Over a decade later, FDR appointed Allen to the U.S. Court of Appeals for the Sixth Circuit, where her colleagues routinely dined without her at their all-male club (Ginsburg and Brill 1995). Judge Allen would retire from the bench before another female, Shirley Hufstedler, was named to the Ninth Circuit by LBJ in 1968. Hufstedler had been a California state trial court judge for five years and then sat on the California Court of Appeals for two years before her nomination to the Ninth Circuit. Eleven years after her appointment to the federal appeals court, Hufstedler left to serve as the first secretary of the Department of Education under President Carter.[1]

Although Florence Allen served well before Shirley Hufstedler, both represented a generation of women "pioneers" who overcame obstacles to pursue professions that were dominated by men. Although the ratio of women to men in law schools is currently close to parity, in 1947, 3.3 percent of enrolled law students were women.[2] By 1970, 8.6 percent of enrolled J.D.'s were women. Over the next decade, the number of women in law schools increased substantially so that by 1980, a little over one-third of enrolled students were women.

Admission to law school would be only the first obstacle faced by those who wished to practice law in the 1950s and 1960s. In 1970, women made up less than 3 percent of the bar. When asked about what it was like to be one of two women in her class at Stanford Law School, Shirley Hufstedler responded, "It never occurred to me to be concerned about it. I knew I was entering a profession that was strictly . . . male. So I had no difference in expectations when that turned out to be what it was."[3] Carter appointee Stephanie Seymour also recalled the gendered nature of private practice during the 1960s. After graduating from Harvard Law School in 1965, Seymour went to work for a private firm in Boston. She recalled, "three percent (of) graduating lawyers the year I graduated were females. So there weren't very many women to go to these law firms. We were a small, but hardy bunch. By then I had really learned to live in a man's world which I had to do."[4]

These comments emphasize the resilience of women who led the way in transforming the appellate bench from an all-male institution. Their shared experiences with differential treatment in law school and the legal profession had a profound effect, for many, in shaping their perspectives on being a federal appeals court judge. In the sections below, we explore legal education and employment underlying the gendered paths to the bench for these women judges, particularly those who were the first to be appointed to a circuit.

LEGAL EDUCATION

Attending a top-tier law school marked the first step for the initial wave of female appointees to the appeals courts. Florence Allen was a graduate of the University of Chicago, whereas Hufstedler received her law degree from Stanford. Both graduated at, or near, the top of their class. In his 1983 study of President Carter's nominees to the lower federal courts, Elliot Slotnick found that 48.5 percent of the women and 39.9 percent of the men nominated were graduates of an elite law school: a difference of about 9 percentage points (1982–83, 286). Carter's female appointees to the appeals court bench had strong academic credentials; they were graduates of Harvard, Yale, Columbia, Michigan, Chicago, Stanford, UCLA, and Washington schools of law. For women judges who attended overwhelmingly male law schools in the 1940s and 1950s, some recalled a chilly reception among students and faculty. As described by Reagan appointee Judge Cynthia Hall, who, like Hufstedler, was one of two women in the Stanford class of 1951, "this was still a time when there were veterans coming back from the Great War and they were still moving through the schools. . . . There was a lot of feeling among the fellow students that I was taking a good man's place . . . and obviously I would just get married and never practice. . . . I was wasting one of the few valuable spots in the law school."[5]

Judges who were among the first women to attend law school recalled that law professors would single them out on specific "Ladies' Days" and, in criminal law classes, calling on women students frequently coincided with discussion of rape cases.[6] By the early 1970s, the climate for women in law schools was changing, but women were still subject to mild forms of hazing by male law students. Judge Rosemary Barkett, one of a handful of women in her class (1970), recalled a practice called "shuffling" in which male students would create noise by shuffling their feet against the wooden floors if a woman walked into a classroom or common room.[7]

Despite their encounters with gender bias, many women judges who were among this first cohort reported that they enjoyed law school. Still, single women enrolled prior to the 1970s found some aspects of law school to be isolating due to gender segregation in housing, a problem at Harvard that was noted by Judge Seymour.[8] Judge Mary Schroeder described "dismal" physical conditions during her first year at the University of Chicago (class of 1965). At that time, the University of Chicago lacked campus housing for female graduate students, requiring that they walk 1.5 miles in bitter cold weather to class.[9]

In addition to shifts in the gender composition of law schools, legal education for more recent women appointees to the circuit courts has broadened to include a mix of public and private institutions. Between 2001 and 2008, George W. Bush appointed women to the circuit bench who graduated from Harvard, University of

Pennsylvania, Duke, UCLA, Emory, Virginia, Tulane, Akron, University of the Pacific, Wayne State, and Baylor. Although studies continue to document gender-based differences in law students' experiences, research generally finds that legal education has a homogenizing effect on students (Guinier et al. 1994).

LEGAL PROFESSION

Upon graduation, many women judges who entered the market in the 1950s and 1960s commented on the limited opportunities, if not outright discrimination, they observed. When asked about employment obstacles following her graduation from law school, Judge Betty Fletcher of the Ninth Circuit responded: "Only when I got out of law school and was looking for a job, prejudice came down on me like a ton of bricks because at first the professor who was supposed to get interviews for graduating students, never got one for me. . . . I was walking down the faculty corridor and I heard his booming voice on the phone: 'Well, you wouldn't consider a woman would you?' "[10]

After her unsuccessful search for work as a lawyer in the late 1950s, Judge Cynthia Hall decided to pursue an LL.M. in tax law. When asked about this decision, Judge Hall explained: "I had talked to a senior partner in a law firm. . . . I asked him what it would take to get him to hire a woman like me. He said, well, if I had a specialty that he desperately needed, he might overlook the fact that I was a woman. So I set out to get a specialty that somebody might desperately need. I went to NYU on a fellowship."[11]

Several judges appointed as part of the initial wave of female circuit court judges experienced their employer's gendered views about working mothers. After being hired by an all-male firm, Judge Mary Schroeder learned that she was expecting a child. When she met with one of the senior lawyers who supported her hiring, he advised her to keep the pregnancy a secret for as long as she could:

> There had been a big blow-up when it had been discovered that they had given me the offer. . . . So I said, "Well, I'll see how long I can stay a little bit pregnant." I did manage to stay a "little bit pregnant" for about 4 more months and then, finally, I had to show up in a maternity dress, and that did not go over very well. I

could see that there was a great deal of buzzing, and talk, and lawyers were kind of closeted together and saying, "We told you so."[12]

Judge Carolyn King of the Fifth Circuit also encountered gender bias while in private practice. The employer who hired her and provided rewards for excellent performance was unwilling to go further as she progressed in her career. King had practiced corporate law in Houston in the late 1960s and early 1970s. After the birth of her second child, a senior partner visited her at home and told her that she was not going to make partner and that she should consider staying home and taking care of her children. King did not initially believe it: she was generating more revenue for the firm and making more money than her male colleagues. After she was turned down for partner, King quit and was offered a better-paying position in another corporate firm that included partnership. Many corporate clients followed her to the new firm and, according to Judge King, "Work life . . . straightened out pretty well . . . [yet] it took me many more years simply to accept the fact that a decision had been made for me that was different than the decision that would have been made for a man."[13]

Balancing motherhood with work was challenging for many in the first generation of women appeals court judges because full-time child care was particularly difficult to find. Several women judges interrupted their studies or deliberately opted out of employment opportunities for family reasons. Like her colleague Ruth Ginsburg, Judge Ilana Rovner of the Seventh Circuit transferred from Georgetown Law in her third year to follow her husband, a doctor who had taken a position in Chicago. After graduating from Chicago-Kent College of Law in 1966, Rovner decided to start a family and waited almost seven years to take the bar exam.

Former D.C. Circuit judge Patricia Wald followed a similar career path. Upon graduating from Yale Law School in 1951, Wald clerked for Judge Jerome Frank of the Second Circuit and married one of her classmates. Her clerkship helped secure a position as the only woman in a new D.C.-based firm: Arnold, Fortas, and Porter. After becoming pregnant with their first child, Wald had four more children and did not return to work for ten years. Whether they temporarily opted out of the practice of law or continued full-time employment, these women faced challenges that ranged from confronting unsympathetic coworkers and friends to feeling the emotional burden of work-family conflicts. When asked about working full time while raising children, Rovner responded that she felt "enormous guilt. You know, worried that we were not there for our children, worrying about having a court appearance and your child was in the play that day."[14]

Opportunities for employment as a lawyer in private practice were extremely limited for many women entering the legal profession during the 1950s and '60s. Not surprisingly, many women judges pursued careers in the public sector. When describing her own experience, Judge Mary Schroeder recalled:

> I say often that when I went to law school in 1962, few women or minorities were stupid enough to go to law school. There were very few of us because in part we couldn't get a job. . . . What happened in 1964 was the Civil Rights Act was passed . . . (and) President Johnson . . . issued an executive order to the government that commanded them to hire women and minorities . . . so all of the agencies then came running to the major law schools to find women and minorities, and there weren't any; so I had my pick of all the best government jobs.[15]

Judge Rovner, a former president of the Federal Bar Association of Chicago, also found the federal government to be more receptive to women lawyers: "Don't forget where women got their first real opportunities. In government and the Federal Bar Association. . . . That's where women had a lot of opportunity."[16] Although more recent female appointees were more likely to have experience in private practice, the federal government continued to be an important employer for women lawyers. Among Clinton's female appointees, about half had careers largely centered in federal and state agencies, and about one-fourth of George W. Bush's female appointees practiced law in the public sector.

JUDICIAL EXPERIENCE

With the exception of the Carter cohort, women appointees often possessed judicial experience, particularly at the trial level (Goldman and Saronson 1994).[17] The first two female appeals court judges, Allen and Hufstedler, had been longtime state court judges prior to their appointment. Two of Ronald Reagan's four female appointees to the appeals courts had previous judicial service, with slightly over half of the male appointees having served on a court. Six of the seven women appointed by George H. W. Bush to the circuit bench were sitting federal district court judges at the time of appointment. In contrast, seventeen of the thirty men appointed by George H. W. Bush had previous judicial experience. Seventy-five percent of Clinton's female appointees and 85 percent of George W. Bush's female appointees had been judges in state or federal court. By comparison, approximately half of the male judges appointed by Clinton and George W. Bush had previous judicial experience.

The effect of these experiences may be a greater appreciation by women judges for the work of the trial court. Judge Rosemary Barkett served as a Florida trial court judge (and then later on the Florida Supreme Court) prior to her appointment to the Eleventh Circuit by President Clinton. When asked about the effect of her trial court experience, Barkett noted: "No, I don't think that I defer more [to the trial court] because I was in that position. But I think I am more empathetic and understanding because I was in that position. I think you understand the process a whole lot better having seen it in action, as it were, instead of only reading about it in a book or a transcript."[18]

AGE

At the time of her appointment, Shirley Hufstedler was among the youngest to be named to the circuit bench. Her relative youth on the bench reflected on an overall trend noted by other scholars: the initial cohort of women federal appeals court judges were younger than their male colleagues at the time of their appointment (Slotnick 1982–1983). Given their relative "youth," this first generation of women judges was more likely to have longer tenure on the bench. For many Carter and Reagan-Bush female appointees who later became the longest serving active judge in their court, these women were offered an opportunity to break another gender barrier as the first female chief judges of their circuit, potentially shaping administrative policy on the courts. For example, during her tenure as chief judge of the Third Circuit, Judge Dolores Sloviter provided organizational support to a task force to study gender bias and was instrumental in ensuring that women were included in the pool of candidates for bankruptcy judicial positions and circuit administrative officers.[19] With longer tenure on the bench, the first generation of women judges was well positioned to alter informal processes associated with judging, a point that we develop further below and in chapter 5. Over time, however, the modest relationship between age and gender has largely disappeared. Under Carter, the average age for a woman appointed to the circuit bench was forty-eight. For those women selected by George W. Bush, the average age was over fifty.

These accounts of women appeals court judges, particularly the experiences of the "pioneer" generation on the bench, suggest their paths to the bench required substantial determination for them to overcome implicit and explicit gender bias in the legal profession. As Judge Hufstedler noted, "every time I wanted to do something, I had to invent a way to do it because there was no path for me."[20] Traditional attitudes about the role of women in the 1950s and 1960s contributed to gender inequality in the legal profession and the judiciary. Over time, attitudes began to shift, but a number of barriers remained for women lawyers. In the remainder of this chapter, we consider these shifts in socializing experiences as we examine whether, and how, women bring a "different voice" to the bench.

Gender and Decision Making: A Framework

In her seminal research on gender and moral development, psychologist Carol Gilligan (1982) published findings that fueled a large body of scholarship across the social sciences. In this study, Gilligan found that males tended to approach moral dilemmas in a manner that emphasized standards of justice and individual rights whereas females often focused on an ethic of care and relationships. Subsequent empirical research testing Gilligan's framework has been mixed in its findings. While studies find that female adolescents are more likely than males to express concern and responsibility for the well-being of others (Beutel and Marini 1995), other scholars have suggested that empirical support for sex differences in morality is minimal and debate the conceptualization and measurement of types of moral reasoning (Jaffee and Hyde 2000).

Given the emphasis on morality and reasoning in jurisprudence, it is not surprising that legal scholars have been drawn to Gilligan's work (Karst 1984; Menkel-Meadow 1985; Sherry 1986; Davis 1992). In one early essay, Kenneth Karst (1984) argued that a woman's "voice" would change existing (male) constitutional values associated with liberty and due process that historically have emphasized a focus on individual freedom from governmental interference. From this view, a "different voice" would emphasize the responsibility of the state to prevent harms (Karst 1984). In her analysis of Justice O'Connor's opinions, Susanna Sherry (1986) suggested that women judges would emphasize connection, subjectivity, and responsibility whereas men would focus on autonomy, objectivity, and rights.

Although theories of gender role socialization advanced by social and developmental psychologists suggest multiple mechanisms through which sex-typed behavior is acquired, recent research provides additional insights on their relationship to social cognition and decision making. According to this line of inquiry, reasoning occurs via a dual process, employing a rapid, intuitive system as well as a deliberative, calculative process. To the extent that stereotypes and attitudes are implicit, they potentially operate under the first, intuitive system (Kahneman 2011). Implicit attitudes that contribute to unconscious responses are rooted at an early age when people first learn to associate and thus form cognitive structures called schemas that help to unconsciously categorize people, objects, and knowledge about the social world (Kahneman 2011).

While research on implicit biases has been largely used to explain racial prejudice, it also may account for gender differences in perception and attitudes associated with equality in the workplace, with women more likely than men to perceive widespread sex discrimination in employment (Negowetti 2014). Women are also more supportive of social welfare, education, and health programs, and of economic policies to assist disadvantaged groups (Shapiro and Mahajan 1986; Marini 1990). Gender differences in opinions dealing with violence and criminal justice have persisted over time, particularly with respect to the death penalty (Smith 1984; Shapiro and Mahajan 1986). Research on gender differences in other areas suggests that women are more likely than men to favor rehabilitation for offenders, but these differences are modest (Applegate, Cullen, and Fisher 2002). To the extent that male and female judges hold policy predispositions similar to those held in the mass public, there is the potential for similar gender differences in judicial decision making. Whereas judging might seem to involve only reasoning processes that are deliberative and calculative, scholars have found that judges are also subject to implicit biases in decision making (Guthrie, Rachlinkski, and Wistrich 2001).

As the number of women judges on the bench has increased, so too has the body of research testing for gender-based differences. Overall, empirical studies suggest more similarities than differences in voting behavior by men and women. In one analysis of decision making on the federal appeals courts, Songer, Davis, and Haire (1994) found that women judges did not vote differently than their male colleagues in two of three issue areas. Their conclusions affirmed the overall portrait suggested by null or mixed findings of earlier research that largely focused on trial court judges (Walker and Barrow 1985; Kritzer and Uhlman 1977).[21]

However, Songer and his coauthors did find that women judges were more likely to support plaintiffs in claims of employment discrimination when compared to voting by their male colleagues. In a comprehensive recent study of federal appeals court decision making in thirteen issue areas, Boyd, Epstein, and Martin (2010) also found that male and female judges did not vote differently from one another with the exception of one case type: employment discrimination. Here, the probability of a vote in favor of the party alleging discrimination increased by about ten percentage points when the judge was female (Boyd, Epstein, and Martin 2010, 401). One former female circuit judge has suggested that women's experiences with discrimination enable them to identify with the position of others in similar positions (Wald 2004). In a survey of Carter appointees, Martin (1990) reported that 81 percent of the women described some form of sex discrimination as the primary challenge facing a woman or man in law (1990, 207). She concluded that the majority of women judges surveyed had to overcome sex discrimination and remained "attuned to the difficulties that other women face in combining family and career as evidenced by their advice to young women lawyers" (Martin 1990, 208).

With the exception of employment discrimination, the large

body of null findings is often attributed to homogenizing influences associated with legal training (Guinier et al. 1994) and paths to the bench, as well as gendered norms and processes that underlie the "classical model of judging" (Solimine and Wheatley 1994–95, 908–11). As a result, gender differences may not emerge as long as the backgrounds and career experiences of female and male judges are similar. And, even with increased diversity in backgrounds, more substantial shifts in the gender composition of the judiciary may be required before a different voice can be detected.

In light of this argument, we extend this line of inquiry and include decisions during a period of time when the number of women judges appointed to the circuit courts increased dramatically and included a substantial number named by presidents of both parties. Initially, we test for gender differences in all cases. Then, heeding research that finds gender differences in public opinion on policies related to the criminal justice system and welfare, we examine whether women judges depart from their male colleagues in appeals brought by criminal defendants and those relating to economic inequality. We also test for differences in cases that may be particularly salient for women: sex discrimination claims. Our analysis of oral histories documented numerous accounts of women judges who recalled their firsthand experience with discrimination in the legal profession during the 1950s and 1960s. As a result, we also test whether the effect of gender on judging in sex discrimination cases varies by birth cohort.

Judicial Policy Outcomes and Gender

As described in the introduction, the observations for our analysis are drawn from two databases on decision making through 2008. After merging case data with judicial background information, we eliminated votes that could not be classified as having any ideological direction with respect to the case outcome. As in the first chapter, the dependent variable for our analysis is the policy outcome supported by the judge's vote. When gender and policy outcome are cross-tabulated, the bivariate analysis reveals a small, statistically significant difference in voting by male and female judges: 39 percent of the women judges' votes supported the liberal position compared to 35.8 percent of the votes by male judges.

By the end of the Reagan administration, most of the women on the circuit bench had been appointed by Democratic president Carter, making it difficult for researchers to separate gender effects from ideology. With more women judges appointed by two Republican presidents (George H. W. Bush and George W. Bush) and another Democrat, Bill Clinton, observations based on voting through 2008 permit us to adequately evaluate the influence of gender after controlling for ideology.

Similar to our analysis of race effects in the previous chapter, we construct voting records for each judge to reflect the degree to which that judge supported the liberal position across all cases in which she or he participated.[22] Restricting the analysis to only those records with at least ten votes, we used boxplots to examine voting behavior by gender and party of appointing president. Boxes represent first and third quartiles of the range, and the band within the box represents the median. "Whiskers" depict dispersion beyond the median, and points beyond these are considered outliers (see figure 4). As these suggest, substantial differences in voting may be attributed

FIGURE 4 Box plots of voting records by judge gender and party of appointing president, 1982–2008

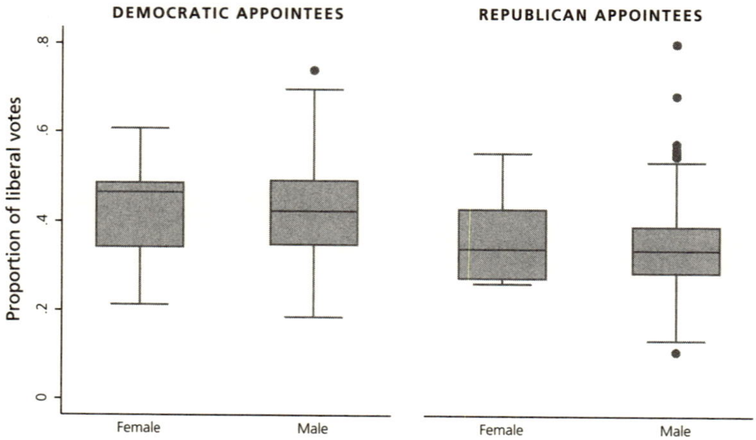

Note: N = 346. Compiled using data from the Multi-User Database on U.S. Courts of Appeals. Includes only appellate judges who cast at least ten votes during the time period of study (1982–2008). Weighted by number of votes cast. All issue areas included.

TABLE 2 Logit model estimates for effect of judge gender on likelihood of a liberal vote

	MODEL 1: ALL CASE TYPES (CONTESTED)	MODEL 2: CRIMINAL APPEALS	MODEL 3: DISTRIBUTIVE POLITICS	MODEL 4: SEX DISCRIMINATION
Female judge	–0.052 (.087)	0.026 (.095)	–0.113 (.140)	0.282* (.153)
N	9,616	7,498	3,271	1,694

Note: *p < .05 (one-tailed test). Robust standard errors in parentheses. Models 1–3 use the Multi-User Database, 1982–2008 votes. Model 4 uses the Epstein, Landes, and Posner (2013) database, 1995–2008 votes. For additional information on estimates for other variables, see table A6.

to the party of the appointing president; however, gender-based differences were minimal. Using voting records as a dependent variable in a regression model, we do not find judge gender to be related to judicial voting after controlling for individual policy preferences.

Because existing scholarship suggests that gender differences may be expected to vary with the issue, we estimated three additional models that take into account other influences on individual votes. Each model measures gender dichotomously, coded "1" if the judge was a female and "0" if a male. The model includes controls for the judge's ideology as well as the policy predisposition of the panel and the circuit. We also include controls for circuit-level variation, the tendency of judges to affirm the lower court, and change over time. In our model of votes in all contested cases, gender is not related to liberal voting. After taking into account other influences on decision making, this model indicates that women judges were no more likely than male judges to support a liberal vote during the time period of our study.[23]

In chapter 1, we found evidence that the effect of a judge's racial and ethnic identity varied with the type of case. We reported modest differences in voting on criminal appeals by African American judges when compared to their Latino and white colleagues. We also found voting by Latino judges in distributive politics cases to be somewhat distinctive. Here, after narrowing the observation set to criminal cases or appeals involving individuals and businesses (that is, distributive politics), we did not find evidence to support the contention that women judges vote differently from their colleagues in these issue areas. Similar to findings reported in previous research, our results suggest that women judges, despite their increasing numbers on the circuit bench, tend to decide cases similarly to their male colleagues, all else being equal (Boyd, Epstein, and Martin 2010).

The single exception to this trend involves issues of sex discrimination. Prior findings and the accounts of employment discrimination experienced by many of these women judges described above led us to estimate a model testing for gender effects in this narrowly defined set of cases. Our analysis in model 4 yields support for this expectation: women judges are more likely to support plaintiffs in sex discrimination cases when compared to the votes of their male colleagues. The predicted probability of a liberal vote is .42 for women judges and .35 for male judges, holding all other variables at their means.

One explanation advanced for the persistent finding of gender differences in cases of sex discrimination focuses on empathic responses to the plaintiff. The ability to adopt the perspective of plaintiffs in sex discrimination cases is likely to be easier for women who have similar firsthand experiences. Scholars have argued that experiences with discrimination will sensitize women judges to these issues (Martin, Reynolds, and Keith 2002). The interview data from oral histories with women judges above suggested the salience of this issue for those who came of age in the 1950s and 1960s, prior to the passage of the Civil Rights Act in 1964. If empathy accounts for gender-based effects, we would expect to see the magnitude of this relationship to be stronger for those women who overcame substantial gender-based obstacles to become successful in the legal profession.

To test whether the effect of gender varies by cohort, we reestimated the same model (with controls for ideology and other factors) and include dummy variables that take into account a judge's gender and birth year.[24] We expect to see the earlier cohort of women judges to be more likely to vote in favor of the plaintiff relative to other cohorts. The estimates reported in table 3 below support our expectations. Relative to the excluded category (male judges born 1945

TABLE 3 Logit model estimates for effect of gender cohort on likelihood of a liberal vote in sex discrimination cases

COHORT	COEFFICIENT (R.S.E.)
Women judges born 1945 or earlier	0.389* (.206)
Women judges born after 1945	0.146 (.189)
Male judges born after 1945	–0.052 (.140)
N	1,694

Note: *p < .05 (one-tailed test). Excluded reference category is male judges born prior to 1946. Includes votes from 1995 to 2008 using the Epstein, Posner, and Landes (2013) database. For additional information on estimates for other variables, see table A7.

or earlier), women judges who were among the first to break down gender barriers are more likely to vote in favor of the plaintiff to a statistically significant degree. Although the estimate for women judges born after 1945 is in the expected direction, the relationship fails to reach statistical significance. Voting by male judges born after 1945 is no different from that by male judges born prior to that time.

To illustrate these differences, we calculate the predicted probability of a liberal vote for each cohort after holding constant all other variables at their means. The probability of a woman judge born in 1945 or earlier to support the plaintiff in a sex discrimination case is .45, whereas the probability for male judges supporting the plaintiff born during the same era is .36. For judges born after 1945, the predicted probability of a vote in support of the plaintiff is .39 for women judges and .35 for male judges.[25]

To recap, the findings reported above reinforce the portrait suggested by earlier studies: women judges' voting behavior is generally similar to that of their male colleagues. In cases involving criminal issues and appeals by individuals in economic redistributive policy areas, women judges' votes are statistically indistinguishable from decisions by male judges. However, like previous studies, we find that women judges are more likely to support the plaintiff in cases related to sex discrimination. When we investigated this result further, we uncovered evidence suggesting that the effect of gender may vary by cohort: women judges who entered the profession during a period of time marked by overt discrimination are also more likely to support the claim of a plaintiff in a sex discrimination case.

Procedural Dimensions of Judging and Gender

Next, we turn our attention to the premise, often advanced in social science research, that gender is related to consensus building, as evidenced by different processes used by men and women in workplace interactions. Based on this line of research, women are believed to emphasize connection, consensus building, and contextual factors, whereas men tend to focus on competition, rules, and individuation (Duerst-Lahti 2002). Experimental research finds that females are more likely than males to prefer universalistic outcomes and group cooperation (Kennedy 2003). Similar findings have been reported in research on political elites. In a study of large-city mayors, Rinehart (1991) found that women adopted a "hands-on" approach that emphasized collegiality whereas men were more likely to adopt a hierarchical approach. A study of state legislative committee chairs also found that women were more likely to act as facilitators (Kathlene 1994, 572). In another study of state legislators, Carey, Niemi, and Powell (1998) similarly concluded that "gender differences are more pronounced with respect to . . . communication and compromise" (101).

Women judges themselves have commented on the potential linkage between gender and consensus building. In an interview with Judge Shirley Hufstedler, the former Ninth Circuit judge offered the following observation: "I think women—not every woman, but many women—have been far more acculturated to understanding, appreciating, and seeing the nuances of other people's behavior. They can be far more effective in trying to harmonize different points of view to work on a collegial court than many men are."[26]

Other women judges have reported on differences between themselves and their male colleagues in administrative and procedural aspects of their work (Tacha 1995; Abrahamson 1984). In this section, we consider dimensions associated with the process of judging where men and women may be expected to differ, focusing on opinion authorship. On any appellate court, writing the majority opinion provides an opportunity for a judge to lead her or his colleagues on the panel in this small group effort. When crafting an opinion, a judge derives satisfaction from efforts designed to enhance her or his reputation while also advancing doctrine consistent with her or his views and those of colleagues on the panel.

How might gender affect a judge's approach to one's colleagues when crafting an opinion? Consistent with the premise underlying a "different voice," we would expect that women judges are more likely to adopt a consensus-building approach as opinion authors and therefore more likely to craft opinions that seek the "middle ground." Interviews with women judges also support that expectation. Drawing an analogy to her successful experience negotiating settlements as a lawyer, Judge Betty Fletcher commented, "I've tried to use that as a judge. The three of us are in it together and we come at the case with sometimes initially not the same result in mind, but then look at the case together—okay now, where are we in common?"[27]

Our empirical test focuses on two approaches to measuring whether an opinion represents the "middle ground" as described by Judge Fletcher. Under the first approach, the content of an opinion is conceptualized along a liberal-conservative policy dimension with "middle-ground" decisions being those in which the policy outcome of the case fell somewhere in between. Consistent with Judge Fletcher's view quoted above, female judges should be more likely to craft an opinion that captures middle-ground policies because they include elements that are attractive to all of the judges on the panel. The second approach focuses on the opinion's treatment of the lower court decision. Lindquist, Martinek, and Hettinger (2007) suggest a number of factors will affect the likelihood of an appeals court panel "splitting the difference" between the litigants (that is, whether the court affirmed in part and reversed in part). Here, we build on their work to test the expectation that women judges will be more likely than their male colleagues to write an opinion that recognizes the legitimacy of the competing claims made by both litigants. As Judge Rosemary Barkett explains, "I worry about the impact of all decisions on people. I worry that wrong decisions can do so much damage. I think we have an obligation to be extraordinarily careful to listen and understand the arguments both sides are making. . . . You have got to put yourself in the shoes of both parties, in order to see the issue from both sides."[28]

To test our expectations, we begin by estimating separate models that capture these two dimensions of "middle-ground" opinions. Our models control for other factors that may affect the likelihood of a mixed treatment or policy outcome, including ideological diversity on the panel. When sitting on panels made up of judges appointed by presidents of different parties, opinion authors are more likely to craft opinions that accommodate the varying views of their colleagues (Maltzmann et al. 2000). In contrast, opinions promoting clear policy outcomes are more likely when one of the litigants is the heavily resourced U.S. government (Lindquist, Martinek, and Hettinger 2007). We also take into account the presence of an amicus brief that may signal a case where organized interests perceive an opportunity to achieve a policy goal. Finally, the models include controls for issue area, circuit-level variation, and change over time. To separate the effect of panel diversity from that associated with opinion author gender, we also include a variable that measures whether one of the other two judges on the panel was a female. The model estimates (reported in table A8) suggest that female opinion authors are more likely than their male colleagues to write decisions that are associated with a compromise policy position; however, this effect is not statistically significant. In a second model (reported in table A8), we find that female opinion authors are no more likely than their male colleagues to author an opinion that affirmed in part and reversed in part.

Recognizing the overlapping but potentially competing tensions between these two dependent variables,[29] we constructed a third dependent variable that combines these two measures and estimates gender effects on the likelihood of an opinion that advocates a mixed policy position *and* resulted in a mixed outcome for the litigants.[30] The coefficient in table 4 strongly supports our expectation: opinions written by women are significantly more likely to be ones that sought the "middle ground" in terms of policy and treatment of the litigants' claims.

This framework also leads to the expectation that majority opinions crafted by women are more likely to be longer as a result of efforts to accommodate the varying views and positions of colleagues and litigants. To test for this effect, we use as a dependent variable the number of pages in signed, unanimously decided cases by

TABLE 4 Logit model estimates for effects of judge gender on likelihood of opinion supporting middle ground position

	COEFFICIENT (R.S.E.)
Opinion author is female	0.307* (0.138)
Female judge on panel (not opinion author)	–0.074 (0.115)
N	6,276

Note: *p < .05 (one-tailed test). Includes only signed majority opinions authored by courts of appeals' judges from 1982 to 2008 using the Multi-User Database. For additional information on estimates for other variables and alternative models, see table A8.

three-judge panels with published opinions. The mean number of pages for opinions authored by male judges was 7.286, compared to the mean of 8.585 for female-authored opinions, a difference that was statistically significant ($p < .001$). Because many factors shape opinion length, we tested for gender effects in a count model that includes controls for whether the appeal was "easy" to resolve (measured as whether affirmed), issue complexity (the number of parties and whether the opinion involved constitutional interpretation), case importance (the presence of amicus and whether there was a previously published opinion associated with the case), ideological diversity on the panel, circuit-level variation in opinion writing norms, and change over time.

Although the effect of gender is modest, the finding does support our theorized expectations. Being a female opinion author increases the estimated opinion length by 7 percent, all else equal. When combined with our findings from the "middle-ground" model, these results suggest that the presence of women on the bench may shape decision making in ways other than the policy outcome—a finding that we explore further in chapters 4 and 5 when we look at decision-making practices at the panel and circuit levels.

Conclusion

Overall, the empirical analyses support the findings reported by other studies that have tested for gender differences in judicial decision making from earlier eras. Men and women on the bench

TABLE 5 Negative binomial regression model estimates for effects of judge gender on opinion length

	COEFFICIENT (S.E.)
Opinion author is female	0.068* (.039)
Female judge on panel (not opinion author)	–0.001 (.019)
N	6,233

Note: *p < .05 (one-tailed test). Includes only majority opinions authored by courts of appeals' judges from 1982 to 2008 using the Multi-User Database. For additional information on estimates for other variables, see table A9.

are quite similar in their voting behavior, with one exception: cases involving sex discrimination. Comments from judge interviews suggested the salience of this issue for those women who were pioneers in the legal profession and the judiciary. Our empirical analysis supports the conclusions of other scholars who suggest that women's experiences, including those associated with being excluded, may affect their perspectives on claims brought by plaintiffs in sex discrimination cases (Kenney 2013, 39). This chapter also highlighted the need to look beyond policy-based voting behavior to test whether gender shapes judicial efforts to develop a consensual position. In the next chapter, we extend our inquiry to consider how gender and race together influence judging.

3

INTERSECTIONALITY AND JUDGING

> *Personal experiences affect the facts that judges choose to see. My hope is that I will take the good from my experiences and extrapolate them further into areas with which I am unfamiliar. I simply do not know exactly what that difference will be in my judging. But I accept there will be some based on my gender and my Latina heritage.*
> —Justice Sonia Sotomayor

As we saw in chapters 1 and 2, characteristics like race and gender can be an important influence on judicial policy making under certain conditions. The evidence from these chapters suggests that personal experiences with differential treatment may lead female and African American judges to engage in substantive representation for women and minorities, respectively. However, there is another valuable perspective on studying diversity: thinking about race and gender not in isolation from one another but as intersecting dimensions. This perspective, known as intersectionality, argues that the interplay of social forces can shape individual identity and experiences in ways not captured by looking at these factors separately (Hancock 2007).

Kimberle Crenshaw was an early leading figure in highlighting the legal dilemmas faced by women of color because of their position at the intersection of race and gender. In a seminal article (Crenshaw 1998), she described how the context of employment discrimination uniquely affected black women. Crenshaw offers examples of several discrimination lawsuits in which judges fail to acknowledge black women's claims because their experience was not representative for all women (that is, white women were not affected) or all blacks (that is, black men were not affected). She further argues that antidiscrimination doctrine, as it currently exists, "creates a dilemma for Black women. It forces them to choose between specifically articulating the intersectional aspects of their subordination, thereby risking their ability to represent Black men, or ignoring intersectionality in order to state a claim that would not lead to the exclusion of Black men" (Crenshaw 1998 [2005], 93). Another critical race theorist has argued that rape has been another area in which black women's experiences differ substantially from those of white women: "The paradigm experience of rape for black women has historically involved the white employer in the kitchen or bedroom as much as the strange black man in the bushes. . . . [And] for black people, male and female, 'rape' signified the terrorism of black men by white men, aided and abetted, passively (by silence) or actively (by 'crying rape') by white women" (Harris 1990, 598–99).

More recently, political scientists have focused on the ways that political institutions can be "race-gendered." Hawkesworth (2003, 531) describes race-gendering as "the production of difference, political asymmetries, and social hierarchies that simultaneously create the dominant and the subordinate." While this framework offers some leverage for understanding the experiences of minority women inside political institutions (Hawkesworth 2003), it has also been used to investigate how the intersection of race and gender affects political candidates who are not minority women (Hancock 2007).

In the following section, we discuss the major findings of empirical research using the frames of intersectionality and race gendering and what these insights may mean for the appellate court context. We then examine patterns in presidential appointments to see whether there are "race-gendered" paths to the bench that point to the existence of different evaluative criteria for minority women compared to white women, minority men, and white men. Building on this discussion, a series of analyses investigates the extent to which minority women judges are marginalized or included in the work of the panel, as it relates to opinion assignment. We conclude by testing whether minority female judges are more likely to engage in substantive representation for gender and race, as previous research on legislators has found.

Studying Intersectionality

From an empirical perspective, there is general agreement that studying intersectionality requires researchers to consider race and gender interactively (Hancock 2007; Simien 2007), as opposed to studying race and gender by themselves or in an additive way. While some feminist scholars have rejected the use of all categories in favor of individualized case-study analyses (see McCall 2009, 52–55), this approach is obviously less useful for large-N research. Other researchers (Reingold and Smith 2012; Best et al. 2011; Collins and Moyer 2008; Orey et al. 2006; Bratton, Haynie, and Reingold 2006) continue to use the categories of race and gender, but do so in a way that attempts to "document relationships of inequality among social groups and changing configurations of inequality" (McCall 2009, 50). For example, Best et al. (2011) test Crenshaw's assertion that antidiscrimination law does not anticipate intersectional claims, finding that nonwhite women are more likely to lose Equal Employment Opportunity (EEO) cases than white women, nonwhite men, and white men.

One question of particular interest for political scientists studying intersectionality has been whether women of color as political elites engage in substantive representation. Pitkin (1967) makes a distinction between descriptive representation ("standing for") and substantive representation ("acting for"). She writes, "The fact that a man or assembly is a very good descriptive representation does not automatically guarantee that they will be good representatives in the sense of acting for, that their activity will really be representing. . . . In the same way, a good symbol need by no means be a good representative when we want activity on our behalf. No matter how enthusiastic we might be about Miss California, few of us would want to elect her to Congress" (Pitkin 1967, 142).

This work on substantive representation and intersectionality builds upon the literature about substantive representation for a single dimension of identity, such as race and ethnicity (Cameron,

Epstein, and O'Halloran 1996; Bratton and Haynie 1999; Haynie 2001; Owens 2005;) or gender. Although "single-axis" substantive representation studies are not without their own challenges (for instance, defining what is "women's interest" legislation), the intersectionality framework poses additional complications in defining what constitutes "representation." Which issues should be counted—those that benefit only minority women, women as a group, or minorities as a group? For instance, Smooth (2011) quotes an African American female legislator who talked about her work on criminal justice policy as a "women's issue"—but because of the effect that incarceration patterns had on the number of single, female-headed households in her urban Maryland district.

The bulk of the empirical research on intersectionality examines the behavior of legislators, primarily at the state level. In a case study of one state legislature (Orey et al. 2006), black women were more likely than Democratic white men and Democratic white women to introduce black interest legislation, and they also introduced women's interest legislation at a higher rate than Democratic white women or Democratic white men. In a broader study of ten state legislatures, Bratton, Haynie, and Reingold (2006) conclude that black women engage in substantive representation for both race and gender by sponsoring more black interest bills than black men and more women's interest bills than white women. More recently, Reingold and Smith (2012) demonstrate that incorporating an intersectional approach to legislative policy making reveals a more nuanced picture of the contributions of white and minority women in shaping welfare policy in the states.

However, Hawkesworth (2003) paints a less optimistic picture in her study of African American women in the U.S. House of Representatives. Through interviews with these representatives, Hawkesworth finds that many women of color experienced "invisibility": they felt ignored by their fellow representatives in committee meetings, as well as frustrated by the many instances in which male colleagues took full credit for their ideas and legislative efforts. Hawkesworth concludes, "As tokens, some women of color are admitted to membership in elite institutions, but their inclusion carries an expectation that they accept the agenda of the dominant members. . . . Women of color are simultaneously pressured to assimilate to the dominant norms of the institution and denied the possibility of assimilation" because of their race and gender (2003, 531–32).

Presumably because of the small number of nonwhite women, we know less about how intersectionality affects the behavior of federal judges than we do in the legislative context. One study that examined the voting behavior of African American and Hispanic female appellate judges (1977–2002) found this group to support the position of the criminal defendant more often than minority men, white women, and white men (Collins and Moyer 2008). The authors speculate that this may be due either to common opinions that emerge from a shared socialization process or to a conscious choice to provide substantive representation. However, they are unable to test empirically either of these explanations. Other work on federal appellate judges (Haire, Moyer, and Treier 2013) demonstrates that the content of the majority opinion is affected both by the race and gender of the opinion author, as well as the demographic makeup of the panel. For instance, black male opinion authors seated with two white men crafted opinions with significantly more points of law than all-white male panels, but no effect was found for black women opinion authors. Taken together, these studies suggest differences among demographic cohorts that may be reflected in judging, but also that there may be variation in how individual judges are received by their colleagues.

A central tenet of intersectional work is that a person's experiences are shaped by the interplay of her or his race and gender (as well as other characteristics). Browne and Misra (2003, 63) argue that "various components of identity often compete and overlap, simultaneously marginalizing and privileging individuals within the same group." For instance, Latinos may be privileged relative to Latinas because of the historical associations between being a man and being a judge.

Because of their unique status at the intersection of race and gender, African American and Hispanic women may take different paths to the appellate bench (compared to their male counterparts and to white women), for a variety of reasons. Different paths may be a result of discriminatory policies or practices that effectively close off certain avenues; this discrimination may be shared by other women, by other minorities, by both, or by neither. Different paths may also be a result of different opportunities and interests for particular groups. For example, as discussed in chapter 1, African American judges on the appellate bench during this time were more likely than white or Hispanic judges to have had some professional involvement in civil rights work prior to their nomination. Finally, elites involved in the federal judicial selection process may also look in particular occupations or sectors for potential judges, and the relative diversity of those places may affect the kinds of individuals nominated to the appellate bench. To explore these possibilities, the next section looks closely at the backgrounds of judges and examines similarities and differences in paths to the bench by both race and gender.

Judges' Paths to the Bench by Race and Gender: Comparisons by Appointing President

Beginning with President Carter, efforts to diversify the federal judiciary beyond white men focused on casting a wide net for qualified women and minority candidates (Goldman 1997). But despite the significant strides Carter made in diversifying the federal bench, his nontraditional appointees to the courts of appeals were almost exclusively white women and minority men: ten out of his eleven female judges were white, eight out of nine African American judges were men, and all of his Hispanic and Asian American appointees were men.[1] The lone minority woman in the group, Amalya Kearse, received a "Well-Qualified" rating from the American Bar Association and, prior to her confirmation to the Second Circuit, had a professional record similar to most white male appointees: she specialized in corporate litigation and worked her way to partner at the law firm of Hughes, Hubbard, and Reed (www.jtbf.org). Unlike most of Carter's nonwhite nominees (see Slotnick 1983–84), Kearse attended an elite undergraduate institution (Wellesley) as well as an elite law school (University of Michigan), where she was an editor on the law review. Kearse might best be understood as a pioneer in terms of race and gender; besides being the first African American woman to be named to the federal courts of appeals, she was the first African American *and* the first woman to make partner at her law firm (www.jtbf.org). However, her path to the bench was not the typical one for women or minorities during the Carter administration—a factor that may have contributed to her selection.

Judicial selection processes under both the Reagan and the George H. W. Bush administrations were characterized by a shift back toward favoring traditional white male candidates, largely as a result of the emphasis on conservative values and the heavy reliance on the senatorial courtesy process to identify nominees (Martin 1999). In contrast to Carter, Reagan's judicial selection procedures did not incorporate any considerations for a nominee's race or gender (Goldman 1997, 289–90). Thus, it is perhaps unsurprising that 92 percent of Reagan's appointees to the appeals courts were white men (Carp, Stidham, and Manning 2014, 123). All four of Reagan's female appointees were white and had spent at least a year in private practice prior to their nomination. During George H. W. Bush's presidency, five of the seven women he appointed to the appellate bench were Reagan appointees that he elevated. Again, all of these women were white, and all but one had private practice experience.

Clinton's presidency represented a watershed moment for the composition of the federal judiciary. For the first time in presidential history, less than half of all appointees to the courts of appeals were white men (Goldman et al. 2001). Over his two terms, Clinton appointed fifteen white women, three African American women, and two Latinas, along with six African American men, five Latinos, and one Asian American man.

Clinton's African American women appointees to the circuit bench (Johnnie Rawlinson, Judith Rogers, and Ann Claire Williams) had in common a background with experience in criminal law, and two of the women (Rogers and Williams) had served as assistant U.S. attorneys prior to their nominations. All three women also shared experience as judges. Both Williams and Rawlinson were U.S. district court judges elevated by Clinton, and Rogers was a judge in the District of Columbia Court of Appeals before she was nominated to fill the vacancy left by Clarence Thomas on the D.C. Circuit.

Both of Clinton's Latina appointees (Sonia Sotomayor and Kim Wardlaw) were elevated from district court judgeships, but also had prior experience in private practice. (Sotomayor had also been a prosecutor before becoming a judge.) These appointments confirm conclusions that other scholars have made about Clinton's female appointees as a whole: namely, that the women were more likely to have been sitting judges and to have had prosecutorial experience (Martin 1999, 125–26).

Overall, Clinton's white male appointees were more often nominated from positions in private law firms (Martin 1999). The African American and Hispanic men appointed largely fit this pattern as well; three of the six African American men were appointed from private practice, and the other three had some previous private practice experience before their appointment. Only one Hispanic man was appointed directly from private practice, but four of the five Hispanic men had spent some time previously in private practice. As with Clinton's female appointees, judicial experience was also very common for minority men. Half of the African American male appointees and all but one of the Hispanic men had served as judges at either the state or federal level. The only Asian American appointee, Atsushi Tashima, was elevated from a district court judgeship, and he had been appointed to that position (by Carter) directly from private practice. With this diverse group, we can see that minority men and women share some similarities, but that gender differences in professional backgrounds also matter.

Unlike his Republican predecessors, George W. Bush made diversity a higher priority for his appointments: only 64 percent of his appellate judges were white men, compared to 70 percent under his father and 92 percent under Reagan. This appointment cohort included fourteen white women, two African American women, one Latina, four African American men, two Latinos, and thirty-nine white men. Of course, George W. Bush also prized conservatism in his judicial appointments (Scherer and Miller 2009) and benefited from a larger pool of conservative women and minorities than either his father or Reagan had available to them. In a study of federal judges associated with the conservative legal organization the Federalist Society, Scherer and Miller (2009, 367) report that out of twenty-three Federalist Society members nominated by George W. Bush to the federal courts of appeals (through 2005), six were women.[2] Notably, one of these women, Janice Rogers Brown, was African American.

The lone Latina, Consuelo Maria Callahan, was nominated to

replace Ferdinand Fernandez on the Ninth Circuit (perhaps signaling that the seat was perceived to be a "Hispanic" seat). Callahan had prior experience as a district attorney and a state court judge in California. In fact, all three Hispanic nominees had experience as state judges prior to their nomination to the appellate bench.

George W. Bush's African American female appointees (Janice Rogers Brown and Allyson Kay Duncan) had experience both as state court judges and in private practice. In comparison, his African American male appointees also all had private practice experience (though two of the four were Clinton appointees to the district court bench that Bush merely elevated). Additionally, both Brown and Duncan had been active in state politics prior to their appointments: Brown had worked for California governor Pete Wilson (a Republican), while Duncan served on a state utilities commission. Only one of the African American men (Lavenski Smith) also had state politics experience; he worked for Arkansas governor Mike Huckabee (a Republican) and also served on the Arkansas Public Service Commission.

All but two of Bush's white female appointees had some experience in private practice. (Sharon Prost of the Federal Circuit and Helene White of the Sixth Circuit were the two exceptions.) Nine of the fourteen also had prior judicial experience at the state or federal level, but only one had prosecutorial experience (Reena Raggi, of the Second Circuit). In comparison, almost all of Bush's white male appointees had private practice experience (only two out of thirty-nine appointees did not). Less than half of Bush's white men (seventeen out of thirty-nine) had any prior judging experience.

To provide some examples, table 6 lists all minority female judges by appointment cohort (from Carter through George W. Bush). The table highlights some of the trends previously discussed, namely that minority women appointees tended to have prior judicial experience as well as experience in government as a prosecutor, elected official, aide to an elected official, or state cabinet member. Five of the nine women had been federal district court judges, while three others had served as state judges in some capacity. Two-thirds had also spent some time in private practice. Notably, none of the African American women attended Howard University, an institution that (as discussed in chapter 1) was very important in shaping the

TABLE 6 Race-gendered paths to the appellate bench?: Minority women appointees to the federal courts of appeals

JUDGE (CIRCUIT)	APPOINTING PRESIDENT AND YEAR	RACE AND GENDER	EDUCATION	PRIVATE PRACTICE EXPERIENCE	JUDGING EXPERIENCE	GOVERNMENT EXPERIENCE
Amalya Kearse (2nd)	Carter (1979)	African American female	Wellesley (BA), Michigan (JD)	Yes	No	No
Judith Rogers (D.C.)	Clinton (1994)	African American female	Radcliffe (AB), Harvard (JD), Virginia (LLM)	No	Yes (federal)	Yes
Kim Wardlaw (9th)	Clinton (1998)	Latina	UCLA (BA), UCLA (JD)	Yes	Yes (federal)	Yes
Sonia Sotomayor (2nd)	Clinton (1998)	Latina	Princeton (BA), Yale (JD)	Yes	Yes (federal)	Yes
Ann Williams (7th)	Clinton (1999)	African American female	Wayne State (BA), Michigan (MA), Notre Dame (JD)	No	Yes (federal)	Yes
Johnnie Rawlinson (9th)	Clinton (2000)	African American female	North Carolina A&T (BS), University of the Pacific (JD)	Yes	Yes (federal)	Yes
Consuelo Callahan (9th)	G. W. Bush (2003)	Latina	Stanford (BA), University of the Pacific (JD)	No	Yes (state)	Yes
Allyson Duncan (4th)	G. W. Bush (2003)	African American female	Hampton (BA), Duke (JD)	Yes	Yes (state)	Yes
Janice Brown (D.C.)	G. W. Bush (2005)	African American female	Cal State–Sacramento (BA), UCLA (JD), Virginia (LLM)	Yes	Yes (state)	Yes

Note: Information drawn from the Federal Judicial Center database. Includes appointees from 1977 to 2008. Government experience includes prosecutorial experience at the state or federal level, elected officials, as well as civil service positions.

group consciousness and professional choices made by a number of the African American male judges. However, Johnnie Rawlinson and Allyson Duncan both attended other historically black colleges or universities (North Carolina A&T and Hampton, respectively). Overall, the educational backgrounds of the women of color appointed to the courts of appeals included attending prestigious academic institutions for undergraduate degrees, law school, or both. Taken together, these factors clearly point to a race-gendered path to the bench for women of color that extends across appointment cohorts.

Discussion

Over the time period from Jimmy Carter to George W. Bush, appointment trends suggest three major factors driving the increased presence of minority women: changing priorities in the nomination process, the available pool, and beliefs about what "diversity" encompasses.

Goldman (1997, 3–4) observed that presidents might pursue a policy agenda, a partisan agenda, or a personal agenda in the judicial nomination process. Pursuing a policy agenda means that the president would make choices about nominees based on their perceived ability to help the president achieve his substantive policy goals; in contrast, a partisan agenda would dictate choices that help solidify political support for a president or the political party. A personal agenda in judicial selection is evidenced by choosing individuals who are close associates or friends of the president. Haire (2006) uses this conceptual scheme to track changes in the selection process for the lower federal courts away from a tendency to further personal agendas or partisan agendas (as was the case through Nixon) and toward a policy agenda when making appointments to the lower federal courts. While Carter and Clinton made a determination that judicial diversity helped to further their substantive policy goals (or served as an end unto itself), Reagan and George H. W. Bush assigned more weight to ideological purity. George W. Bush's appointment strategy to the courts of appeals is reflective of both a desire to fill vacancies with proven, legal conservatives as his father did (Goldman et al. 2005) but also an interest in looking beyond white men for conservative nominees. It should be noted that George W.

Bush's cabinet choices were substantially more diverse than previous presidential administrations, Republican or Democratic (http://usatoday30.usatoday.com). Among his cabinet appointees were two African Americans (Colin Powell and Condoleeza Rice), an Asian American woman (Elaine Chao), and two Hispanic men (Alberto Gonzales and Carlos Gutierrez). White women also led the Environmental Protection Agency (EPA) (Christine Todd Whitman), Department of Education (Margaret Spellings), Department of Agriculture (Ann Veneman) and Department of the Interior (Gale Norton).

Additionally, increasing numbers of minority women in law school and in the legal profession aided Carter, Clinton, and George W. Bush in their attempts to fill judicial vacancies. All three of these presidents benefited from a "pipeline" of minority women already serving as judges: every single minority woman appointed by either George W. Bush or Clinton had prior experience as a judge. (In contrast, Carter's lone nonwhite woman had a profile very similar to his white male appointees.) As other scholars (Martin 1999; Slotnick 1983–84) have noted, white male appointees have generally been more likely to come out of private practice than out of positions as judges. The differences in professional backgrounds of minority women, compared to other groups, suggests that these individuals may be subject to higher expectations than the traditional white male nominee; that is, a minority woman must "prove herself" as a judge in a lower court before she is considered a serious candidate for an appellate judgeship. Moreover, such candidates may have to overcome systematic bias toward women and minorities in the evaluative process used by the American Bar Association to rate judicial qualifications (Sen 2014).

Third, it is evident that each presidential administration viewed "diversity" somewhat differently. While Carter was very explicit about his priorities with respect to diversity, his appointments reflect an understanding of diversity that includes only white women and African American men. In the next two administrations, less attention was paid to the appointments of nonwhite men, and so diversity in this context meant white women. It was not until Clinton and then George W. Bush that minority women really were included in "diversification" efforts: Clinton appointed five minority women to the bench, while George W. Bush appointed three. Clinton and George W. Bush also looked beyond African Americans in their appointments, the former appointing seven and the latter appointing three Hispanic individuals to the bench. However, white women have been (by far) the most common "nontraditional" choice made by any of these presidents.

Testing for Invisibility and Marginalization

Next, we test Hammonds's claim (1997, 182) that "intersectionality is manifested in invisibility, otherness, and stigma." On appellate panels, there are several ways that we might observe the marginalization of minority women. First, women of color may be less likely than other colleagues, all things being equal, to be assigned the majority opinion by their colleagues in important cases. Being assigned the majority opinion allows a judge to exert a disproportionately large influence on the content of the opinion, even allowing for input by other members of the panel (Choi and Gulati 2007).[3] Research on performance expectations in small groups suggests that both women and African Americans (compared to men and whites, respectively) are associated with lower standards for competence (e.g., Biernat and Kobrynowicz 1997), which can affect assessments of their work. Given these (subconscious) assumptions about competency, a minority woman may be at a disadvantage when a case is viewed as being of greater importance. Indeed, research on opinion assignments in state supreme courts suggests that, under some institutional conditions, African American men and white women are less likely to be assigned to write the majority opinion (Christensen, Szmer, and Strich 2012). Other work on the federal courts of appeals points in a different direction, finding that female judges are significantly more likely to be assigned to write the opinion in sexual harassment cases, perhaps as a result of consensual assignment norms that involve women actively asking to write these opinions (Farhang, Kastellec, and Wawro forthcoming).

Additionally, when minority women are the presiding judges on a panel (with the power to assign the majority opinion), their decision to assign the opinion to themselves could also indicate a reaction to feeling "invisible" within the institution. Allen and Wall (1993) have argued that female judges might react to their relative isolation in very different ways, depending on their role orientation. For instance, they might choose to modify their behavior to conform with the dominant group (as a "token"), or alternatively, they may reject group norms altogether (Allen and Wall 1993, 158–59). In the context of sexual harassment cases, Farhang, Kastellec, and Wawro (forthcoming) find no evidence that women are more likely than men to self-assign opinions. However, because no existing work looks at the intersection of race and gender in opinion assignment, the literature does not give us clear directional expectations for self-assignment. Minority women may go out of their way to assign opinions to others when they are the presiding judge, or they might be particularly assertive in assigning opinions to themselves.

OPINION ASSIGNMENT

From 1982 to 2008, the diversification of the federal courts of appeals has resulted in a moderate decline in white male judges' influence as majority opinion authors. Breaking out three distinct time periods (1982–92, 1993–2000, and 2001–8) that correspond with presidential administrations of the same party, white males make up a decreasing proportion of all majority opinion authors in our sample. In the first period, white men authored 78.5 percent of signed, published opinions, dropping to 71.2 percent in 1993–2000 and 65 percent in 2001–8. Among nontraditional judges, white women have been the most influential as opinion authors, moving from 7.43 percent of all opinions in the first period to 16.9 percent in the most recent time period. African American men authored close to 4 percent in all three periods, while Hispanic men's percentage grew from 1.38 in the first era to just under 5 percent during 2001–8. In contrast, minority women lagged far behind white women and minority men overall and in each era (with the exception of Asian men, who wrote less than half a percent of majority opinions in each time period). African American women wrote less than 1 percent of majority opinions between 1982 and 1992 and only 2.62 percent from 2001 to 2008. Hispanic women's percentage stayed under 1 percent over the entire period of observation.[4] Of course, this limited opinion writing is a reflection of the small number of African American and Hispanic women on the bench, as well as the sample of cases under study. But it is yet another reminder that white women and African American men have been the largest beneficiaries of presidential attempts to diversify the judiciary and that this preference has implications for whose voices are heard through judicial opinions.

Moving beyond aggregate numbers, next we look at opinion-assignment trends in individual cases. Are minority women systematically overlooked when it comes to opinion assignment by other judges? To answer this question, we examine the frequencies for opinion authorship under a variety of conditions.[5]

Minority women were present in the following circuits during the period of our study: the Second, Third, Fourth, Seventh, Ninth, and D.C. Of these, the Second and the D.C. Circuits had the highest percentage of opinions written by minority women in our sample (7 percent and 6.6 percent, respectively). In the Second Circuit, two minority women wrote opinions during this time: Amalya Kearse (an African American) and Sonia Sotomayor (a Latina). In the D.C. Circuit, there were two African American women during our time period: Judith Rogers and Janice Brown. Both courts are about the same size, as the D.C. Circuit had twelve authorized judgeships through 2008 and the Second Circuit had eleven through 1983 and thirteen after 1984. (The number of judgeships is relevant to understanding opinion-writing opportunities because the rotating panel system and random assignment to panels affects how often a panel is constituted with a minority female member.) The other circuits with minority women had significantly lower percentages of opinions authored by this group in our sample. In the Ninth Circuit (the court with the largest number of judgeships), 2.1 percent of opinions were written by minority women, followed by 1.9 percent in the Seventh Circuit, 1.3 percent in the Fourth Circuit, and less than 1 percent in the Third Circuit.

To investigate our expectation that women of color will be less likely than other judges to be assigned to write majority opinions in important cases, we examined the percentage of cases in which a minority woman was seated on the panel, was eligible to write the majority opinion, and was not assigned the opinion, compared to those where she was assigned. Here, only signed published opinions from three-judge panels are included (1982–2008), and instances in which the minority women assigned the opinion to herself and when she was not part of the majority coalition are omitted. A variable, *Important Case,* was coded as a "1" if any of the following conditions were met in a case: publication of the district court opinion, presence of any amicus briefs, a constitutional claim, death penalty cases, or remands from the Supreme Court. Cases that lacked all of these factors were coded as a "0." We also coded whether the case was unanimously decided ("1") or if there was a dissent ("0").

To evaluate whether marginalization in opinion assignment exists, we examined the frequencies for minority women opinion authors in important cases, excluding instances in which minority women could self-assign (as the presiding judge on the panel) and cases in which they were not in the majority. The Chi-squared test fails to reach conventional levels of significance, indicating that minority women are no more or less likely to be assigned the majority opinion in important cases relative to less important cases.

Dissensus is another indicator of case salience, as it suggests that the case represents something other than a "routine" appeal in which all three judges can easily come to agreement on the resolution (Hettinger, Lindquist, and Martinek 2006); the presence of a dissenting opinion is a predictor of en banc review (Giles, Walker, and Zorn 2006) and can also make Supreme Court review more likely. Here, women of color were actually more likely to be assigned the majority opinion in non-unanimous cases than unanimous cases.[6] The raw numbers are quite small, but minority women were assigned the opinion in 24 percent of non-unanimous cases, compared to less than 3 percent of unanimous cases. (The Chi-squared test is significant at $p < .001$.) By definition, being in the majority in a non-unanimous decision makes it more likely that a judge will write the majority opinion. (The presiding judge has only two options for opinion assignment, rather than three.) However, there does not appear to be a systematic effort to marginalize women of color in these salient cases. While it is prudent to be cautious in drawing strong conclusions here, because we cannot control for competing explanations, these findings do not provide any evidence in support of the marginalization hypothesis.[7]

Moving beyond opinion assignment, the next analysis investigates whether minority women are more or less likely to self-assign opinions when they are the presiding judge.

For this model, opinion authors were grouped into race-gender cohorts: white women, African American men, African American women, Hispanic men, Hispanic women, and Asian American men (white men were the excluded reference category). We can determine whether an opinion is self-assigned by calculating each judge's years of active service on that circuit to determine who is the most senior, eligible judge; visiting judges from district courts and other circuits, as well as senior judges from within the circuit, cannot assign opinions—though they can write them. If an eligible judge with the most seniority wrote the opinion, we can ascertain that she assigned it to herself.

The logit model for self-assignment includes fixed effects for circuits as well as time. We examine only unanimous, signed decisions because our interest is in identifying patterns in the most common type of disposition (unanimous decisions) in which the presiding judge has the largest choice set available in terms of assigning the opinion (two other judges besides herself or himself). Controls were included for the ideological distance between the opinion writer and the panel median, the ideological direction of the outcome, issue area (civil rights, criminal), and the treatment of the lower court decision.

Shown in table 7, the results from the self-assignment model highlight the utility of examining race and gender in an intersectional way. Using white men as the comparison group, white women, Hispanic women, and Hispanic men were significantly more likely to self-assign the majority opinion; the coefficients for African American women and men are both positive but fall far outside conventional levels of significance. To help assess the magnitude of this effect, predicted probabilities were calculated for the significant race-gender cohorts, holding continuous variables at their means and dichotomous variables at their modal values. These probabilities reveal considerable gender differences within racial/ethnic groups. For example, white men's probability of self-assignment was .11, while white women's probability of self-assignment was .19. The gender differences among Hispanic judges were even more substantial: the probability for Hispanic men was .23 and a whopping .49 for Hispanic women.

Although these findings are certainly affected by the relative se-

TABLE 7 Logit model estimates for effects of judge race and gender on likelihood of self-assignment of majority opinion

RACE AND GENDER OF PRESIDING JUDGE	COEFFICIENT (S.E.)
White woman	0.682** (.199)
African American woman	0.661 (.492)
Hispanic woman	2.05** (.334)
African American man	0.356 (.342)
Hispanic man	0.867* (.393)
Asian American man	0.389 (.595)
N	7,088

Note: *p < .05 (two-tailed test); **p < .01 (two-tailed test). White men are the excluded reference category. Unanimous signed decisions from 1982 to 2008 using the Multi-User Database. For additional information on estimates for other variables, see table A11.

niority of each race-gender cohort (which affects how often a judge will have the opportunity to self-assign), they do point to some interesting differences in judicial behavior among race-gender cohorts. First, the African American women and Latina judges in our sample exhibit different assignment tendencies, despite their shared status as "double minorities." Latina judges were the most proactive subgroup among both all women and all racial and ethnic groups, assigning nearly half of all eligible cases to themselves. Among the three Latina judges, however, there is a great deal of variation in terms of connection to their Hispanic heritage. For instance, Kim Wardlaw's mother was the American-born daughter of Mexican immigrants, and Wardlaw's father was of Scottish heritage (http://ms-jd.org). Sonia Sotomayor was raised in New York City by Puerto Rican immigrants (Bazelon 2013). In contrast, Consuelo Callahan's Hispanic heritage comes from one set of grandparents from Spain (www.sacbar.org). While this variation and the small number of Hispanic women suggests we should be cautious in making generalizations about Latinas, it is notable that both Hispanic men and women engaged in self-assigning behavior more often than white men or white women. In the next section, we examine the voting behavior of minority women judges relative to other race-gender cohorts.

VOTING BEHAVIOR

Apart from the general observation that the intersection of race and gender may create distinctive experiences and disadvantages, what do we know about differences in attitudes across and within groups that might be reflected in judicial voting? The empirical research on race-gendered differences in attitudes is relatively scant, due in part to data limitations related to obtaining too few minority women in large, national samples. Additionally, public opinion polls do not always ask Hispanic respondents their nationality, which can affect generalizability of results as well. Yet the research that does exist sheds some light on this question.

In attitudes toward the judicial process, the legal system, and criminal justice issues, scholars have uncovered gender differences among African American respondents as well as among Hispanic respondents. For instance, Brooks and Jeon-Slaughter (2001) find that economically better-off African Americans and African American women have lower confidence in courts than do poor blacks and black men, respectively. Along these same lines, Sun and Wu (2006) find that black women hold more negative attitudes about the fairness of court procedures and outcome than do black men. Compared to Hispanic women, black women hold more negative attitudes as well. Bedolla, Monforti, and Pantoja (2006) find that Latinas are much less supportive of the death penalty than white women and Latino men. This fits with earlier public opinion studies that found Latinas to hold more liberal attitudes than Latinos.

Research on gender differences among members of the Hispanic community has noted that it may be problematic to ignore national origin when disaggregating the data. Montoya (1996) notes that individuals of Mexican ancestry differ from those from Puerto Rico and Cuba, though men and women from each subgroup have few differences. The only area where she finds a strong gender difference across all three nationalities is in attitudes about women's social and political roles, where Mexican women hold more modern views about women's roles than Puerto Rican women or Cuban women.

Finally, studies of elected officials and legislators suggest that minority women may view their roles as representatives in a more expansive way than minority men or white women. Fraga et al. (2006) interviewed Latina and Latino state officials in Arizona, California, Texas, and New Mexico and found that Latinas tended to prioritize building consensus and representing multiple minority groups more than Latinos. Two different studies of state legislators (Orey et al. 2006 and Bratton, Haynie, and Reingold 2006) indicate that African American female legislators are active in proposing both women's interest legislation as well as legislation that benefits African Americans.

To examine differences in voting behavior across different race and gender cohorts, we follow the approach taken in earlier chapters and construct a liberalism score for each circuit judge who participated in at least ten cases during the time period.

Figure 5 shows box plots of mean liberalism scores (weighted by the number of votes used to calculate the score) for each group, with higher values indicating greater liberalism and smaller values indicating greater conservatism in voting. Among all women, white women have the largest range of three female subgroups. While their median value (.4) is equivalent to African American women, the latter group has much less variance and a smaller interquartile range. The three Hispanic women, on the other hand, are substantially more liberal in their voting than any other subgroup among women or men. In fact, the most striking contrast between men and women of the same race is between Hispanic women and Hispanic men, who are the most conservative group on average. This gender gap in liberalism among Hispanics is consistent with public opinion findings in the literature (e.g., Bedolla, Monforti, and Pantoja 2006), though the liberalism of the particular Latinas included here is probably more a function of the judicial selection process than a reflection of Latinas in the general population.

Extrapolating from this research, as well as from the overall liberalism of the African American and Hispanic female judges during this time period, we hypothesize that women of color will be more likely than white women, minority men, or white men to take the liberal position in gender and race salient cases. To test this expectation, we utilize the Sunstein et al. (2006) dataset expanded

FIGURE 5 Box plots of voting records by race and gender cohorts, 1982–2008

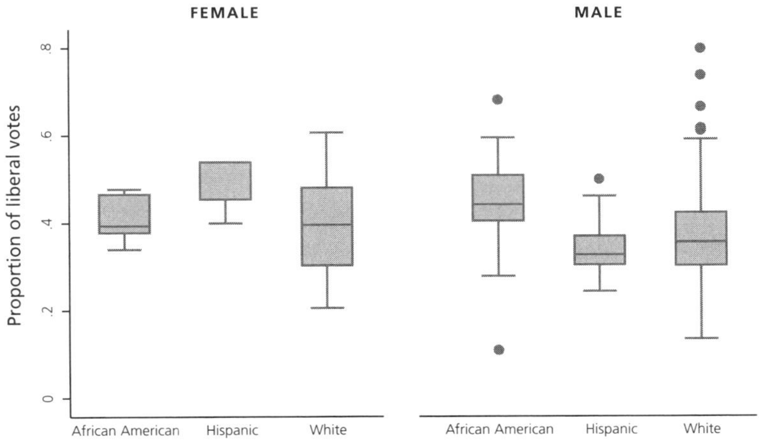

Note: N = 346. Data from the Multi-User Database on Decisions of the U.S. Courts of Appeals. Includes only appellate judges who cast at least ten votes during the time period of study (1982–2008). Weighted by number of votes cast. All issue areas included.

by Epstein, Landes, and Posner (2013), which includes published decisions from all circuits in several issue areas from 1995 to 2008. Despite the more limited time span compared to the Multi-User Database, these data include more observations from each issue area and more observations of nontraditional judges (something that is critical given the small numbers of black and Hispanic women on the bench).[8] We operationalize gender salience as sex discrimination cases and race salience as Title VII race cases and estimate separate logistic regression models on each of these case types.[9] The dependent variable in both models is a dichotomous measure indicating whether the judge cast a liberal (1) or a conservative (0) vote. To test the intersectional hypothesis, a series of dummy variables indicating both the race and gender of the judge was created, with white men as the excluded reference category.

In addition, a variety of ideological controls accounts for individual judge ideology (Giles, Hettinger, and Peppers [2001] liberalism scores), the composition of the remainder of the panel (Democrat-

TABLE 8 Logit model estimates for effects of judge race and gender on likelihood of liberal vote in salient cases

JUDGE RACE AND GENDER	GENDER-SALIENT MODEL	RACE-SALIENT MODEL
White woman	0.321* (.158)	0.117 (.176)
African American woman	0.599* (.364)	0.136 (.361)
African American man	0.332 (.242)	0.871** (.233)
Hispanic woman	0.195 (.559)	—
Hispanic man	0.251 (.303)	–0.010 (.335)
N	1,727	1,609

Note: **p < .05 (two-tailed test); *p < .05 (one-tailed test). Robust standard errors in parentheses. White men make up the excluded reference category. Both models use the Epstein, Landes, and Posner (2013) database, 1995–2008 votes. Hispanic women are dropped from race-salient model due to small numbers and insufficient variation. For additional information on estimates for other variables, see table A12.

Democrat, Democrat-Republican, with Republican-Republican as the excluded category), and the ideological preferences of the circuit (median Judicial Common Space score for the circuit-year). We expect that, all things being equal, more liberal judges, panels, and circuits will be positively associated with a liberal vote cast in a given case. Another variable controls for the ideological direction of the lower court decision (1 = conservative, 0 = liberal), which should be negatively related to a liberal vote. Finally, fixed effects for circuit and time were included.

Beginning with the gender salience model, we find mixed support for the expectation that minority women will be more likely to support the position of the plaintiff. Compared to white males, African American women are significantly more likely (at $p < .05$, one-tailed) to cast a liberal vote, as are white women. Holding all other variables at their modal or median values, the probability of a black woman casting a liberal vote while on a panel with two other Democrats is .49, compared to .42 for a white woman.[10] However, the coefficient for Latinas fails to achieve significance, against our expectations. There is also not a significant effect seen for African American men or Latinos.[11]

Next, in the race salience model, our hypothesis receives less support. The only demographic variable to achieve statistical significance is the variable for African American men, who are more likely to cast a liberal vote. The few observations with Latinas do not vary in this issue area, so this variable is dropped from the model. Alternative specifications that included capital punishment cases and affirmative action cases, alongside Title VII, yielded substantively identical results for our key variables. The control variables perform largely as expected.[12]

Overall, the findings from the voting models diverge somewhat from the conclusions of the legislative literature on women of color: namely, that minority women are especially active in "representing" both women's interests and the interests of their racial group. On the one hand, we find that African American female judges are especially likely to support the position of female plaintiffs in sex discrimination cases, suggesting that they view these claims differently than do African American men, Hispanic men and women, and white men. On the other hand, no sex difference appears in cases dealing with racial discrimination. One interpretation of these results is that black judges may engage in substantive representation for the issues most salient for them personally: for black women, this may be sex discrimination, while for black men, it may be discrimination based on race. More broadly, this underscores arguments made by intersectionality theorists that representation by minority women is not necessarily the sum of racism plus sexism, but rather a more nuanced and contextual process.

Conclusion

The diversification of the federal appellate courts has reflected an evolving understanding of what "diversity" itself means. White women have been the biggest beneficiaries of efforts to diversify, followed by African American men, Hispanic men, and then minority women. Indeed, by the end of George W. Bush's presidency in 2008, there had only been nine nonwhite women appointed to the federal appellate bench and no Asian women. The Latinas appointed did not have much in common in terms of a shared ethnic background (each had a very different connection to their Hispanic heritage), but as a group they were far more liberal in their voting behavior than their Latino counterparts. Nearly all of the minority women appointed had very similar professional backgrounds that include attending elite schools, government or public service, and prior judicial experience. This profile differs substantially from the typical career paths for white male judges (in which private practice experience plays a larger role) and suggests that minority women, like white women and minority men, may have to climb a different career ladder to prove their mettle—and ultimately, minority women may be lower priority appointees because being "female" is essentialized to mean a "white woman" and "minority" is essentialized to mean a minority man.

Moving next to our hypotheses about invisibility and marginalization, there is no clear evidence of marginalization of minority women, but we do find that certain race-gender cohorts of judges were especially assertive about assigning themselves the majority opinion. Hispanic women, Hispanic men, and white women were all significantly more likely to self-assign than white men. Self-assignment behavior may be an indicator of confidence and possibly career ambition, so one possible inference that may be drawn is that the individual judges in these groups are especially driven to make a name for themselves.

Building on chapters 1 and 2, we revisit the argument that judges will engage in substantive representation in salient cases. Here, we investigated whether African American and Hispanic women would be especially active in their support for women in sex discrimination cases and plaintiffs in race discrimination cases, as the legislative literature suggests. While both white and African American women were significantly more likely than white men to cast liberal votes in sex discrimination cases, the size of the effect for black women was much greater when compared to the effect for white women. In race discrimination cases, African American men (but not African American women) were more likely to cast liberal votes. While these results do not square with the conclusions of legislative scholars who find that black women engage in representation for both sex and race, they do offer strong support for an intersectional approach to studying substantive representation generally: race does not affect men and women in precisely the same way, and not all women react to sex discrimination claims in an identical manner. We believe that these are important contributions that judicial scholars should account for in future studies of judicial behavior.

Moving forward, the next chapter ties together the arguments raised in chapters 1, 2, and 3 by examining the ways that small-group dynamics on the panel are affected by the extent of diversification. Specifically, we examine competing perspectives on how heterogeneity affects small-group decision-making processes.

4

DIVERSITY ON THE PANEL

We are there to engage in a discussion; to explain why an argument is being rejected or a position is being espoused as logically preferable or at least, viable. That's the point of having three people on a panel . . . the idea is to subject an argument to multiple views. Each judge should engage in testing his or her position against the logic being advanced by another.

—Judge Rosemary Barkett

By having three judges decide an appeal together, different perspectives will be brought to bear on the panel as it examines claims of legal error and establishes binding precedent for the circuit. Because federal appellate judges must sit with one another repeatedly over the course of their time on a circuit, judges have pointed to the importance of collegial norms, which help "to create the conditions for principled agreement by allowing all points of view to be aired and considered" (Edwards 2003, 1645).

How might gender and racial diversity on an appellate panel affect these processes and their outputs? In the preceding chapters, we have identified a variety of conditions under which these demographic characteristics shape the individual behavior of judges, both in terms of their voting behavior and the opinions they write. But what, if anything, changes in the small group dynamic when there is diversity among the judges on the panel?

In this chapter, we test several perspectives advanced by social psychologists to explain these dynamics. One perspective suggests that stereotypes affect group members' expectations of each other and shape their interactions and evaluations of individual performance (see Correll and Ridgeway 2006). The resulting status hierarchies within a small group may undermine the ability of women and minorities to participate and diminish their influence as equals on the panel. A second perspective suggests that demographically mixed panels result in a broader range of viewpoints being aired. With more robust deliberative processes, panels should produce more thorough opinions due to more information processing among judges and the consideration of tradeoffs among alternatives (Suedfeld and Tetlock 1977; Gruenfeld 1995; Gruenfeld, Thomas-Hunt, and Kim 1998). Are these accounts mutually exclusive? Scholarship suggests that they are not; attribution processes and decision-making rules may condition the information exchanges in a small group. For instance, in groups where nontraditional judges make up a majority, deliberative norms can be more inclusive and facilitate information processing (Sommers 2006; Karpowitz, Mendelberg, and Shaker 2012).

The next section begins by explaining why appellate panels are appropriately conceptualized as small groups. Then, building on these insights, we investigate how well the theoretical perspectives on small group diversity mentioned above explain three kinds of legal outputs: separate opinions, the content of the majority opinion, and variability in judicial voting.

Small Group Decision Making on the U.S. Courts of Appeals

Though there are a number of variations in how each circuit court manages caseloads, the process by which a case comes before a panel is relatively similar, starting with the random assignment of three judges to the panel. Exceptions are made to this general practice, particularly when cases are related to each other in terms of issues, litigants, or facts (Cohen 2002). For cases that are orally argued, interchamber communication over a case typically does not take place prior to that point.[1] Judges may pose questions to attorneys during argument that convey their own ideas about the legal issues (Wasby 1977). Following oral argument, the judges meet in conference for a face-to-face discussion of the case. After conference, the presiding judge typically drafts a memo that outlines the positions of the members of the panel with an indication of their collective judgment (Cohen 2002). The presiding judge next assigns the opinion to a member of the panel. Once the majority opinion has been drafted, it is circulated to members of the panel, who then respond to the draft (Cohen 2002). D.C. Circuit Judge Edwards observed that "coming to a multi-judge agreement is not a straightforward matter of voting for one side or another. Rather, it is a complex interplay of reasoning that may be overlapping, continuous, related, or opposed, and which must, if we do our job well, ultimately distill to a clear holding that tells the parties and future litigants what the law is" (2003, 1662).

In a thoughtful essay on the utility of conceptualizing appellate panels as small groups, Martinek (2010) lays the foundation for adopting this approach in studies of federal courts of appeals' decision making. First, she notes that circuit judges interact on a regular basis and value their collegial ties with one another (see also Cohen 2002; Howard 1981; Edwards 2003; Baum 2006, 56–57). For example, one circuit judge explained, "With the advent of email, we are constantly in touch, back and forth. It could be about educational seminars, it could be about our cases, it could be about our families" (Moyer 2008, 199). Another judge emphasized the importance of good relations with colleagues, given the strains of being a federal judge: "There's a great deal of collegiality in this business, and if there weren't, it'd be a horrible job. The judges, of necessity . . . do sort of have to get . . . cloistered, away from all the good old buddies and lawyers we've all enjoyed so much. So we have to work with each other, and we can disagree without being disagreeable about it. Usually, we can do it heatedly if necessary, because we're serious about it, but then get together for lunch. It's a family" (Moyer 2008, 199–200).

Second, the institutional environment of these appellate courts and decision-making practices promotes adherence to shared legal norms that guide three-judge panels as they render a collective judgment (Martinek 2010). Judge Frank Coffin has characterized such rules and conventions as "centripetal craft forces": various appellate rules of procedure, rules of evidence, stare decisis, and canons of statutory construction (1994, 259–60). Although various methods of legal reasoning may not operate to limit judicial discretion (Posner 2008), they do provide a common frame of reference for the appellate panel as the judges formulate the *ratio decidendi* underlying their decision.

Finally, Martinek (2010) emphasizes that appellate review on a collegial court requires behavioral interdependence through the exercise of majority rule. One appeals court judge described the opinion-writing process in these terms: "Let me tell you what the most important skill in the procedure of writing an opinion is. It's being able to count to three. You're not writing an opinion unless you get a majority" (Moyer 2008, 195). Another judge echoed these comments when asked whether judges wrote their opinions for any particular audience: "First, of all, for my colleagues. To persuade them. They have to be the primary audience. And if I manage to persuade them, then everything follows" (Moyer 2008, 195). As these quotes suggest, judges recognize the importance of majority rule; however, this rule may only reinforce an existing interest in persuading one's colleagues (Baum 2006, 60).

All members of an appellate panel share a common identity as circuit judges and value norms, such as collegiality and adherence to precedent, that reinforce the status quo. Yet within each panel, other social identities like those associated with race and gender are also likely to shape influence and deliberations on the panel. In the next section, we elaborate on the theoretical perspectives about diversity mentioned in the introduction to the chapter and subject these perspectives to empirical tests.

Theoretical Perspectives on Diversity

DIVERSITY, STATUS, AND EXPECTATIONS

Expectation states theory posits that status hierarchies, including those based on race and gender, emerge in those situations where individuals are focused on accomplishing a collective goal or task. The shared focus on the group's goal heightens expectations for individuals themselves as well as for others regarding their contributions to the work of the group (Correll and Ridgeway 2006; Martinek 2010). These expectations may be based on external status characteristics in our society, such as gender and race, which have been used to shape widespread beliefs about an individual's performance (Correll and Ridgeway 2006). In support of this theory, research finds that women and minorities are frequently undervalued in surveys that ask respondents to compare them to white men in terms of opportunities to perform, performance evaluations, and influence (Lucas and Baxter 2012, 54). Examining behavior rather than thought, this perspective also emphasizes how the iterative nature of these status-generalizing processes generates widespread societal patterns of inequality not limited to interactions with those individuals who hold prejudicial beliefs (Correll and Ridgeway 2006). In experiments, scholars find that subjects' propensities to accept influence from a partner are affected by the status characteristics of their partner relative to themselves. This is true for gender (Pugh and Wahrman 1983) and race (Webster and Driskell 1978). In another experimental setting, racial minorities had to demonstrate higher levels of competence than whites in order for participants to consider them as able to carry out a task successfully (Biernat and Kobrynowicz 1997).

As noted earlier, attempts to persuade others are frequent occurrences among those sitting on three-judge panels. Expectation states theory suggests that these attempts will be shaped by stereotypes that reflect status-generalizing processes. According to this account, on diverse panels, judges will hold negative performance expectations for those with lower relative status (for example, female and minority judges) compared to those with higher status (for example, white male judges).

Ideally, a test of expectation states theory would utilize data on interchamber communications; however, because panel deliberations take place outside of public view, we can only evaluate the explanatory power of this perspective using proxy measures, such as the outputs of decisional processes.

DIVERSITY AS SUPERADDITIVITY

While expectation states theory predicts that small group diversity may negatively affect group functioning (by causing individuals to rely on stereotypes that devalue the contributions of women and minorities), a second theoretical perspective that we refer to as superadditivity (Page 2007) emphasizes the information-processing benefits that can result from diversity within a group.

Supported by social science research on demographically diverse groups (Schweiger, Sandberg, and Rechner 1989), scholars have found that group attempts to brainstorm yield better ideas when the group is racially mixed (McLeod, Lobel, and Cox 1996). Research also suggests that the expression of a minority viewpoint promotes more thorough decision making, whereas homogenous groups are less likely to identify and consider alternatives (Stasser and Birchmeier 2003; Nemeth 1986; Janis 1972). When a group is composed of like-minded individuals, members tend to focus on shared information and reach consensus on a position that potentially fails to identify errors (Sunstein 2003).

Jury studies suggest potential decision-making benefits for demographically diverse groups. Comparing racially mixed and all-white mock juries, Sommers (2006) found the diverse jury deliberated longer, with more citations to case facts and fewer errors in fact finding. Another study reports that this effect is not due to the expression of views by minorities; instead, the effect is associated with different information processes used by white participants in racially mixed groups (Sommers, Warp, and Mahoney 2008). Small, integrated work groups can also enhance the performance of African American members—compared to their performance in segregated work groups (Ruhe and Eatman 1977).

Together, these studies suggest an account of group performance in which the overall dynamic of the group is something more than the contributions of the component members (Page 2007; Gruenfeld and Hollingshead 1993; Sommers, Warp, and Mahoney 2008). Described by scholars as group cognition, "individuals in social interaction . . . engage in active reconciliation and integration processes, leading to the emergence of ideas, representations, solutions, and arguments . . . that no individual had to begin with" (Gruenfeld and Hollingshead 1993, 385). Having a variety of backgrounds and experiences represented among members is expected to facilitate group cognition (Jehn, Northcraft, and Neale 1999, 741–42).

As applied to the context of decision making on the federal courts of appeals, the superadditivity account predicts that diverse panels should follow deliberative processes characterized by greater information acquisition due to varying demographic traits. The degree to which diversity affects deliberations should then be related to the range of backgrounds on the panel.

Analyzing the Link between Panel Diversity and Separate Opinions

The theoretical accounts reviewed above offer vastly different views on diversity and small group decision making as it applies to appellate panels. To evaluate each of these perspectives empirically, we first investigate whether one visible output of panel decision making, separate opinion writing, is linked to the composition of the panel.

Following deliberations, a member of the panel may disagree with the majority's decision and inform panel members of his or her intent to file a dissenting opinion (in whole or in part). Very rarely, a judge may file a concurring opinion in which he or she agrees with the outcome of the majority but writes separately to record a preference for a holding on different legal grounds, to discuss limits in the majority opinion, or to expand on the reasoning in the majority opinion (Hettinger, Lindquist, and Martinek 2006, 18). But could the decision to write separately also be shaped by perceptions of, and reactions to, the identity of the majority opinion author, as suggested by expectation states theory? Are panels made up of demographically homogenous judges (that is, white males) more likely to agree on the holding, consistent with the superadditivity account?

First, if expectations about poor performance and status generalizing processes operate on the panel, there should be a higher incidence of concurring and dissenting opinions filed by white males when the majority opinion is written by a nontraditional (that is, minority and/or female) judge. To test this hypothesis, we identified all white male participations (excluding those as opinion author) in cases decided by three-judge panels from 1982 to 2008 in the Multi-User Database of Decisions of the U.S. Courts of Appeals. In a cross-tabulation of these participations, however, we did not find a statistically significant relationship between the demographic identity of the majority opinion author and the incidence of separate opinions authored by white men on the panel.

But because dissenting and concurring opinions have different effects on collegiality (Hettinger, Lindquist, and Martinek 2006), a dichotomous measure of the decision to file a separate opinion may obscure differences that appear when the two types of opinions are disaggregated from each other. Moreover, we need to control for other influences on decisions to write separately including those associated with the judge's policy preferences, the judge's age, the salience of the issue area, and position of the judge on the court below. To account for these factors, we construct two statistical models that also adjust for the relative rarity of a concurring or dissenting opinion.[2]

The results for most control variables (as reported in table A14 in the appendix) are statistically significant and signed in the expected direction. For instance, a white male is less likely to file a separate opinion when the majority opinion advocates a policy outcome that is consistent with his ideology. He is also more likely to disagree with the position of the majority opinion when seated with two judges of the opposing party, and when the appeal resulted in a reversal or raised questions of constitutional interpretation. Nevertheless, the estimates from both models for our variables of interest support our conclusion from the bivariate analysis: white male judges' decisions to disagree with the majority are not related to the gender or race of the majority opinion author. In other words, we find no evidence that this aspect of judicial behavior reflects lower performance expectations for nontraditional judges. While performance expectations may affect other aspects of the deliberative process, separate opinion writing appears to be driven by other considerations.

Next, we turn to the second perspective on diversity in small groups we described earlier: superadditivity. This is the premise that diversity introduces a range of differing viewpoints into small group decision-making processes. While much of the literature on superadditivity emphasizes the positive aspects of having different perspectives represented, in the context of an appellate panel needing to reach a decision by majority rule, this may also present challenges.

One way that this dynamic might be observed is by looking at whether the panel was able to reach a unanimous decision. With more perspectives represented, it should be more difficult for three judges to come to agreement. Thus, demographically homogenous panels should be more likely to come to unanimous decisions, while highly heterogeneous panels should be more likely to yield nonunanimous decisions.

To assess these expectations, we first calculated the proportion of decisions with a separate opinion for three-judge panels that included only white male circuit judges. We then compared those proportions to those for heterogeneous panels on which no judge was seated with his or her demographic match in terms of race and gender. For example, a heterogeneous panel would be one that had a white male, African American female, and Hispanic male because no two judges match on race and gender. On panels made up of three white male judges, the proportion of decisions that included a concurring or dissenting opinion was 13 percent. Decisions by heterogeneous panels were slightly more likely to yield a separate opinion at 16 percent. However, because these figures do not account for other influences on separate opinion writing, we then estimated two rare event logit models of separate opinions and dissenting opinions, including controls. (The results of these models appear in the appendix, table A15.)

Recall that the superadditivity account suggests that heterogeneous panels should be associated with a higher likelihood of separate opinion writing because of all the perspectives generated during the group decision-making process. As the estimates from both models indicate, heterogeneous panels were no more likely than other panels to produce a separate opinion.[3] Thus, it seems that greater panel diversity does not result in the formal expression of divergent views through separate opinions.

Analyzing Deliberative Outputs in Unanimous Cases: Majority Opinions

Having seen that panel dynamics related to diversity do not appear to exert much of an influence on non-unanimous decision behavior, we turn now to the deliberative outputs that are the most common in the federal courts of appeals: unanimous decisions. What role does panel diversity play in these decision-making processes? In this section, we focus on processes related to the content of the majority opinion and empirically test predictions from both the expectation states and superadditivity accounts.

Research consistently shows that courts of appeals judges are responsive to the preferences of their colleagues on the panel (Kim 2009; Kastellec 2007; Farhang and Wawro 2004; Sunstein et al. 2006). For instance, panels that include judges with diverging ideological predispositions yield outcomes that are more moderate than what one would predict by the position of the median judge (Sunstein 2003; Spitzer and Talley 2013; Cross and Tiller 1998). With respect to demographic diversity, scholars have also observed that male judges on the courts of appeals are systematically affected by the presence of a female judge on the panel when deciding employment discrimination claims (Boyd, Epstein, and Martin 2010; Farhang and Wawro 2004; Peresie 2005). Recent research also finds that panels are more likely to support affirmative action if an African American judge is seated on the panel (Kastellec 2012).

Evaluating panel influences on case outcomes is relatively straightforward because the votes of judges are recorded in published opinions; however, because of the closed nature of the judicial process, scholars have struggled to identify how much (and what types of) interaction occurs during the opinion-writing stage in unanimous cases. There are, however, a few studies that have generated insights on panel deliberations.[4] In their analysis of an extensive private archive of a retired D.C. Circuit judge, Black and Owens (2013) find that about three-fourths of responses by panel judges to draft opinions were indications that the judge would join; however, 13 percent of the responses were suggestions or requests to delay. The remaining responses were indications by the judge that he or she intended (or threatened) to write separately. Appellate judges themselves also chronicle the robust give-and-take that occurs in the process of trying to hash out a unanimous majority opinion (Edwards 2003; Tacha 1996; Coffin 1994).

Building from this discussion, this set of analyses uses the theoretical perspectives highlighted earlier in the chapter to generate hypotheses about how panel diversity will affect the number of points of law in the majority opinion. We begin with the claim associated with the superadditvity account that the inclusion of different perspectives will produce greater information acquisition in the deliberative process. Therefore, the degree to which diversity affects deliberations should be related to the range of backgrounds on the panel. Decisions by demographically homogenous panels should be characterized by a limited range of viewpoints (and fewer points of law) than decisions by demographically mixed panels.

We test this prediction following the approach taken by Haire,

Moyer, and Treier (2013) in their analysis of majority opinion content.[5] They estimate models using a measure of the points of law in the majority opinion, which is based upon Westlaw's case headnotes (also called the "key number system"). When any appellate court issues an opinion for publication, trained attorneys at West Publishing analyze the opinion and identify the points of law that are presented in the final published form as headnotes. The entire system of key numbers covers roughly 400 major topics and many more subtopics, and is relied upon by both legal academics and practitioners (including judges) engaged in legal research.[6] This measure, available in the Multi-User Database only for 1997–2002, provides an indicator of the number of points of law addressed in the court's opinion. (It does not, however, speak to whether an opinion is qualitatively "better" in terms of doctrine, as this is a very subjective determination and outside our scope of inquiry.)

Limited to unanimous decisions by three-judge panels of circuit court judges (that excludes panels with non–appeals court judges, including district court judges sitting by designation), the data used here are a subset of those analyzed by Haire, Moyer, and Treier (2013). The distribution of this variable does not vary substantially by issue area; it is positively skewed and ranges from 0 to 86, with a mean of 10.8 and the median value falling at 9.

If, as suggested by the superadditivity account, information processing increases with the range of views and backgrounds on the panel, we would expect to see fewer points of law in opinions generated by all white male panels and higher points of law associated with panels where there was at least one nontraditional judge. Panels on which each judge brings a different demographic background should yield opinions with the highest number of points of law.

A comparison of the average points of law for these various panel configurations provides modest support for that premise. The mean number of points of law for an all white male panel opinion is 10.6; for demographically mixed panels, the figure is 10.9. Panels made up of three judges who did not share a demographic identity (with respect to race and gender) yielded opinions with an average of 11.4 points of law.

Because many factors influence the attention to issues in a majority opinion, we estimate a statistical model that includes a measure of demographic diversity, as well as controls for ideological diversity on the panel, circuit level dissensus and variations in opinion-writing practices, and other case-level factors (Haire, Moyer, and Treier 2013). Because the dependent variable is a count (the number of points of law) rather than a continuous variable, an ordinary least squares model is inappropriate. For this reason, we estimate a negative binomial regression model to account for unobserved heterogeneity among observations.

Our first model evaluates the impact of mixed panels (that is, at least one judge is a female or minority) against all white male panels in unanimous decisions that were heard by three courts of appeals judges. Then, in a second model, we examine the effect of panels where no judge has a demographic match in terms of race and gender, compared to all other panels.

Table 9 shows the coefficients (and standard errors) for the effects of demographically mixed (model 1) and heterogeneous panels (model 2). Although the effect for demographically mixed panels is not statistically significant, the effect of demographic diversity in model 2 has a positive and marginally significant effect, as predicted, on the number of points of law ($p = .054$). We use the estimates from model 2 to predict points of law for heterogeneous panels, comparing their outputs to those of panels where at least two judges were from the same demographic cohort. The predictions are calculated for decisions by the Sixth Circuit, a court that was demographically diverse during this time period. The predicted number of points of law for a Sixth Circuit panel where at least two judges match on

TABLE 9 Negative binomial regression model estimates for effects of demographic composition of panel on points of law

	MODEL 1: MIXED PANEL	MODEL 2: HETEROGENEOUS PANEL
Coefficient (S.E.)	0.050 (.04)	0.099+ (.062)
N	1,294	1,294

Note: +p < .10 (one-tailed test). Includes only unanimous cases decided from 1997 to 2002 using the Multi-User Database. For additional information on estimates for other variables, see models 1 and 2 in table A16.

race and gender is 10.6. In comparison, the predicted number of points of law for decisions by a completely heterogeneous panel in the Sixth Circuit is higher, 11.7.

Connecting back to theoretical perspectives on small group diversity, the results from these two models provide only partial support for the superadditivity account. Namely, heterogeneous panels are associated with more points of law, but demographically mixed panels are not; what this tells us is that not all diverse panels have a significant impact on deliberative outputs. In terms of expectation states theory, the nonfinding for demographically mixed panels is consistent with the premise that the presence of a single nontraditional judge (with respect to gender or race) on the panel would *not* lead to more robust deliberations because the contributions of such individuals would not be solicited or valued.[7]

Thus far, our examination of deliberative outputs in unanimous decisions yields puzzling findings where we do not observe similar effects across demographically mixed panels. Why? In this next section, we consider an alternative perspective to account for these diverging findings. During this deliberative process, we posit that it is relevant to consider who is in the demographic majority of the panel in order to understand fully the effects of diversity on deliberative outputs. Given the dominance of white males in positions of power and the historical underrepresentation of women and minority officeholders in political and legal institutions, one would expect that norms guiding small group deliberations, including those associated with information processing, will reflect these status hierarchies. The influence of a single female or minority may be particularly limited in contributing to group deliberations because norms of interaction are defined by the majority group: white males (Kanter 1977).

Being in the numerical minority in a small group may compound the effects of status. For example, Johnson and Schulman (1989) found that women's influence is rated lower when they are in a numerical minority and that the effect of numerical minority status is greater on women than on men. A more recent study of influence in small group deliberations (Karpowitz, Mendelberg, and Shaker 2012) also found that women are disadvantaged when they are the lone female member of their group and that men are not similarly disadvantaged when they are the only member of their gender group. However, increasing representation of women altered these dynamics. Overall, women did not have the same level of voice and authority when compared to male participants, but the gender disparity plummeted when the proportion of women in the deliberating group exceeded 50 percent (Karpowitz, Mendelberg, and Shaker 2012, 542).

Applied to the context of appellate panel decision making, this research suggests that nontraditional judges may be more influential when constituting a numerical majority on the panel because the norms of interaction are defined by women and minorities rather than by white males. According to Karpowitz and colleagues, "getting the relevant facts, insights, and perspectives into the deliberation is not enough for substantive representation; it is also necessary that many members of the disadvantaged group air those facts, insights, and perspectives and that they do so more than once" (2012, 545). In small groups, like appellate panels, where decisions are made by majority rule, the gender gap in influence narrowed only when the proportion of women exceeded a majority (Karpowitz, Mendelberg, and Shaker 2012). For similar reasons, we expect a smaller effect when the level of diversity on a panel is at its minimum (that is, one nontraditional judge) and greater when the number of women or minority judges on the panel increases to the point that there is a shift in the demographic majority on the panel (that is, two nontraditional judges).

Below, we initially evaluate this prediction by examining the mean points of law for varying panels, beginning with the baseline, three white male judges, and increasing numbers of nontraditional (female and/or minority) judges. The mean number of points of law for opinions issued by panels with all white males was 10.7. In comparison, the mean for panels made up of two white males and one nontraditional judge was almost identical, 10.8. When the panel majority shifts to nontraditional judges, the mean points of law in the opinion is somewhat higher (11.2).

To assess this difference when other factors are controlled for, we estimate a model as highlighted in table 10. The estimated coefficient evaluating the effect of a single nontraditional judge on the panel (relative to the excluded category, all white male panels) is not statistically significant and suggests that a token nontraditional

TABLE 10 Negative binomial regression model estimates for effects of varying levels of demographic diversity on points of law

	COEFFICIENT (S.E.)
Single nontraditional judge on panel	0.038 (.042)
Demographic majority is nontraditional	0.095* (.058)
N	1,294

Note: *p = .05 (one-tailed test). Includes only unanimous cases decided from 1997 to 2002 using the Multi-User Database. For additional information on estimates for other variables, see models 3 and 4 in table A16.

judge on the panel does not affect the deliberative content of the majority opinion. Panels with three white males and panels with token diversity produce opinions with very similar issue coverage: an estimated 10.1 versus 10.4 points of law, all else equal. In comparison, the effect of panels made up of two or more nontraditional judges suggests that this demographic shift matters. Holding control variables at their means, panels made up of two nontraditional judges are estimated to produce majority opinions that address about 10 percent more points of law (11.1) than opinions from all white male panels. Taken together, these figures lend modest support to the proposition that status-based processes minimize the potential contributions of token women and minority judges in panel deliberations. When the makeup of the panel majority shifts away from white males, status quo decisional norms may begin to shift as well, resulting in greater attention to issues in the majority opinion.

In their analysis of the effects of panel diversity on the coverage of issues in the majority opinion, Haire, Moyer, and Treier (2013) sorted panels into groups based on the demographic traits of the majority opinion writer compared to the other two members of the panel. Panels comprised of all white males wrote majority opinions with the fewest number of points of law. Relative to this baseline, each of the other combinations wrote opinions that were more thorough in their coverage of the issues. Moreover, their results found that the presence of a token nontraditional judge on the panel can result in more points of law, but only if that judge is the majority opinion writer.

Panel Diversity and Variability in Voting

Lastly, we return to white male judges and their reactions to panel diversity. In the first section of the chapter, we found no evidence that white men reacted to opinions authored by nontraditional judges by penning separate opinions. In the second section, the results pointed to the continued influence of deliberative norms shaped by white males, unless nontraditional judges make up the majority on the panel or are the majority opinion writer. The final aspect of panel diversity we now turn to is the impact of nontraditional judges (and the different perspectives they bring) on the voting behavior of white male judges.

As discussed earlier, scholarship on "panel effects" in the courts of appeals has found that male judges are more likely to adopt a pro-plaintiff position in sex discrimination cases when seated with a female judge (Boyd, Epstein, and Martin 2010) and that the presence of African American judges has a similar effect on white judges' decisions in affirmative action cases (Kastellec 2013). Underlying these findings is the view that judicial diversity may be expected to shift the decision making employed by white males who are responding to the presence of women and minority judges. If these shifts are changes in decision-making processes used by white males, we would expect them to exhibit less consistency in their votes—regardless of the issue area—when seated on panels with women and minorities.

Scholarship increasingly suggests that understanding the dynamics surrounding judges' decisions requires greater attention to those factors that shape the consistency of judicial choice (Collins 2008, 2011; Bartels 2011). We follow the approach taken by recent research that analyzes variability in judicial voting and employ a heteroskedastic probit model of decisions by white male judges (Kaheny, Haire, and Benesh 2008).

The theoretical perspectives discussed in this chapter advance differing predictions about the connection between panel diversity and white male voting. Recall that under the superadditivity account, diverse groups bring in more alternatives and engage in more thorough information processing as they make collective decisions. The effect of diversity is more than just the sum of the individual parts:

it affects the decisional processes of all members of the group. Thus, this perspective predicts that white males' voting behavior should be more variable when they sit on panels with women and/or minority judges. In contrast, expectation states theory suggests that white male judges' voting behavior will not be responsive to the presence of one (or more) female or minority judges.

Our review of existing scholarship, and findings above, also emphasized the importance of taking into account the demographic composition of the majority (Karpowitz, Mendelberg, and Shaker 2012; Johnson and Schulman 1989). From this perspective, the effects of panel diversity on a white male judge will be different depending on whether he is in the demographic majority on the panel (that is, seated with other white males) or in the demographic minority (that is, seated with two women and/or minorities).

To test these expectations, we specify a model of judicial choice advanced in our earlier chapters and restrict the observations to votes by white males. Following the approach taken by recent scholarship (Kaheny, Haire, and Benesh 2008; Collins 2008), we utilize an error variance model to investigate why judges have greater underlying and unobserved variability in their voting behavior. Specifically, this allows us to test whether white male judges' votes are more variable when sitting on panels with minority or female judges.

In looking at the model of vote choice—whether a judge supports a liberal or conservative outcome—the results reinforce findings reported in previous research. White male judges' decisions are influenced by their ideology, the preferences of colleagues on the panel, the policy predisposition of the circuit, and other case-level and institutional factors (Kaheny, Haire, and Benesh 2008; Songer, Sheehan, and Haire 2000).[8] Turning our attention to the variance model, we include predictors identified from previous research as factors that influence consistency of vote choice, such as career stage, ideological extremism, and circuit size (Collins 2008; Kaheny, Haire, and Benesh 2008). Table 11 presents results for our variables of interest about the effects of the demographic composition of a panel on the error variance.

The results of the variance model indicate that white males' voting is indeed less predictable when sitting on panels that are demographically diverse. This supports the expectation from superaddi-

TABLE 11 Error variance model estimates for effects of panel diversity on consistency in voting

	COEFFICIENT (S.E.)
White male in the majority: sitting with one nontraditional judge	0.029 (.043)
White male in the minority: sitting with two nontraditional judges	.182* (.109)
N	11,625

Note: *p < .05 (two-tailed test). The reference category is a white male seated with two white males. Detailed results of heteroskedastic probit model appear in table A17.

tivity theory and is in opposition to what expectation states theory suggests. However, there is a caveat: voting by white male judges became less predictable in the presence of women and minorities to a statistically significant degree only when there were no other white males on the panel. This is consistent with our earlier findings that suggest status-generalizing processes can mitigate the influence of a single minority or female judge on the panel.

Conclusion

This chapter approached the issue of diversity from a different angle than previous chapters: the small group dynamics of panel decision making. We focused on testing theoretical perspectives about the impact of heterogeneous and homogeneous panels on legal outputs and the behavior of the dominant demographic group: white males.

In the first section, our analysis of separate opinion writing by white men did not uncover any evidence that this behavior was a reaction to lower status and performance expectations of women and/or minority opinion authors. However, in the third section, we do find that white males were affected by the demographic composition of their panel. The error variance analysis shows that white men became more variable in their voting behavior when seated on heterogeneous panels, which suggests that the input from judges with different backgrounds shifts their own voting tendencies. This finding lines up with other research showing that men are more likely to support plaintiffs in sex discrimination cases when seated with women judges (Boyd, Epstein, and Martin 2010) and that white judges are more likely to cast liberal votes in affirmative action cases when seated with African American judges (Kastellec 2013).

Superadditivity theory, which argues that heterogeneity can stimulate more robust small group decision-making processes, receives some support in our analyses. Compared to panels of three white males, those panels on which no judge matched another with respect to race and gender produced opinions reflective of more thorough deliberative processes, as indicated by the number of points of law. While expectation states theory did not emerge as a strong explanation for the panel behaviors tested here, the results from this chapter do provide some support for the premise that numbers and status within the group matter when it comes to influencing legal outputs. For instance, the presence of a single nontraditional judge did not increase the number of points of law in the majority opinion, unless that judge was the opinion author (Haire, Moyer, and Treier 2013). Likewise, the consistency of white males' voting behavior was unaffected when only one nontraditional judge was seated on the panel. As Mansbridge (1999, 636) observed, "in theory, deliberation seems to require only a single representative, or a 'threshold' presence, in the deliberation to contribute to the larger understanding . . . [but] in practice . . . disadvantaged groups often need the full representation that proportionality allows."

Drawing from these insights about diversity at the aggregate level, the next chapter considers how shifts in the overall demographic composition of each circuit have contributed to changes in judicial policy making and court norms.

5

DIVERSITY WITHIN THE CIRCUITS

It was a very exciting time for the federal judiciary. . . . It shocked a lot of people when we had our first ceremonial sitting of the Ninth Circuit. There was a Hispanic judge with a beard and a black robe sitting right in the middle of the first row.

—Judge Mary Schroeder

As the federal judiciary began to experience changes in the kind of individuals appointed to the appellate bench, this transformation was felt differently in each circuit. Some courts, like the Ninth Circuit, saw a relatively rapid influx of nontraditional judges, as presidents appointed women and minority judges to new or vacant seats in quick succession. In other circuits, change was slower or limited to either (white) women or minority (male) judges, but not both. From the previous chapters, we have seen that the level of diversity on a panel can have important effects on the behavior of judges individually and collectively on the panel. But were judges similarly affected by factors like the overall percentage of nontraditional judges in the circuit, or the presence of a female or minority chief judge?

Below, we begin by describing major theoretical perspectives about diversity within organizations and discuss their applicability to the court environment. We then test several expectations suggested by these perspectives about the impact of courtwide diversity on legal outputs. In particular, we build on the findings from chapter 2 that point to differences between men and women judges in promoting consensus, and findings from chapters 1 and 2 that identify issue areas where women and racial minorities vote in distinctive ways.

Theoretical Perspectives on Diversity within Organizations

CRITICAL MASS

Probably the most commonly used framework for analyzing the impact of diversity at the organizational level is the concept of "critical mass." A foundational study for research in this area is Rosabeth Moss Kanter's 1977 book, *Men and Women of the Corporation.* In this book, Kanter argues that when those from minority groups reach a certain proportion, they become individuals who are distinguished from one another and can form coalitions that affect the organization's culture (1977, 209). The flip side of this assertion is that when the levels of women or minorities in an organization fall below this point, individuals may try to downplay their differences, or they may simply have less success in accomplishing their goals because of their small numbers (e.g., Saint-Germain 1989; Thomas 1991, 1994; Grey 2002; but see Bratton 2005; Wolbrecht 2000). Tokens within an organization can experience heightened performance pressures, isolation, or role entrapment into particular stereotypes for their group (Childs and Krook 2006).

In 1988, Dahlerup adapted Kanter's framework to the legislative context in her study of women's representation in Scandinavian countries. Dahlerup identified a range of possible effects that could result from changing the proportion of female legislators: changes in the reaction to women politicians, changes in the performance and efficiency of women politicians, changes in political culture and discourse, policy changes, and the empowerment of women (2006, 513). It should be noted that while the term "critical mass" has become fairly widespread both in academic and policy circles (see Dahlreup 2006 for an overview), the term is sometimes construed to mean that policy change occurs at a specific critical mass point (for example, 15 or 30 percent) and in other places used to emphasize behavioral differences that occur at multiple levels of proportionality (Beckwith 2007).

Most empirical applications of the critical mass perspective focus on the representation of women in corporations, bureaucratic agencies, and legislative institutions, rather than courts. Indeed, the limited amount of scholarship about critical mass within judicial institutions draws largely from theories articulated in the legislative literature (Moyer 2013; Collins, Manning, and Carp 2010; McCall 2008). For this reason, we begin by drawing from research examining nonjudicial organizations and then discuss the insights most relevant for the federal courts of appeals.

Critical mass studies of legislative institutions raise important questions for thinking about diversity in the federal appellate court context. For example, is a certain level of women or minorities necessary for changes in institutional outputs to be observed? Answers to this question in the legislative context have been largely dependent on measurement, with the most common threshold used for critical mass being 15 percent.[1] However, some scholars have found evidence that a critical mass may occur at points both higher and lower than 15 percent. Bratton (2005) shows that in "skewed" state legislatures (where the percentage of women falls below 15 percent), women are able to be as effective as men in accomplishing their legislative agendas. Looking at race and critical mass in educational organizations, Meier and Stewart (1992) find that 25 percent seems to be the relevant tipping point for seeing an impact on student performance, but that this is true only at the management level.

A related question is whether the increasing presence of an "out-group" (such as women and minorities) can trigger negative reactions from individuals that represent the dominant group within the organization (here: white men). Viewed this way, the more diverse an institution becomes, the less effective minority individuals will be in accomplishing their goals. This "backlash effect" has been discussed in the context of women's participation within legislative institutions (Yoder 1991; Kathlene 1994) and courts (Kenney 2013), though others dispute this interpretation (Thomas 1991, 1994).

Another question raised in the critical mass literature has to do with the outcome being studied. What precisely does it mean to "make a difference"? A central claim of the critical mass literature, as applied to political institutions, is that greater representation of women or minorities should lead to substantive policy outcomes that benefit those groups. However, there is disagreement within this literature about which policy areas count as substantive representation, particularly in terms of women's representation (see Childs and Krook 2006, 526). For instance, some dispute the inclusion of abortion rights as a "women's issue," and prefer to call it a "feminist" issue (see Bratton 2005 for an overview). As we have discussed in chapter 3, the intersection of race and gender (as well as other characteristics) can also lead varying interpretations of what substantive representation means (Smooth 2011). And beyond substantive policy outputs, others have argued that increased gender and racial diversity within an organization can change the culture and norms of the organization, as well as its performance (Pitts 2005, 617–18). As we have already seen in chapter 4, a mixture of gender and racial diversity on panels is associated with outputs that are consistent with increased deliberation on the panel.

While only a few studies have applied the critical mass framework to the court context, they all share in common an emphasis upon gender and less so on racial and ethnic diversity.[2] Both McCall (2008) and Collins, Manning, and Carp (2010) find that increases in the number of women judges serving in state supreme courts and federal district courts are linked to an increased likelihood that an individual female judge will make a liberal decision in a criminal case. Moyer (2013) focused on the federal courts of appeals and found that the more often a mixed sex panel was comprised within a circuit, the more likely both male and female judges were to side with plaintiffs in civil rights cases. However, this result only held in the 1982 to 1994 time period, before all of Clinton's appointees had joined the appellate bench.

Like state supreme courts (McCall 2008), the federal courts of appeals utilize multimember panels to decide cases. However, unlike state supreme courts, the practice of using rotating panels with random assignment effectively guarantees that every judge in the circuit will sit with every other judge at some point (more often in smaller circuits, less often in larger ones). Additionally, judges become acquainted with one another through court meetings, en bancs, and social events hosted by the legal community. Through all of these interactions, women and minority judges were able to gauge the reactions of their colleagues to the increasing diversification of the court. Oral histories and interviews with nontraditional appointees offer a vivid picture of specific experiences and suggest a causal mechanism behind the critical mass argument. How, precisely, can an outsider change the organizational culture of a court?

As each circuit was diversified, newcomers confronted existing norms and traditions that reflected a bench comprised of only white men.[3] For instance, Kenney (2013, 141) writes that when Florence Allen was first appointed to the Sixth Circuit, "Allen's male colleagues did not welcome her and had in fact opposed her appointment. Three judges failed to write a customary letter of congratulation [and one] took to his bed." In the early 1980s, attorneys were not accustomed to seeing judges who were not white men on the bench. New appointees used a variety of strategies to respond to organizational cultures that were directly or indirectly unwelcoming to women and minorities.

One approach that some female and minority judges adopted was to use humor as a way to broach sensitive issues related to diversity. For instance, as the lone female on her court, Shirley Hufstedler described how she made light of job requirements challenged as discriminatory to get her male colleagues to see things from her perspective:

> There were moments when I realized that my colleagues, not universally, but some of them, not because of me, but because of issues that came before the court, had a hard time seeing the world the way it really is. For example, I had always been opposed to such things as insisting on weight limitations for women, for carrying, that were irrelevant. I used to have some fun with them [the male judges] about it. I would say, "Heavens, you mean a woman isn't able to work for UPS because she picks up packages? Have you ever picked up a package that kicked? Women with children pick them up dozens and dozens and dozens of times and they are not as supine as a parcel."[4]

Likewise, Judge Reynaldo Garza of the Fifth Circuit used humor to push back against ethnic stereotypes when he was the first Mexican American appointed to the federal appellate bench. Garza made this joke when a flight delay caused him to be late to court on his first day as a federal district court judge: "When I got on the bench, I said, well, I'm starting my career as a judge in regular

Mexican style, late for my first court session. That broke the ice and everybody laughed."[5]

Another kind of response to existing traditions and norms was to insist on changes to those traditions. Judge Mary Schroeder was shocked when she learned that the club where the Ninth Circuit held its annual holiday party did not admit women. (Women had to go in through the side entrance, not the front door.)

> And so I called Shirley Hufstedler. I said, "Are you going? This club doesn't admit women." And she said, "Well I'm going. I'm going. I've gone every year. And it's a wonderful dinner." And so we had quite a discussion among the newer judges as to whether or not we should go and I think we all decided that we would go, but we got the agreement of the Chief Judge that we would never go to the Bohemian Club again. We never did.[6]

Similarly, Dolores Sloviter encouraged her colleagues to reconsider their decisions to attend events held at all-male clubs, making a public statement (picked up in the local newspaper) about her refusal to attend a reception: "I very publicly said, 'Thank you very much, but the Union League doesn't accept women as members, and I couldn't really celebrate this in a facility that doesn't think I'm good enough to be a member'" (www.law.upenn.edu). She noted that most of her colleagues also declined to attend the event, and ultimately the event was moved to a different facility.

Sometimes, giving up old traditions within a circuit led to the creation of new traditions that memorialized the struggles of the "pioneer" generation judges. For instance, in the Sixth Circuit, the table that Florence Allen lunched at alone while her male colleagues dined without her is now passed down to new female judges in the circuit.[7]

For the nontraditional judges appointed by Carter, coming into their position as part of a cohort helped to ease the transition. One female judge commented that the two other women appointed along with her were also mothers and had husbands in the law. "We all had a lot in common, so I didn't feel isolated at all. We all came on together and were very wary and were made to feel very welcome by all our colleagues."[8] Another of Carter's female appointees, Mary Schroeder, fondly recalled how she was part of the so-called "Big Ten" and had her picture taken, along with the other female district court judges, at the White House.[9] These sentiments were echoed by female judges from outside the Ninth Circuit as well. In the Third Circuit, Dolores Sloviter commented that "the women [in the Big Ten] felt a camaraderie that has lasted until this day" despite the fact that they were spread out across a number of different circuits.[10]

As discussed in chapter 2, experimental research has documented gender differences in decision-making processes, with women being more likely than men to act as facilitators (Kathlene 1994) and to emphasize cooperation and communication (Kennedy 2003; Carey, Niemi, and Powell 1998).[11] Other experimental work has shown that all-female groups are advantaged, relative to men, in their ability to read nonverbal cues and use that information to foster consensus (Hannagan and Larimer 2010).

Comments by several female judges seem to echo these findings and suggest that the integration of women into a circuit often led to some changes in the organizational culture of the court particularly with respect to the processes and norms that govern collective interactions. Prior to Carter's push for diversity, the existing organizational culture in each circuit had grown out of a broader legal culture and court settings that were dominated by white men. While it is quite likely that some newly appointed women tried to fit into the existing organizational culture, others resisted. For instance, Judge Stephanie Seymour observed that she and the other female judge on the Tenth Circuit (Judge Deanell Tacha) did not adopt the established male dynamic of the circuit but rather tried to take a different approach: "From a female perspective, she and I are different from the guys in the sense that we don't have any testosterone. When the fellows are going at each other in an en banc conference, for example, Deanell and I are the ones who are usually the peacemakers or trying to figure out some way to negotiate a solution to the problem as opposed to joining the fray."[12] In the Ninth Circuit, Judge Betty Fletcher commented that despite the ideological differences among the women on the court, the female judges all seemed to share "a women's culture or process. . . . At meetings, we like to consult, look at all sides of questions" rather than just vote and move on, as the male judges seemed to prefer to do.[13] Another Ninth Circuit judge observed that she was "always asked to talk about collegiality" at circuit retreats and that she believed these conversations had created "a little bit of peer pressure" to cut down on sharply worded dissents and emails on the court. She added, "It's been sort of fun to see, like in law school, we have a lot of highly ego-ed people and how they soften, just given a chance."[14]

Sometimes, female judges complained to one another that their male colleagues did not always treat them as peers in group settings. Judge Betty Fletcher recounted an occasion when Judge Pam Rymer (whom she described as not generally very supportive of sex discrimination claims) told her, "You know, if I make a good suggestion about anything at the court meeting, if the men pick up on my idea, it's all their idea and no longer mine."[15] Justice Ruth Bader Ginsburg has made similar comments in reference to her time in the legal profession before being appointed to the Supreme Court: "It was a routine thing [in the past] that I would say something and it would just pass, and then somebody else would say almost the same thing and people noticed. I think the idea in the 1950s and '60s was that if it was a woman's voice, you could tune out, because she wasn't going to say anything significant. . . . I've talked to other women in high places, and they've had the same experience" (Bazelon 2009). Ginsburg then went on to observe that this dynamic would likely be different on courts where there were multiple women and women in leadership roles (Bazelon 2009).

From these anecdotes, we can see some potential causal mechanisms behind critical mass, though nothing that suggests a particular threshold is needed for organizational change or substantive representation to occur. We now turn to an alternative theoretical perspective that links diversity within an organization to outputs: the critical actor argument.

CRITICAL ACTORS

Some scholars argue that we should look beyond critical mass to identify institutional factors that make substantive representation more likely to occur. Childs and Krook (2006, 527–28) contend that individuals who act on the behalf of other women (or minorities) may be as or more important than the proportion of such individuals. These critical actors "may operate alone, [but] they may also stimulate others to act, setting in motion a momentum for policy change, or alternatively, provoking a backlash among those opposed to fundamental reform" (Childs and Krook 2006, 528). Such individuals are not necessarily members of the groups they are representing (that is, they may be any race or gender). Previous work (Moyer 2013) has found some evidence that the gender and race of the chief judge are related to pro-plaintiff outcomes in civil rights cases, though the small number of nontraditional chiefs in the analysis limits this finding. Because of the limited empirical research about critical actors within courts, we next turn to statements made by circuit judges to identify examples of what critical actors do.

As the first woman appointed to the U.S. Supreme Court, Sandra Day O'Connor is often identified as a groundbreaking figure for women in the law. While political scientists and legal scholars have debated whether she engaged in substantive representation for women while she served on the bench (Sherry 1986; Davis 1993), O'Connor can be seen as a critical actor in terms of the changes she was able to make to the existing organizational culture at the Court. Specifically, O'Connor appears to have been intentional about making the Court a more inclusive institution for both justices and law clerks.[16] Her 8 a.m. exercise class for clerks, herself, and any other justices wishing to join was a direct response to the existing tradition of basketball games at the so-called "Highest Court in the Land," which tended to exclude women (Supreme Court Historical Society 2012, 4–5). O'Connor also started a tradition of the justices eating lunch together after conferences, and, according to Clarence Thomas, she would personally visit him if he went more than a couple of days without attending (*The Supreme Court* 2009).

As the administrative leaders for their circuit (Hettinger, Lindquist, and Martinek 2003), chief judges can have tremendous influence on the priorities and organizational culture of their court (Wasby 2003) and as such can serve as critical actors.[17] Among the judges with oral histories, several women made reference to the actions (or inactions) of chief judges as important factors in their transition to the appellate bench. For instance, one female judge cited Chief Judge Jim Browning of the Ninth Circuit as being pivotal in the successful integration of nontraditional judges:

> He did an absolutely fabulous job of welcoming all of these new judges, who didn't look like any judges that had ever sat on that court before . . . Jim Browning never bothered to make any special welcome to anybody. New judges just kept coming in and the meeting room for the court got bigger. They added 13 new judges during his tenure including the ten new judgeships. He just kept adding chairs to the table. He didn't make a big deal of it. We were just all there as judges doing our business. It was quite amazing.[18]

However, not all chief judges were comfortable with the changing appearance of their circuit, even if they were not overtly hostile. Shirley Hufstedler noted that when she began her appointment in 1968, "I could tell that he [the chief judge] was very uncomfortable. I could tell that he was deeply concerned that all of a sudden he might find a female who might want to redecorate the court in chintz. It was all I could do to stop running from the other side of the desk to say, 'There, there . . . I'm not going to ruin your court.' Took him awhile to adjust, I think."[19]

As nontraditional judges gained more seniority within their circuits, the position of chief judge began to be occupied by individuals who were not white males. For instance, both the first female to serve on the appellate bench and the first African American served as chief judges (Florence Allen in the Sixth Circuit and William Hastie in the Third Circuit).[20] Certain circuits have had both gender and racial diversity in their chief judges, such as the Third Circuit and the D.C. Circuit, although no circuit through 2008 had a minority woman as chief judge. The Fifth Circuit has had either a woman or a minority as chief continuously from 1999 to 2013.

Some of these chief judges took explicit actions to make both their court and the legal profession more inclusive. Probably the clearest example of such an individual is Dolores Sloviter, a Carter appointee to the Third Circuit. Prior to and during her time as chief judge, Sloviter was intentional about addressing formal and informal barriers encountered by women and minorities, making her a clear example of a critical actor.

Immediately upon joining the Third Circuit, Sloviter became concerned about the underrepresentation of women and minority attorneys at the annual Third Circuit Judicial Conference. The policy in place allowed judges to invite one attorney as a "delegate" to the conference (a prestigious honor for any attorney), and Sloviter noticed that "judges tended to appoint their mirror images as their delegates, so that attorney representation at the Judicial Conference was exclusively white male."[21] At her first conference, Sloviter read a statement at the end of the judges' meeting outlining her concerns about the "gross underrepresentation of women and minorities among attorney delegates to the Conference."[22] As she returned to her seat, Sloviter heard "a noticeable number of hisses—from the judges."[23] However, the year following her statement, the manner in which attorney delegates were chosen was altered, and under Chief Judge A. Leon Higginbotham (an African American), the rule was permanently changed, with the effect of improved diversification.[24] Like Sloviter, Higginbotham was also a firm believer in the importance of an inclusive judiciary.[25]

Later, when she became chief judge of the circuit, Sloviter was intentional about seeking out female candidates for openings within the circuit and accommodating law clerks whose family responsibilities necessitated that they work part-time or leave early to pick up their children (www.law.penn.edu). She also established a Task Force on Equal Treatment to investigate the status of women and racial minorities in the courts. According to Sloviter, the report found that minority women perceived that they were treated unfairly, so Sloviter planned a series of focus groups to find out how to change that perception. However, her actions were not universally supported. Consistent with Childs and Krook's assertion that critical actors can provoke backlash, the long-term impact of the task force was mitigated by Sloviter's successor. Sloviter observed, "The problem was that, when I ceased being Chief Judge, the next Chief Judge, Becker, thought the whole thing was ridiculous and disbanded everything. And so there it ended."[26]

It should be emphasized, however, that not all nontraditional judges who served as chief judge took up the mantle of substantive representation in an administrative position. Some clearly enjoyed their work leading their circuit and sought to make an impact in other ways. For instance, as chief judge of the Fifth Circuit, Carolyn King organized efforts to bring resources to overwhelmed magistrate and district court judges who served along the southwestern borders of the United States.[27] While she saw her appointment by Carter to (by itself) be a symbolic service to women and to the profession, she did not articulate a desire to be especially proactive on diversity issues in her capacity leading the circuit: "When I was asked to take this job, it was because President Carter thought it was important to appoint a woman to the western half of the Fifth Circuit. There had not been any women appointed to the Fifth Circuit at all before his tenure as president. So there was good to be accomplished by doing that. . . . I did it because that was a way of being of service to women and to my community. And I'm glad that I did that."[28] While this type of representation (symbolic representation) is not generally what critical actor scholarship is concerned with (because the focus is primarily on acts), individuals like Judge King did offer evidence through their service that women and minorities could be effective court leaders.

However, as significant as these judges were in making changes to the preexisting cultures of their circuits, it is important to emphasize that diversification did not take place at the same rate or to the same extent in every circuit. The next section describes the pockets of diversity that emerged across the federal courts of appeals and then empirically tests some propositions derived from the critical mass and critical actor perspectives.

Pockets of Diversity

The uneven distribution of women and minorities throughout the federal courts of appeals is largely a function of the dynamics surrounding the judicial selection process for lower court judges. The selection of circuit judges reflects not only the priorities of the appointing president but also the preferences of home state senators in circuits where there are vacancies or new seats (Steigerwalt 2010; Giles, Hettinger, and Peppers 2001; Goldman 1997). In the modern era of judicial appointments, presidential and senatorial preferences are informed by the demands of both party and issue activists (Scherer 2005b, 23). In addition, Solberg (2006) argues that circuit size and prestige, the presence of new seats, the political culture and ideology of the states comprising the circuit, and the heterogeneity of the available pool of nominees all can influence the extent of diversification within a circuit.

FIGURE 6 Racial and ethnic diversity on the federal courts of appeals, 1978–2008

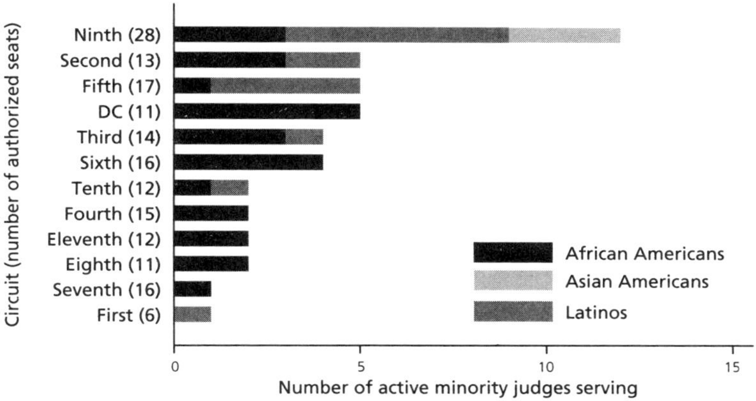

Note: Number of authorized seats based on 2008 figures. Most circuits increased during this time period, with two exceptions. The D.C. Circuit lost one seat in 2007. The Fifth Circuit lost seats to the Eleventh Circuit, which was created in 1981.

When we examine the regional distribution of minority judges, several interesting observations come to light. First, as of 2008, the Ninth Circuit was the only circuit in which Asian Americans were appointed.[29] California has the largest Asian population of any state, and Hawaii, which is also in the Ninth Circuit, has historically had a high proportion of residents who identify as Asian (www.census .gov).

Latino judges have also been appointed primarily to circuits containing states with a large Hispanic population. A total of six Latino judges have been appointed to the Ninth Circuit (through 2008), reflecting an available pool of nominees drawn from states like California and Arizona with large Hispanic populations.[30] Similarly, the Fifth Circuit, which includes Texas, has had four Hispanic judges in its history.[31] Puerto Ricans are represented on both the Second Circuit and the First Circuit; the former circuit includes New York (a state with a large Puerto Rican population in New York City), and the latter includes Puerto Rico in its jurisdiction.

While African Americans have been more evenly represented across the circuits, relative to Hispanic judges, racial politics has played a major role in impeding the representation of African Americans within particular circuits. Goldman (1997, 272) quotes Mississippi senator John Stennis as saying, "There are no black lawyers of judicial timber in Mississippi . . . the good ones leave." In the Fifth Circuit, a court with a reputation as a leader in civil rights cases, the first African American appointee was Joseph Hatchett, who filled a Florida seat on the circuit. After the Fifth Circuit was split in 1981 and Hatchett was reassigned to the new Eleventh Circuit, it took more than a decade for another African American (Carl Stewart) to be appointed to the Fifth Circuit by President Clinton. It is worth noting that Stewart was from Louisiana, a state that voted for Clinton in both 1992 and 1996. In contrast, five African Americans were appointed to the Sixth Circuit (Kentucky, Michigan, Ohio, and Tennessee) through 2008, more than any other circuit.

Perhaps the most well known example of racial politics affecting African American appointees to the federal appellate bench is the Fourth Circuit, comprising North and South Carolina, Maryland, West Virginia, and Virginia. Despite the fact that the Fourth Circuit is the court with the highest proportion of African Americans in its jurisdiction, it contained no black judges until President Clinton used a recess appointment at the end of his second term to get Roger Gregory on the court. Previously, Clinton had nominated four African Americans (including Gregory), but their nominations had all languished in the Senate without a vote.[32] One news account of Gregory's nomination quoted Clinton as saying he had "tried for five years to put an African American on the 4th Circuit" and insinuated that Senator Jesse Helms (R-NC) was to blame for the obstruction of his nominees ("Helms Won't Block Black Judge"). As Black and Black (2002, 103–11) write, Helms had "virtually no support among North Carolina blacks" and gained notoriety for racially charged political advertisements that ran against his 1990 challenger, Harvey Gantt, an African American.[33] Goldman (1997, 273) also recounts an earlier instance in which President Carter's attempt to nominate two African Americans to the Fourth Circuit was scuttled by both North Carolina senators (Helms and Robert Morgan, a conservative Democrat). For these reasons, the Fourth Circuit proved slow to diversify (at least in terms of race), although as we discuss in the conclusion, President Obama has reversed this trend with his appointments to the court.

FIGURE 7 Female judges on the federal courts of appeals, 1978–2008

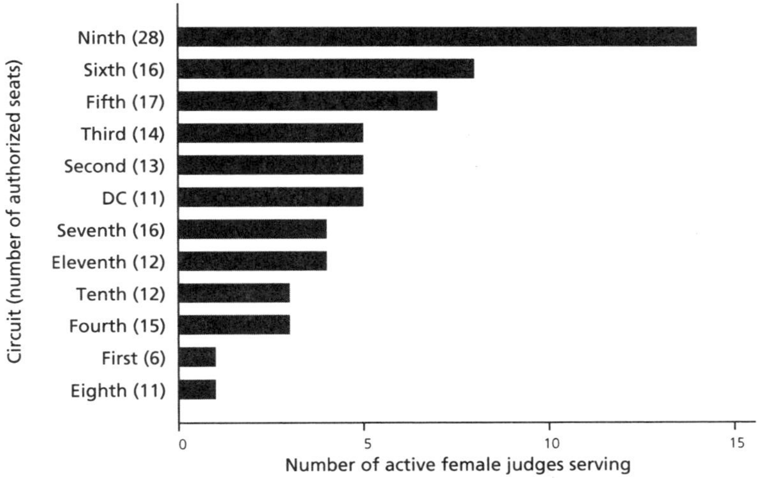

Note: See note to figure 6 for details about changes in the numbers of authorized seats. Minority women are included in figure 6 and also appear here.

In terms of the appointment of women, empirical evidence has shown that female nominees to the circuit courts experience more difficulty in the nomination process than similarly situated men (Steigerwalt 2010). Additionally, women are generally less likely to be chosen for circuits with fewer authorized judgeships and even less so if the court has already been diversified (Williams 2007; Bratton and Spill 2002). To give an illustration, the First Circuit (with only six authorized seats) only had one woman (Sandra Lynch) appointed through 2008. In contrast, the Ninth Circuit, with twenty-eight authorized seats, has had the largest number of women appointed of any circuit (thirteen in its history through 2008). Across all circuits, the number of women serving on a circuit in a given year and the number of seats on the court is highly correlated ($r = .71$) and statistically significant at the .001 level. Thus, greater numbers of women within a given circuit tend to be associated with more densely populated regions that have been apportioned a larger number of judgeships.

The appointment of women to particular circuits has also been affected by abortion politics in those states. To appease pro-life groups,

Reagan, George H. W. Bush, and George W. Bush nominated conservative women to appellate positions (Scherer 2005b, 82).[34] Some of these were opposed by pro-choice groups (for example, Priscilla Owen in the Fifth Circuit), in part because the states in the Fifth Circuit (Louisiana, Texas, and Mississippi) were perceived as especially likely to have restrictive abortion laws challenged in federal court (Steigerwalt 2010).

Court Size, Diversity, and Legal Outputs: Dissensus

With a clearer understanding of how different courts came to be diversified through the politics of the appointment process, our discussion next moves to a consideration of the relationship between judicial diversity and court dissensus. There is wide variation across the circuits in terms of the number of authorized seats, ranging from six (in the First Circuit) to twenty-eight (in the Ninth Circuit). Moreover, the use of senior judges to keep up with rising caseloads and vacancies means that many judges continue to work alongside their active status colleagues (sometimes for many years) after they have taken senior status. To gain an overall sense of how circuit-level diversity has varied over time, figures 8–10 show trends in circuit composition with respect to women, minorities, and both women and minorities for the time period 1989–2008.[35] For reference, each graph includes a line representing the overall circuit average for each measure over the entire time period.

Looking at the graph of women's presence first (figure 8), there is a clear upward trend over time in almost all circuits. The Third and Ninth Circuits remain at or above the overall average for the entire time period, and there is a sharp increase in the Fifth Circuit as a result of George W. Bush's female appointees.

In comparison, figure 9 shows that proportion of minority judges lags behind the proportion of women both in an absolute sense and in terms of growth over time. While the Ninth Circuit clearly has remained highly racially diverse during the 1989–2008 period (hovering around 20 percent), it is the Fifth Circuit that shows the biggest increase over time (from being all-white in 1989 to about 20 percent nonwhite in 2008). Finally, figure 10 considers race and gender together and displays the proportion of all judges who are not white males. The courts with the highest levels of diversity, measured this

FIGURE 8 Gender diversity of active and senior status judges by circuit, 1990–2010

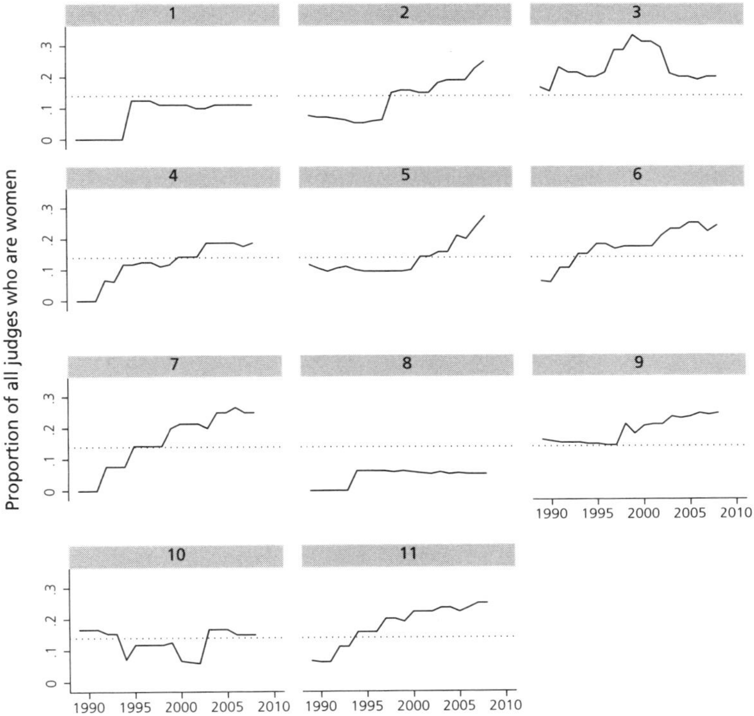

Note: Dotted line denotes combined average for all circuits over the time span. Compiled from data made available at the Federal Judicial Center's History of the Federal Judiciary web site.

way, are the Third, Fifth, Sixth, and Ninth Circuits; the Second, Fourth, and Eleventh Circuits also show clear upward trends toward greater diversity. At the other end of the spectrum, the Eighth Circuit remains well below average for the entire time period.

Given the substantial variation seen, what effect has circuit diversification had on cohesion within each court? Both the literature on group composition and comments by female judges suggest our first hypothesis that, at the aggregate level, increased representation of women within a circuit should produce less disagreement, as evidenced by lower dissent rates. However, others argue that "token"

FIGURE 9 Racial diversity of active and senior status judges by circuit, 1990–2010

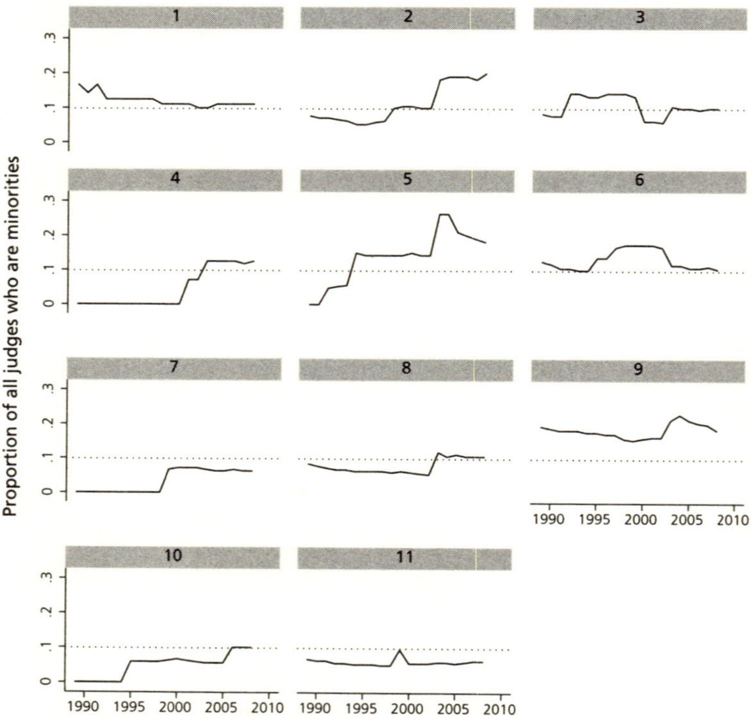

Note: Dotted line denotes combined average for all circuits over the time span. Compiled from data made available at the Federal Judicial Center's History of the Federal Judiciary web site.

representation is not sufficient to see changes in behavior within an organization, but instead, a particular threshold (or critical mass) must be reached for change to take place. Therefore, we advance a second hypothesis that a decrease in a circuit's dissent rates will not be achieved until the numbers of women in the circuit reach a critical mass.

To test these hypotheses, we construct several different measures that tap into women's relative presence within a circuit. First, we calculate a simple proportion of the total number of judges (active and senior status) who are female within the circuit. We include

FIGURE 10 Combined gender and racial diversity of active and senior judges by circuit, 1990–2010

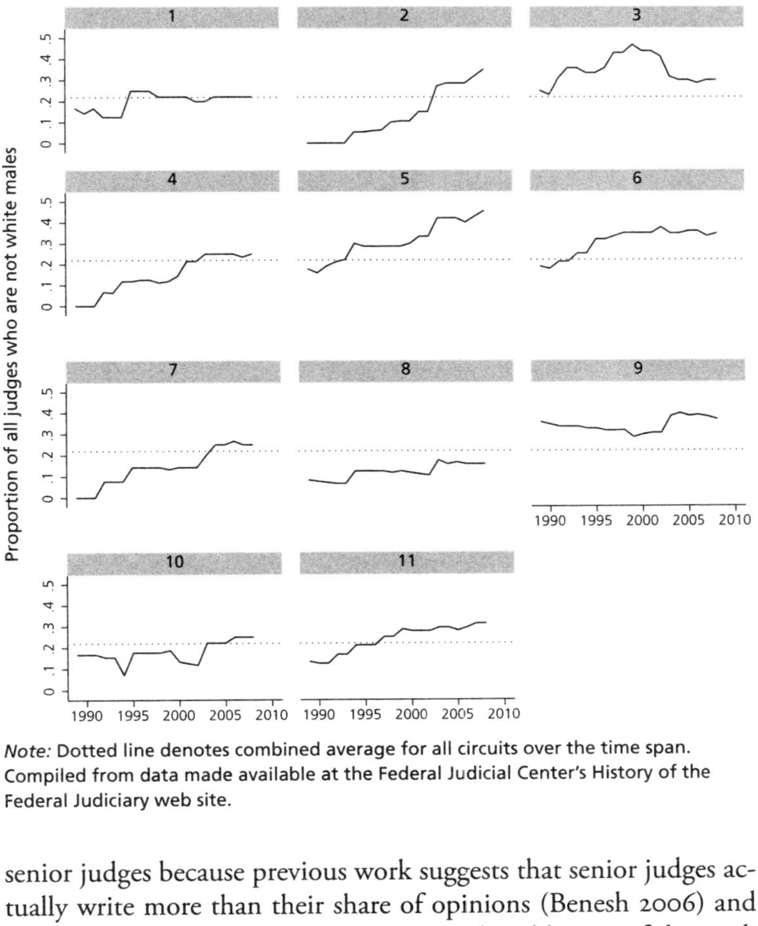

Note: Dotted line denotes combined average for all circuits over the time span. Compiled from data made available at the Federal Judicial Center's History of the Federal Judiciary web site.

senior judges because previous work suggests that senior judges actually write more than their share of opinions (Benesh 2006) and that they continue to be an important and visible part of the work and organizational culture of the circuit (Moyer 2013; Yoon 2005). This variable ranges from a minimum of 0 to a maximum of .33 (mean = .14, SD = .074). Next, we test for the presence of a critical mass by using a series of threshold dummy variables for 10, 15, 20, 25, and 30 percent. (Each of these is coded as a "1" if the proportion of women in a circuit equals or exceeds the threshold and "0" if it does not.) We also operationalize Kanter's concept of tokenism by constructing three dummy variables that indicate whether there are no women, one woman, or more than one woman in the circuit.

The dependent variable, circuit dissent rate, comes from Epstein, Landes, and Posner (2013) and is calculated as a proportion of all merits terminations. This variable ranges from .005 to .06, with a mean value of .025. Because OLS regression is not appropriate for a dependent variable that is bounded by 0 and 1, we estimate a generalized linear model using the binomial distribution and the logit link function with robust standard errors (McDowell and Cox 2004; Papke and Wooldridge 1996).[36]

We also control for other factors that Epstein, Landes, and Posner (2013, 293) found to be related to a circuit's dissent rate. The greater the caseload, the less likely judges may be to add to their workload by dissenting, so we include the authors' measure of annual circuit caseload. The number of authorized seats in a circuit may also affect norms about disagreement, as it will affect how often judges interact with each other.[37] In addition, courts in which the members are ideologically distant (as measured by the standard deviation of ideology) may have more reason to disagree than courts that are ideologically homogeneous. Finally, fixed effects for circuits and time are included. Additional information for all models is included in the appendix.[38]

In table 12, we summarize the results of the GLM analyses, focusing on the central concept of interest: the presence of women within a circuit. Consistent with our first hypothesis, we find that as the proportion of women rises within a circuit, the dissent rate in that court declines. Next, a series of models evaluate differing thresholds for critical mass. Interestingly, the only thresholds to achieve statistical significance are 10 and 15 percent.[39] While this is lower than the more commonly used thresholds in the legislative literature (generally 15 or 30 percent), it is consistent with Bratton (2005), who finds that a "critical mass" can occur at much lower thresholds than previously argued. When the critical mass perspective is operationalized differently by considering whether there are no women, one "token" woman, or more than one woman in a circuit in a given year, we find that dissent rates decrease only when there are multiple women: one "token" is not enough to affect the circuit dynamics with respect to dissent. As Kanter argued, tokens within an organization may

TABLE 12 Summary of GLM model estimates for effects of women's presence on circuit dissensus

MODEL	DIRECTION OF EFFECTS
Proportion of women	Negative
10% threshold	Negative
15% threshold	Negative
20% threshold	N.S.
25% threshold	N.S.
30% threshold	N.S.
Token woman	N.S.
Two or more women	Negative
N	208

Note: Data from Epstein, Posner, and Landes (2013). Results shown are statistically significant at $p < .05$ (one-tailed test), unless denoted as "N.S." (not significant). For additional information, see tables A19 and A20.

try to minimize their differences with the dominant group and, in this situation, adopt the existing norms about dissent within the circuit.[40] However, there may be "safety in numbers" when it comes to changing consensual norms within a circuit.

Voting Behavior

Next, we build on our analyses of voting behavior from chapters 1 and 2 to see whether court-level diversity and the presence of nontraditional chief judges affect votes in salient cases. The critical mass perspective suggests that individuals will be more likely to engage in substantive representation as their relative numbers rise within an organization.

Drawing from our earlier findings, we examine two issue areas in which we found there to be strong differences between African American judges and other judges (Title VII race cases) and between men and women (sex discrimination cases). The underlying issue, discrimination, is a theme that reappeared frequently in oral histories and judge interviews, suggesting that it was highly salient for nontraditional judges. Therefore, we expect that as a circuit grows more diverse, African American judges will be more likely to support the position of plaintiffs in race discrimination cases. For the same reason, we expect that increasing diversity at the circuit level will also increase the likelihood of a female judge supporting the position of plaintiffs in sex discrimination cases.

To evaluate our expectations for African American judges' voting, we test two different types of circuit-level diversity: racial diversity (as measured by the proportion of all judges who are nonwhite) and racial and gender diversity (as measured by the proportion of all judges who are not white males). For our analysis of women judges' votes, we use both the latter measure as an indicator of circuit diversity as well as a measure of gender diversity (the proportion of women). As in chapters 1 and 2, all models control for judge and circuit ideology, the partisan composition of the panel, and the ideological direction of the lower court ruling, and include fixed effects for circuit and time with full model results reported in the appendix (see table A21).

However, the results of the judge-level voting analyses offer no support for a critical mass explanation of individual behavior. Regardless of how we operationalize circuit diversity, no significant interactive effects are found for African American judges in criminal or Title VII cases, or women in sex discrimination cases.[41] This is consistent with Moyer (2013), who found that circuit composition did not affect female judges' votes in sex discrimination cases or in civil rights cases after 1994.

Finally, we investigate one other aspect of circuit diversity. Several of the statements from judges earlier in this chapter pointed to the importance of chief judges in leading the circuit's response to increasing diversification. As critical actors, nontraditional chief judges could affect the climate in a circuit in several ways. They may be able to influence a court's inclusiveness directly (as Judge Sloviter did when she organized the taskforce on discrimination) or indirectly, by raising their colleagues' awareness about racial or gender discrimination.[42] Other judges in the circuit may simply become more attuned to issues of discrimination because they come to understand the very real struggles faced by their chief judge. Moreover, when a nontraditional judge occupies the circuit's key leadership position, this may hold special significance for other nontraditional judges in the circuit, spurring them to engage in more substantive representation.

These arguments suggest two hypotheses. First, we expect that the presence of a nontraditional chief judge (alone) will be positively related to liberal votes in sex or race discrimination cases throughout the circuit (that is, an additive effect). Second, we expect that nontraditional judges will respond to the presence of a nontraditional chief judge in their votes on cases that raise issues of sex or race discrimination (that is, an interactive effect).

To test these hypotheses, we again build from the individual-level voting models, utilizing the same battery of controls. For the additive model, we first add a dummy variable indicating whether there was a female chief judge serving in the year of the opinion (in sex discrimination cases), or whether there was a minority chief judge (in race discrimination cases). Then to test whether nontraditional judges are responding to that presence (the interactive effect), one model includes a multiplicative term between the sex of judge and the sex of chief judge; another model interacts the variable for African American judges with whether the chief judge was a minority. Finally, we interact judge sex with a dummy variable for a nontraditional chief judge (1 = chief was not a white male, 0 = chief was a white male), and do the same for judge race.[43]

We find support in both issue areas for the proposition that the presence of nontraditional chief judges, by itself, is associated with support for plaintiffs in discrimination cases (see table 13). This is true for female chief judges in sex discrimination cases and for minority chief judges in Title VII racial discrimination cases.[44] In both race discrimination and sex discrimination models, the effect for chief judge identity is also robust to alternative specifications, such as whether the chief judge is a white male. One interpretation of these results is that having a nontraditional chief judge contributes to all judges in the circuit being more aware and responsive to issues of discrimination. This is consistent with scholarship at the panel level, finding that white and male judges' behavior alters with the presence of minorities and women, respectively (Kastellec 2013; Boyd, Epstein, and Martin 2010). In some circuits, this additive effect may be driven by overt leadership actions taken by chief judges, while in others it may be a function of all judges (including white

TABLE 13 Logit model estimates for additive effect of chief judge's identity on likelihood of a liberal vote in salient cases

MODEL AND VARIABLE	COEFFICIENT (R.S.E.)
Race-salient cases, minority chief judge	1.04* (.406)
Gender-salient cases, female chief judge	.767** (.269)

Note: N = 1,556 (Race-salient cases); N = 1,658 (Gender-salient cases). *p < .05 (two-tailed test); **p < .01 (two-tailed test). Data from Epstein, Posner, and Landes(2013): 1995–2008. For additional information on estimates for other variables, see table A22.

males) coming to better understand the realities of discrimination through the life experiences of their chief judge.

We also predicted that the presence of nontraditional chief judges would increase the propensity of women and African American judges to support plaintiffs in sex and race discrimination cases, respectively. The results as graphed in figure 11 offer some support for this hypothesis (see table A23). In sex discrimination cases, female judges were more likely to cast a pro-plaintiff vote in circuits with a sitting woman as chief judge. Holding all other variables at their median or modal values, the probability that a female judge would support the plaintiff increased from .14 to .37. However, this effect was not seen when the diverse chief judge variable was operationalized more broadly to include both race and gender. In race discrimination cases, African American judges were much more likely to support plaintiffs when the chief judge was not a white male.[45] All else equal, an African American judge's probability of supporting the plaintiff increased from .51 to .78 in circuits where the chief judge was a woman and/or a minority.[46] The magnitude of these effects shows that diversity in circuit leadership can greatly affect substantive representation by African American judges and women in cases related to sex and race discrimination, making a real impact on legal outcomes. As above, this effect may be a result of explicit actions taken by chief judges to confront inequality within the legal culture or circuit, or it may occur through more informal processes that change the organizational culture of a circuit.

Of course, our ability to evaluate the impact of critical actors is limited because of our exclusive focus on nontraditional chief

FIGURE 11 Effect of chief judge identity on substantive representation

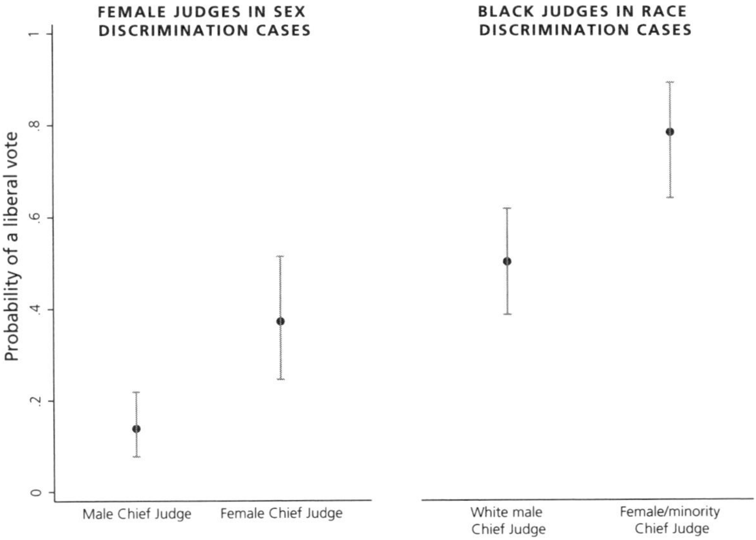

Note: Data drawn from Epstein, Landes, and Posner (2013). All other variables held at their median value (for continuous measures) or modal value (for dichotomous measures). See table A23 for detailed results.

judges. Not all women or minorities behave as critical actors, and moreover, it is highly likely that some white men should be considered critical actors. Furthermore, critical acts do not necessarily have to be undertaken by individuals with the official title of chief judge. Other judges or administrative personnel (such as the circuit executive) may serve as leaders in making a court a more inclusive and welcoming institution. Unfortunately, without a reliable record of such behavior by individuals in all circuits, it is difficult to systematically evaluate these claims. What is clear, however, is that circuits, as organizations, have experienced tremendous changes in personnel and leadership, and some of these changes have led to measurable impacts in how these courts function and decide cases.

Conclusion

Efforts to diversify the lower federal courts were experienced differently by each circuit. The politics of the selection process, regional characteristics, and the existence of new seats (or vacancies) all affected the extent to which each circuit added judges who were not white males. This diversification did not occur at the same rate or in the same manner across courts, which led to vastly different circumstances for new, nontraditional appointees. As white women, minority men, and minority women joined a circuit, they were often faced with institutional norms and traditions that reflected the old status quo: white males.

Conscious of their outsider status, newcomers to a court reacted in a variety of ways. Some insisted they were not bothered by the existing exclusionary traditions, like holding official circuit meetings at private clubs that did not admit women. Others tried to change discriminatory practices indirectly (for example, engaging their other colleagues through humor), while still others were more assertive in identifying such practices and demanding that the circuit become more inclusive. Comments from oral histories indicate that judges often found solace in the connections they made with other nontraditional appointees to the bench, but also that they felt they were generally well received by the white males in their respective circuits.

With respect to the concept of critical mass, we find that having multiple women (active or senior status) serving in a circuit does affect consensual norms on a court. This is consistent with our findings from chapter 2 and experimental research that finds women to put a higher premium on collegiality and consensus building in decision making. Interestingly, this effect appears at a low threshold: two or more women. Once the barrier for a "token" is broken, the ability for women to impact the norms of the court becomes much greater. Generally, the overall level of diversity on a court did not produce greater levels of substantive representation for women or racial minorities.

However, the presence of a critical actor did matter. When the chief judge of the circuit was a female and/or an African American, substantive representation in gender- and race-salient cases increased. It is unclear whether this effect is a function of the "pioneer" judges who served as chiefs during our time frame of study—like what we saw with the first wave of female judges in chapter 2—or whether it points to something more enduring. Given how institutions tend to resist changes to the status quo, and how even marginalized groups can unconsciously reinforce practices that institutionalize their inferior status (Jost, Banaji, and Nosek 2004), it may be relevant that changes in legal outputs and court norms appeared only after some "tipping point" (like the appointment of more than one woman or the selection of a nontraditional chief judge) was reached.

Taken together, these results underscore the importance of contextual factors in understanding how the mix of appellate judges affects the legal outputs of a court. As we found in chapter 4, we uncover more evidence that institutional structures (such as majority rule or the role of chief judge) affect whether and how much diversification will affect the work of a court. Our findings here also shed new light on more recent trends in judicial appointments that have taken place in the Obama administration. It is to these developments that we turn in the conclusion.

CONCLUSION

> *The president wants the federal courts to look like America. He wants people who are coming to court to feel like it's their court too.*
> —Kathryn Ruemmler, White House counsel to President Barack Obama

Significant changes in the composition of the federal appellate judiciary have occurred since the beginning of President Carter's administration. Prior to 1977, the courts of appeals were composed entirely of white males, with only six exceptions (two white women and four African American men) in the entire history of the federal judiciary. In contrast, by the end of the George W. Bush administration, over a quarter of the sitting circuit judges were women, and 15 percent were African American or Hispanic.

But have these changes actually affected judicial policy making in these courts? In a word: yes. According to the analyses presented in this volume, greater heterogeneity has affected both the processes and outcomes of judicial decision making at the individual, panel, and court levels. We begin this chapter by reviewing the major empirical findings of each chapter and then consider the implications of our findings in light of the dramatic shifts in the federal judiciary under the Obama administration. We conclude by identifying directions for further inquiry.

Synopsis of Major Findings

RACIAL IDENTITY AND MINORITY CLEAVAGES: AFRICAN AMERICANS AND LATINOS ON THE BENCH

Building on a framework that emphasizes the centrality of linked fate in evaluating the impact of racial identity, our analysis finds that judges' votes vary by race; however, these effects are modest. Race and ethnicity effects in decision making are stronger in salient issues, such as employment discrimination, where we find African American judges are more likely than whites and Latinos to support the liberal position. This finding, along with comments from black judges, suggests that a sense of shared experiences with racial prejudice provides a powerful frame that potentially shapes judicial perceptions of civil rights issues. On matters of criminal justice policy, we find some support for our expectation that African American judges would be more skeptical of positions taken by the prosecution in appeals before their court. We did not observe similar patterns in decision making by Latino judges. Consistent with findings reported in research on state legislators, Latino judges do not share the same decisional tendencies as African American judges; in fact, they are more likely to support a conservative outcome in civil rights and criminal justice policy areas when compared to voting by black judges. However, Latino judges are not uniformly conservative in their voting. Although the estimated relationship just missed conventional levels of statistical significance, the analysis suggests that Latino judges are somewhat more supportive of the liberal position in distributive politics cases when compared to voting by white and African American judges.

WOMEN ON THE BENCH: EMPATHY AND CONSENSUS BUILDING

The analysis in chapter 2 describes the experiences of those women judges who blazed a trail and pursued careers in a profession largely dominated by men. Not surprisingly, our empirical analysis finds that this trail-blazing cohort of women judges is substantially more likely to empathize with plaintiffs in sex discrimination cases. In other issue areas, however, judicial voting by women and men was quite similar. The importance of gendered socializing experiences also motivated the expectation that women will bring a "different voice" to the process of judging. The empirical findings and oral histories indicate that women opinion authors are more likely than their male colleagues to forge consensual positions and pen opinions that are longer, a finding that we argue stems from their efforts to explain outcomes to losing litigants and accommodate the views of their colleagues.

INTERSECTIONALITY: VARIATION WITHIN AND ACROSS RACE-GENDER COHORTS

Early efforts to diversify the bench resulted in greater attention given to the appointment of white women and minority men with little recognition given to the potential contributions of minority women. Consequently, there have been fewer minority women on the appellate bench than white women or minority men. Examining the backgrounds of appointees, we found evidence of a race-gendered path to the bench: with only one exception (the first minority woman appointed), every other woman of color appointed to the circuit bench by 2008 had previously been a judge. Comparisons within racial groups revealed some differences in voting patterns between men and women. For instance, Latinas had a much higher percentage of liberal votes than Latinos, as did white women when compared to white men; however, African American men were slightly more liberal than African American women. While we found no evidence that women of color are systematically marginalized by their colleagues in opinion assignment, significant differences in self-assignment behavior did emerge, with Latina judges more likely to self-assign than any other race-gender cohort. In voting analyses of discrimination cases, we find that African American women have a very high propensity to support plaintiffs in sex discrimination cases but not in race discrimination cases; the converse is true for African American men.

PANEL DYNAMICS: THE SUM IS GREATER THAN THE PARTS

Proponents of judicial diversity often emphasize how heterogeneity can enhance the robustness of information processing in appellate deliberations. Our empirical findings offer some support for that perspective. More viewpoints are brought to bear in deliberations with highly heterogeneous panels, where no judge matches another with respect to race and gender. White males also appear to shift their voting tendencies when seated on heterogeneous panels by becoming less consistent, suggesting that they are influenced by the contributions of their female and minority colleagues. However, the results suggest that it is not simply the range of viewpoints that is important to enhancing deliberative outputs. The presence of a single female or minority judge did not alter the attention to issues in the majority opinion. But when two nontraditional judges were seated with a white male judge, expanded issue coverage in the majority opinion was more likely. White men were more variable in their voting when seated on panels where they were the demographic minority; however, they did not respond negatively to nontraditional majority opinion authors by writing concurring or dissenting opinions.

COURT-LEVEL DIVERSITY: CHANGING NORMS AND CRITICAL ACTORS

Taking the circuit as the unit of analysis, diversification has not occurred evenly or in the same way in all courts. Pockets of diversity are evident in certain regions of the country, consistent with the demographics of those regions (for example, Asian American appointments to the Ninth Circuit), but the racial politics associated with appointing African American judges mean that the representation of blacks has not always mirrored demographic trends, particularly in the South (for example, the Fourth Circuit). For many years, the involvement of southern senators with prosegregationist views in confirmation processes contributed in part to the underrepresentation of blacks in specific circuits. In more recent years, the inclusion of women and minorities into formerly all white male courts had the effect of changing certain court traditions and norms, as evidenced by the judges' comments. The makeup of a circuit, with respect to women, can affect consensual norms within that court; however, this is limited to circuits that have more than one female judge (active or senior status). This is consistent with our finding at the panel level that merely having a "token" female or minority was insufficient to affect issue coverage in the majority opinion. While the level of diversity in a court does not affect substantive representation by female or minority judges in salient cases, we do find support for the argument that critical actors can stimulate substantive representation by others through their leadership. Specifically, the presence of nontraditional chief judges increases the propensity of women and minorities to support plaintiffs in discrimination cases.

President Obama and Judicial Diversity

Running on a theme that emphasized how he would bring change to government, presidential candidate Barack Obama, a former law professor and member of the Senate Judiciary Committee, understood well the important role of judicial appointments and recognized the demographic disconnect between the makeup of the federal courts and the citizenry. The 2008 Democratic Party platform explicitly highlighted the importance of judicial diversity: "We will select and confirm judges who are men and women of unquestionable talent and character, who firmly respect the rule of law, who listen to and are respectful of different points of view, and who represent the diversity of America."[1]

After his election, Obama was slow to nominate individuals to fill vacancies on the lower federal courts (Wheeler 2012), but ultimately fulfilled this promise with a record number of minority and female appointees, including two such appointments to the Supreme Court. By the end of Obama's first term, he surpassed Clinton's record for the lowest percentage of white male appointees, and the overall proportion of nontraditional judges on the courts of appeals stood at 42.5 percent (Goldman et al. 2013). Moreover, judicial selection during the Obama administration has yielded a record number of nominees who are "diverse" on multiple dimensions. For instance, of the seventy women appointed by Obama to the federal courts, 39 percent are women of color. Another groundbreaking shift has been Obama's appointment of a broad range of racial and ethnic minorities. In just one term, Obama appointed twelve Asian Americans to the federal courts—three more than the total number appointed between 1981 and 2008—including the first Asian American woman ever appointed to the federal courts of appeals (Jacquelyn Nguyen). Beyond racial diversity, Obama has appointed three openly gay individuals to the federal bench (Goldman et al. 2013) as part of a broader effort to appoint qualified lesbian and gay individuals to various executive branch positions, such as ambassadorships and Justice Department positions (Eilperin 2013).

Obama has also been successful in reshaping the composition of individual courts of appeals, such that three circuits (Second, Fourth, and Sixth) now have a majority of nontraditional judges (relative to white males). Perhaps the most compelling transformation is that of the Fourth Circuit, once known both for its conservatism and its lack of diversity. Table 14 compares the composition of the circuit in 2008, when Obama first took office, to 2012, using a seat-by-seat comparison.

With six appointees to the U.S. Court of Appeals for the Fourth Circuit, including Judges J. Harvie Wilkinson and J. Michael Luttig, Presidents Ronald Reagan and George H. W. Bush ensured judicial policy for this court would tend to be conservative during and after their administrations. As discussed in chapter 5, this circuit was one of the last to be racially integrated, with no African Americans on the bench until 2000. Stymied in his four efforts to appoint an African American to this court, Clinton eventually prevailed, giving Roger Gregory a recess appointment in the final days of his administration. In a show of bipartisan support, George W. Bush made that appointment permanent. Throughout the 1980s and 1990s, the conservative reputation of the Fourth Circuit had been well documented, particularly in analyses of death penalty appeals brought before this court (Blume 2010).

In 2003, Deborah Sontag wrote an article for the *New York Times Magazine* on the Fourth Circuit, profiling the court as it grappled with a sexual harassment case brought by Lisa Ocheltree (*Ocheltree v. Scollon Productions*). The en banc court was reviewing the majority decision by a divided three-judge panel. Judge Karen Williams, a Bush appointee, wrote the panel decision overturning the jury verdict in favor of Ocheltree. In her observations of oral argument, Sontag noted that Judge Gregory clearly understood the subject of discrimination: "Title VII is not about sex or race, he said; it's about power."

When she published her article in 2003, Sontag did not know the outcome of the en banc decision and hinted that the conservative, largely white male court would not be changing in the near future. History would suggest otherwise. Ocheltree prevailed in a

TABLE 14 The transformation of the Fourth Circuit, 2008 and 2012

	2008		2012		
	RACE AND GENDER	APPOINTING PRESIDENT		RACE AND GENDER	APPOINTING PRESIDENT
J. Harvie Wilkinson	White male	Reagan	Same occupant	—	—
Paul Victor Niemeyer	White male	G. H. W. Bush	Same occupant	—	—
Karen J. Williams	White female	G. H. W. Bush	Henry Franklin Floyd	White male	Obama
M. Blane Michael	White male	Clinton	Stephanie Dawn Thacker	White female	Obama
Diana Motz	White female	Clinton	Same occupant	—	—
William Traxler	White male	Clinton	Same occupant	—	—
Robert King	White male	Clinton	Same occupant	—	—
Roger Gregory	Black male	Clinton/G. W. Bush	Same occupant	—	—
Dennis Shedd	White male	G. W. Bush	Same occupant	—	—
Allyson Duncan	Black female	G. W. Bush	Same occupant	—	—
G. Steven Agee	White male	G. W. Bush	Same occupant	—	—
Vacancy since 2000	—	—	Andre M Davis	Black male	Obama
Vacancy since 2007	—	—	Barbara M. Keenan	White female	Obama
Vacancy since 1994	—	—	James A. Wynn	Black male	Obama
Vacancy since 2007	—	—	Albert Diaz	Hispanic male	Obama
Totals	7 white males 4 women and/or minorities 4 vacancies			7 white males 8 women and/or minorities	

9–2 decision, and the next few years ushered in dramatic changes in the composition of this court. In 2003, George W. Bush appointed an African American female, Allyson Duncan, to the Fourth Circuit. He then named two more judges to this court, but was unable to fill other vacancies. With three long-term vacancies and three more Republican-appointed judges leaving the bench in 2006–7, the Obama administration found itself in the position of being able to appoint six judges to this circuit in its first term. Of the six, only one was a white male. From 2008 to 2012, the Fourth Circuit went from having 60 percent of its active judges as white males down to 47 percent. In a 2012 article published in the *Richmond Times-Dispatch* on recent appointees to the Fourth Circuit, University of Richmond law professor Carl Tobias remarked, "They are diverse in terms of gender and ethnicity . . . [and] I think we're beginning to see some opinions that probably look different than they would have before those judges came on the court."[2]

The push for judicial diversity during the Obama administration attracted some opposition to selecting a bench that "looks like America." In response to Justice Sonia Sotomayor's "wise Latina" remark, several Republican senators suggested that judges were not being impartial if they allowed their ethnic background to influence decision making.[3] Following the Sotomayor confirmation, one Republican senator queried a D.C. Circuit nominee on "how diversity does, or should, influence adjudicating cases or the outcome of a case."[4] Kenney (2013, 18) points out that such criticisms overlook the perspectives that white males themselves bring to deciding cases and (inaccurately) conflate the white male experience with judicial neutrality.

In evaluating this debate, it is important not to overstate the empirical findings about the influence of demographic diversity on judicial voting. Our results are consistent with those of other scholars who find that, in most issue areas, there are not significant differences *in voting* across judges of different races or of different sexes. If past trends hold, Obama's judges will likely exhibit decisional tendencies on par with white males appointed by Democrats, *except in cases dealing with discrimination.* And in these types of cases, the presence of women and minorities will be expected to affect the voting behavior of white males (Boyd, Epstein, and Martin 2010; Kastellec 2013). We add one caveat to this prediction. Our analysis of judge gender and decision making found that the more senior cohort of women on the circuit bench offered more support for plaintiffs in sex discrimination cases than their younger female colleagues who were appointed by more recent presidents. Women judges appointed by Obama have not had to deal with formal barriers to legal employment faced by those who entered the profession in the 1950s and 1960s. As a result, we would not be surprised if women and men appointed by Obama to the circuit bench are more alike than different in their decision making across all issue areas, including sex discrimination.

However, with so much attention focused on whether there are differences in voting, this overlooks what may be the more important impact related to diversifying the bench: changes in the norms and decisional processes of judging. The findings from this book demonstrate how judges, as individuals, are affected by their colleagues, and how these working relationships can change entrenched traditions and operating procedures. Certainly, in many circuits the inclusion of a greater variety of people has changed an organizational culture that was previously dominated by white males and often was overtly discriminatory in practice. As the meaning of "diversity" continues to evolve over time, we expect to see more of these changes in established norms and practices. And as long as demographic traits serve as a proxy for diversity of information or different experiences (Jehn, Northcraft, and Neale 1999, 741–42), the representation of women, various racial and ethnic minorities, and other types of diversity such as sexual orientation will likely alter deliberative procedures in a manner that accommodates a wider range of perspectives. Indeed, the presence of such diversity makes undesirable decisional tendencies of small groups (such as group-think) less likely. In this respect, impartiality on the courts will be strengthened, rather than weakened, by the presence of nontraditional judges.

Will diversification continue? As we document, Democratic presidents have generally made the appointment of women and minorities a higher priority than Republican presidents, but the George W. Bush administration also made significant inroads in the appointment of underrepresented groups. The extent to which this trend will continue depends on a great many factors: presidential priorities, the political environment for judicial selection, changes in the legal pipeline, societal shifts in attitudes toward certain groups (for example, gays and lesbians), and the effect of the economic recession on who enters the legal profession. At the time this book went to press, the full extent of Obama's impact on diversifying the federal judiciary was yet to be determined. But we know from the Carter female appointees that coming in with a cohort of other "outsiders" can make the transition to becoming a circuit judge less isolating and intimidating. There will be a large, diverse Obama cohort, and this will almost certainly affect the judiciary that future judges enter.[5]

While this book focused on the judges in the federal courts of appeals, our conclusions about judicial diversity may apply more broadly to other judicial institutions that are structured similarly: specifically, appellate courts with multiple judges that have high workloads and low discretion. Future research should explore whether and how decision-making processes in other types of courts are influenced by the diversity of judges. In different judicial contexts, including those in other countries, constraints related to the institution and composition of the docket will likely affect the extent to which all manners of judicial diversity will shape legal policy making and create observable changes in those institutions. To better understand the causal mechanism, scholars should continue to document the experiences of nontraditional judges through oral histories—a rich source of information that is valuable to scholars and policy makers alike. Taken together, these approaches can help to create a holistic understanding of the connections between traits, group identity, and behavior in the legal realm.

APPENDIX

Introduction

TABLE A1 Women and minority appeals court judges through 2008, by circuit

	FEMALE JUDGES	AFRICAN AMERICAN OR HISPANIC JUDGES
First Circuit	Sandra Lynch (Clinton, 1995)	Juan Torruella (Reagan, 1984)
Second Circuit	Amalya Kearse* (Carter, 1979)	Thurgood Marshall (JFK, 1962)
	Rosemary Pooler (Clinton, 1998)	Amalya Kearse* (Carter, 1979)
	Sonia Sotomayor* (Clinton, 1998)	Lawrence Pierce (Reagan, 1981)
	Reena Raggi (G. W. Bush, 2002)	Sonia Sotomayor* (Clinton, 1998)
	Debra Livingston (G. W. Bush, 2007)	Jose Cabranes (Clinton, 1994)
		Barrington Parker (G. W. Bush, 2001)
Third Circuit	Dolores Sloviter (Carter, 1979)	William H. Hastie (Truman, 1950)
	Carol Mansmann (Reagan, 1985)	A. Leon Higginbotham (Carter, 1977)
	Jane Roth (G. H. W. Bush, 1991)	Timothy Lewis (G. H. W. Bush, 1992)
	Marjorie Rendell (Clinton, 1997)	Theodore McKee (Clinton, 1994)
	Maryanne Barry (Clinton, 1999)	Julio Fuentes (Clinton, 2000)

TABLE A1 *continued*

	FEMALE JUDGES	AFRICAN AMERICAN OR HISPANIC JUDGES
Fourth Circuit	Karen Williams (G. H. W. Bush, 1992)	Roger Gregory (Clinton/Bush, 2001)
	Diana Motz (Clinton, 1994)	Allyson Duncan* (G. W. Bush, 2003)
	Allyson Duncan* (G. W. Bush, 2003)	
Fifth Circuit	Carolyn King (Carter, 1979)	Reynaldo Garza (Carter, 1979)
	Phyllis Kravitch (Carter, 1979, after 1980, 11th)	Joseph Hatchett (Carter, 1979, after 1980, 11th)
	Edith Jones (Reagan, 1985)	Carl Stewart (Clinton, 1994)
	Edith Clement (G. W. Bush, 2001)	Emilio Garza (G. H. W. Bush, 1991)
	Priscilla Owen (G. W. Bush, 2005)	Fortunato Benevides (Clinton, 1994)
	Jennifer Elrod (G. W. Bush, 2007) Catharina Haynes (G. W. Bush, 2008)	Edward Prado (G. W. Bush, 2003)
Sixth Circuit	Florence Allen (FDR, 1934)	Wade McCree (Johnson, 1966)
	Cornelia Kennedy (Carter, 1979)	Damon Keith (Carter, 1977)
	Alice Batchelder (G. H. W. Bush, 1991)	Nathaniel Jones (Carter, 1979)
		Ransey Guy Cole (Clinton, 1995)
	Martha Daughtrey (Clinton, 1993)	Eric Clay (Clinton, 1997)
	Karen Moore (Clinton, 1995)	
	Julia Gibbons (G. W. Bush, 2002)	
	Deborah Cook (G. W. Bush, 2003)	
	Susan Neilson (G. W. Bush, 2005)	
	Helene White (G. W. Bush, 2008)	
Seventh Circuit	Ilana Rovner (G. H. W. Bush, 1992)	Ann Williams* (Clinton, 1999)
	Diane Wood (Clinton, 1995)	
	Ann Williams* (Clinton, 1999)	
	Diane Sykes (G. W. Bush, 2004)	
Eighth Circuit	Diana Murphy (Clinton, 1994)	Theodore McMillan (Carter, 1978)
		Lavenski Smith (G. W. Bush, 2002)
Ninth Circuit	Shirley Hufstedler (Johnson, 1968)	Arthur Alarcon (Carter, 1979)
	Betty Fletcher (Carter, 1979)	Jerome Farris (Carter, 1979)

TABLE A1 *continued*

	FEMALE JUDGES	AFRICAN AMERICAN OR HISPANIC JUDGES
	Dorothy Nelson (Carter, 1979) Mary Schroeder (Carter, 1979) Cynthia Hall (Reagan, 1984) Pamela Rymer (G. H. W. Bush, 1989) Susan Graber (Clinton, 1997) Margaret McKeown (Clinton, 1998) Kim Wardlaw* (Clinton, 1998) Marsha Berzon (Clinton, 2000) Johnnie Rawlinson* (Clinton, 2000) Consuelo Callahan* (G. W. Bush, 2003) Sandra Ikuta (G. W. Bush, 2006)	Cecil Poole (Carter, 1979) Ferdinand Fernandez (G. H. W. Bush, 1989) Kim Wardlaw*(Clinton, 1998) Johnnie Rawlinson* (Clinton, 2000) Richard Paez (Clinton, 2000) Consuelo Callahan* (G. W. Bush, 2003) Carlos Bea (G. W. Bush, 2003)
Tenth Circuit	Stephanie Seymour (Carter, 1979) Deannell Tacha (Reagan, 1985) Mary Briscoe (Clinton, 1995)	Carlos Lucero (Clinton, 1995) Jerome Holmes (G. W. Bush, 2006)
Eleventh Circuit	Phyllis Kravitch (Carter, transferred from Fifth, 1981) Susan Black (G. H. W. Bush, 1992) Rosemary Barkett (Clinton, 1994) Frank Hull (Clinton, 1997)	Joseph Hatchett (Carter, transferred from Fifth, 1981) Charles Wilson (Clinton, 1999)
D.C. Circuit	Patricia Wald (Carter, 1979) Ruth Ginsburg (Carter, 1980) Karen Henderson (G. H. W. Bush, 1990) Judith Rogers* (Clinton, 1994) Janice Brown* (G. W. Bush, 2005)	Spottswood Robinson (Johnson, 1966) Harry Edwards (Carter, 1979) Clarence Thomas (G. H. W. Bush, 1990) Judith Rogers* (Clinton, 1994) Janice Brown* (G. W. Bush, 2005)

Note: *Denotes female minority judge.

TABLE A2 Indicators and data sources

INDICATORS	ATTRIBUTES	DATABASE/SOURCE
Judge level		
Race	African American; Latino; White; Asian American	Federal Judicial Center
Gender	Female/Male	Federal Judicial Center
Race and gender	White male; White female; African American male; African American female; Latino male; Latina female; Asian American male	Federal Judicial Center
Nontraditional judge	Minority and/or female judge	Federal Judicial Center
Appointment information	Year of confirmation; Identity of appointing president	Federal Judicial Center
Age	Year born	Federal Judicial Center
Ideology	Judicial Common Space score—higher scores indicate more conservative views	Epstein et al. (2007), updated
Ideological extremism	Absolute value of Judicial Common Space score	Epstein et al. (2007), updated
Case level		
Policy outcome	Whether majority opinion advocates a liberal, conservative, or mixed policy (or cannot be coded in liberal/conservative dimension)	Multi-User Database; Epstein, Landes, and Posner (2013)
Mixed treatment	Affirmed/reversed in part	Multi-User Database
Mixed policy	Policy advocated in opinion is mixed between liberal and conservative	Multi-User Database

Separate opinion	Whether a judge on the panel wrote a concurring or dissenting opinion	Multi-User Database
Criminal issue area	Appeal by criminal defendant or prisoner petition focused on conviction	Multi-User Database
Distributive politics	Appeal pits individual against business in private civil case	Multi-User Database
Race discrimination	Claim based on Title VII, employment discrimination based on race	Epstein, Landes, and Posner (2013)
Sex discrimination	Claim based on sex discrimination	Epstein, Landes, and Posner (2013)
Constitutional challenge	Case involved constitutional interpretation	Multi-User Database
Prior publication	Previously published opinion associated with this case	Multi-User Database
Death penalty	Death penalty issue raised in case	Multi-User Database
Supreme Court review	Case was remanded by U.S. Supreme Court	Multi-User Database
Dissenting opinion	Whether a judge filed a dissenting opinion (includes those that concur in part/dissent in part)	Multi-User Database
Concurring opinion	Concurring opinion filed	Multi-User Database
Lower court deference	Ideological directionality of lower court decision	Multi-User Database; Epstein, Landes, and Posner (2013)
U.S. government's position	Ideological position (liberal/conservative) of United States, when a party in case	Multi-User Database
Litigant resources	U.S. government is appellant or respondent; individual is appellant or respondent	Multi-User Database
Legal inputs provided by counsel	Total number of attorneys representing appellants and respondents	Multi-User Database

TABLE A2 *continued*

INDICATORS	ATTRIBUTES	DATABASE/SOURCE
Both sides contest outcome below	Cross appeal filed	Multi-User Database
Amicus	Amicus brief filed on behalf of appellant or respondent	Multi-User Database
Panel level		
Heterogeneous panel, diversity	No judge is sitting with a demographic match (both race and gender) on the panel	Multi-User Database
Token diversity, panel	One judge on panel is female and/or minority; the other two judges on panel are white males	Multi-User Database
Nontraditional majority, panel	Two or more judges on panel are female and/or minority	Multi-User Database
Policy predisposition of colleagues on panel	Two other judges on panel are Republican appointees (RR); two other judges on panel are Democratic appointees (DD); two other judges on panel are Democratic and Republican appointees (DR)	Multi-User Database; Epstein, Landes, and Posner (2013)
Panel ideological heterogeneity	Panel made up of judges who were appointed by presidents of different parties	Multi-User Database
Ideological distance from panel	Ideological distance from opinion author to panel median, using Judicial Common Space scores	Epstein et al. (2007), updated

Circuit level variables		
Circuit liberalism	Median Judicial Common Space score among active judges, by circuit year, higher scores indicate more conservative circuits Standard deviation of Judicial Common Space scores, by circuit year	Epstein et al. (2007), updated
Circuit level differences	Dummies for individual circuits (excluded reference category is D.C. Circuit)	Multi-User Database; Epstein, Landes, and Posner(2013)
Workload	Number of published opinions divided by the number of active judgeships, by circuit year	Administrative Office of the U.S. Courts
Size of circuit	Based on number of authorized judgeships	Administrative Office of the U.S. Courts
Dissensus	Dissent rate as reported by Westlaw, by circuit year	Epstein, Landes, and Posner (2013)
Demographic identity of chief judge	Female chief judge; minority chief judge; nontraditional chief judge (not a white male)	Federal Judicial Center
Gender makeup of circuit	Percent of all serving judges (active and senior) who are female by circuit year	Federal Judicial Center
Thresholds	10%, 15%, 20%, 25%, 30% or more of all serving judges (active and senior) are female, by circuit year	Federal Judicial Center

Chapter 1

TABLE A3 Descriptive statistics for key variables in analysis of judge race

VARIABLE	DATASET	DESCRIPTIVE STATISTICS
Liberalism	Multi-User Database: voting records, minimum 10 votes, 1982–2008	Range: 0–1 Median: .371 SD: .273 N = 346 African American: 8% Hispanic: 4% White: 88%
Liberal vote	Multi-User Database: votes by U.S. Courts of Appeals judges in three-judge panels	54%, contested (N = 9,566) 20.7%, criminal (N = 7,460) 38%, distributive politics (N = 3,258)
Race of judge	Multi-User Database: votes (contested cases)	White: 88.8% African American: 7.7% Hispanic: 3.4% (votes by Asian Americans excluded)
Liberal vote	Epstein, Landes, and Posner (2013): race discrimination cases (Title VII)	35% (N = 1,589)
Race of judge	Epstein, Landes, and Posner (2013): race discrimination cases (Title VII)	White: 88% African American: 9.1% Hispanic: 3%

TABLE A4 Logit model estimates for effects of judge race and other influences on likelihood of a liberal vote

	MODEL 1: ALL CASE TYPES (CONTESTED)	MODEL 2: CRIMINAL APPEALS	MODEL 3: DISTRIBUTIVE POLITICS	MODEL 4: RACE DISCRIMINATION
African American	0.066 (.093)	0.156⁺ (.106)	0.092 (.149)	0.674** (.204)
Latino	–0.129 (.173)	–0.249 (.224)	0.258⁺ (.163)	–0.187 (.289)
Controls				
Ideology of judge	–0.649** (.075)	–0.559** (.104)	–0.463** (.109)	–0.211⁺ (0.166)
Seated with RR	–0.056 (.049)	–0.035 (.068)	–0.221* (.083)	0.042 (0.151)
Seated with DD	0.111* (.061)	0.181* (.091)	0.165⁺ (.116)	0.277⁺ (0.190)
Circuit ideology	–0.236** (.118)	0.175 (.194)	–1.179** (.260)	–1.513** (0.622)
Lower court decision	—	–0.693** (.080)	–1.026** (.089)	1.570** (0.182)
Criminal case	–0.482** (.056)	—	—	—
U.S. gov't supports conservative pos.	0.399⁺⁺ (.050)	—	—	—
U.S. gov't supports liberal pos.	–0.545⁺⁺ (.083)	—	—	—
Constant	.133 (.097)	–0.513 (.165)	1.174 (.254)	–1.415 (.396)
N	9,566	7,460	3,258	1,589

Note: ⁺⁺p < .05 (two-tailed test); ⁺p < .10, *p < 0.05; **p < .01 (one-tailed test). Models significant at p < .01. Robust standard errors in parentheses, clustered by judge. Models 1–3 use the Multi-User Database, 1982–2008 votes. Model 4 uses the Epstein, Landes, and Posner (2013) database, 1995–2008 votes. Whites are the excluded reference category; votes by Asian American judges are excluded. Contested cases (model 1) are those where panel reversed (in full or in part) the court below and/or a panel judge did not join the majority opinion. Output for time and circuit variables omitted for space reasons. In a model estimated for all cases (contested and noncontested), the effects for the U.S. government are signed and significant in the expected direction. In models 1, 2, and 4, the difference between African American and Latino judges is statistically significant. In models 1–3, the lower court decision variable indicates a conservative lower court decision; in model 4, the variable indicates a liberal lower court decision.

Chapter 2

TABLE A5 Descriptive statistics for key variables in analysis of judge gender

VARIABLE	DATASET	DESCRIPTIVE STATISTICS
Liberalism	Multi-User Database: voting records, minimum 10 votes, 1982–2008	Range: 0–1 Mean: .371 SD: .273 N = 345 Female: 15% Male 85%
Liberal vote	Multi-User Database: votes by judges on three-judge panels made up of appeals court judges, 1982–2008	54%, contested cases (N = 9,617) 20.7%, criminal (N = 7,498) 38.2%, distributive politics (N = 3,271)
Mixed policy outcome/ treatment	If opinion advocates a position in between liberal and conservative/if court affirms in part and reverses in part	13.4% mixed policy (N = 7,995) 13.6%, mixed treatment (N = 8,586) 9.0% mixed treatment and mixed policy (N = 7,075)
Opinion length	Multi-User Database: signed unanimous opinions authored by appeals court judge, 1982–2008	Range: 0–54 Mean: 7.454 SD: 5.008
Sex of judge	Multi-User Database: votes (contested cases)	Women: 14.9% Men: 84.1%
Liberal vote	Epstein, Landes, and Posner (2013): sex discrimination cases	38.2% liberal (N = 1,694)
Sex/birth cohort of judge	Epstein, Landes, and Posner (2013): sex discrimination cases	Women born before 1946: 8.3% Women born 1946 and later: 8.4% Men born before 1946: 67.2% Men born 1946 and later: 8.4%

TABLE A6 Logit model estimates for effects of judge gender and other influences on likelihood of a liberal vote

	MODEL 1: ALL CASE TYPES (CONTESTED)	MODEL 2: CRIMINAL APPEALS	MODEL 3: DISTRIBUTIVE POLITICS
Female judge	–0.052 (.087)	0.026 (.095)	–0.113 (.140)
Controls			
Ideology of judge	–0.672** (.087)	–0.572** (.097)	–0.502** (.113)
Seated with RR	–0.061 (.049)	–0.038 (.043)	–0.222** (.084)
Seated with DD	0.100* (.060)	0.171* (.090)	0.157 (.116)
Circuit ideology	–0.228* (.119)	0.167 (.194)	–1.179** (.260)
Lower court decision	—	–0.687** (.080)	–1.027** (.088)
Criminal case	–0.488** (.055)	—	—
U.S. government supports conservative position	0.399+ (.049)	—	—
U.S. government supports liberal position	–0.557+ (.083)	—	—
Constant	0.167 (.098)	–0.490 (.166)	1.243 (.260)
N	9,616	7,498	3,271

Note: +p < .05 (two-tailed test); *p < 0.05; **p < .01 (one-tailed test). Models significant at p < .01. Robust standard errors in parentheses, clustered by judge. All models use the Multi-User Database, 1982–2008 votes. Contested cases (model 1) are those where panel reversed (in full or in part) the court below and/or a panel judge did not join the majority opinion. Output for time and circuit variables omitted for space reasons. In a model estimated for all cases (contested and noncontested), the effects for the U.S. government are signed and significant in the expected direction.

TABLE A7 Logit model estimates for effects of judge gender cohort and other influences on likelihood of a liberal vote in sex discrimination cases

INDEPENDENT VARIABLE	COEFFICIENT (R.S.E.)	COEFFICIENT (R.S.E.)
Female judge	0.282* (.153)	
Female judge born 1945 or earlier	—	0.389* (.206)
Female judge born after 1945	—	0.146 (.189)
Male judge born after 1945	—	–0.052 (.140)
Controls		
Ideology of judge	–0.655** (.142)	–0.662** (.142)
Seated with RR	–0.174* (.115)	–0.177* (.114)
Seated with DD	0.401* (.185)	0.396* (.185)
Circuit ideology	0.789 (.652)	0.798 (.651)
Liberal lower court decision	1.10** (.131)	1.10** (.132)
Constant	–1.762 (.366)	–1.149 (.300)
N	1,694	1,694

Note: *p < .05; **p < .01 (one-tailed test). Models significant at p < .001. Robust standard errors clustered by judge. Male judges born 1945 or earlier are the excluded reference category. Models use the Epstein, Landes, and Posner (2013) database, 1995–2008 votes. Output for time and circuit variables omitted for space reasons.

TABLE A8 Logit model estimates for effects of judge gender and other influences on likelihood of supporting middle ground position

	MODEL 1: MIXED POLICY	MODEL 2: MIXED TREATMENT	MODEL 3: MIXED POLICY AND MIXED TREATMENT (TABLE 4)
Opinion author is female	0.186+ (.129)	0.027 (.122)	0.307* (.138)
Female judge on panel	–0.101 (.093)	–0.097 (.100)	–0.074 (.115)
Controls			
Ideologically heterogeneous panel	0.005 (.085)	0.059 (.084)	–0.075 (.104)
Case appealed by both sides	0.911** (.116)	1.373** (.108)	0.670** (.144)
Individual litigant	–0.431 (.372)	–0.668* (.366)	–0.557 (.512)
U.S. government is appellant	–0.488** (.181)	–0.406* (.177)	–0.758* (.267)
U.S. government is respondent	–0.185** (.083)	–0.207* (.080)	–0.059 (.094)
Amicus	–0.216 (.164)	–0.209* (.147)	–0.521** (.217)
Civil rights	–0.040 (.104)	0.367** (.099)	0.160 (.122)
Civil liberties	0.276 (.230)	0.224 (.221)	0.018 (.280)
Prior publication	0.092 (.088)	0.161* (.086)	0.230** (.096)
Constant	–2.049 (.202)	–2.186 (.184)	–2.880 (.224)
N	6,276	6,748	6,276

Note: +p < .10; *p < .05; **p < .01 (one-tailed test). Robust standard errors in parentheses, clustered by judge. Models significant at p < .001. Includes only signed majority opinions from the Multi-User Database, 1982–2008. Mixed policy equals "1" if opinion adopted a position between liberal and conservative. Mixed treatment equals "1" if court affirmed in part and reversed in part. For model 3, outcome equals "1" if both mixed policy and mixed treatment. Output for time and circuit variables excluded for space reasons.

TABLE A9 Negative binomial regression estimates for effects of judge gender and other influences on count of number of pages in majority opinion

INDEPENDENT VARIABLE	COEFFICIENT (S.E.)
Opinion author is female judge	0.068** (.023)
Female judge on panel	–0.001 (.018)
Controls	
Ideologically heterogeneous panel	–0.014 (.016)
Treatment (if affirmed)	–0.147** (.014)
Number of parties	0.0003 (.0003)
Amicus	0.226** (.029)
Constitutional challenge	0.210** (.018)
Prior publication	0.117** (.016)
Constant	2.262 (.033)
N	6,233

Note: $^{+}p < .10$; $^{*}p < .05$; $^{**}p < .01$ (one-tailed test). Model significant at $p < .001$. Includes only majority opinions authored by courts of appeals' judges from 1982 to 2008 using the Multi-User Database. Output for time and circuit variables omitted for space reasons.

Chapter 3

TABLE A10 Descriptive statistics for key variables in analysis of intersectionality

VARIABLE	DATASET	DESCRIPTIVE STATISTICS
Dependent variables		
Liberalism	Multi-User Database: voting records, min. 10 votes, 1982–2008	Range: 0–1 Median: .371 SD: .273 N = 346 African American women (2%), Hispanic women (1%), white women (12%), African American men (6%), Hispanic men (3%), white men (76%).
Self-assigned opinion	Multi-User Database: majority opinions 1982–2008	15% self-assigned (N = 7,088)
Liberal vote	Epstein, Landes, and Posner (2013) 1995–2008	44% liberal (N = 6,146)
Independent variables		
Sex and race of judge	Epstein, Landes, and Posner (2013)	N = 13,781 votes 73% white male 15% white female 4.2% African American male 2.2% African American female 4% Hispanic male 0.5% Hispanic female
Sex and race of opinion author	Multi-User Database	N = 7,930 opinions 72% white male 12% white female 4.2% African American male 1.3% African American female 2.9% Hispanic male 0.3% Hispanic female 0.4% Asian American male

TABLE A11 Logit model estimates for effects of judge race-gender and other influences on likelihood of self-assignment of majority opinion

INDEPENDENT VARIABLES	COEFFICIENT (R.S.E.)
White woman	0.682** (.199)
African American woman	0.661 (.492)
Hispanic woman	2.05** (.334)
African American man	0.356 (.342)
Hispanic man	0.867* (.393)
Asian American man	0.389 (.595)
Controls	
Ideological distance	0.406 (.251)
Criminal case	–0.139+ (.077)
Civil rights	–0.117 (.094)
Affirm	0.029 (.069)
Constant	–2.21** (.282)
N	7,088

Note: +p < .10 (two-tailed test); *p < .05 (two-tailed test); **p < .01 (two-tailed test). Model significant at p < .001. Robust standard errors clustered by judge. Includes only signed unanimous decisions from the Multi-User Database, 1982–2008. Output for time and circuit variables omitted for space reasons.

TABLE A12 Logit model estimates for effects of judge race-gender and other influences on likelihood of a liberal vote in salient cases

	GENDER SALIENT MODEL	RACE SALIENT MODEL
White woman	0.321* (.158)	0.117 (.176)
African American woman	0.599* (.364)	0.136 (.361)
African American man	0.332 (.242)	0.871** (.233)
Hispanic woman	0.195 (.559)	—
Hispanic man	0.251 (.303)	–0.010 (.335)
Controls		
Judge ideology	–0.644** (.164)	–0.277 (.184)
Seated with DD	0.568** (.170)	0.275 (.191)
Seated with DR	0.176 (.116)	–0.030 (.126)
Circuit ideology	0.838 (.533)	–1.17** (.510)
Conservative lower court decision	–1.05*** (.128)	–1.53*** (.161)
Constant	–0.368 (.299)	0.306 (.437)
N	1,727	1,609

Note: *p < .05 (one-tailed test); **p < .05 (two-tailed test); ***p < .01 (two-tailed test). Robust standard errors in parentheses. Models are significant at p < .001. White men are the excluded reference category. Uses the Epstein, Landes, and Posner (2013) database, 1995–2008 votes. Hispanic women are dropped from the model because of small numbers and insufficient variation. Output for time and circuit variables omitted for space reasons.

Chapter 4

TABLE A13 Descriptive statistics for key variables in analysis of panel diversity

VARIABLE	DATASET	DESCRIPTIVE STATISTICS
Separate opinions	Multi-User Database, 1982–2008: three-judge panels, excludes those with non–appeals court judges	14% with separate opinion (N = 6,242) 10% with dissent (N = 6,242)
White male participation (excluding opinion authorship)	Multi-User Database, 1982–2008: three-judge panels, excludes those with non–appeals court judges	5.2% wrote separate opinion (N = 11,280) 4.3% wrote dissent (N = 11,171)
Demographic composition of the panel	Multi-User Database, 1997–2002: three-judge panels, excludes those with non–appeals court judges	10% heterogeneous: no demographic match 37% homogenous: all white male (the only other homogenous panel—all white female panels—were too rare to estimate an effect) 62% mixed: with at least one nontraditional judge 47% token: with only one nontraditional judge 16% nontraditional majority: two or more judges are minority/female (N = 1,294)
Points of law	Multi-User Database, 1997–2002: three-judge panels, unanimous cases: number of headnotes, signed majority opinions	Range 0–86 Median 9 Mean 10.83 S.D. 8.68 (N = 1,294)
Voting by white males	Multi-User Database: U.S. Courts of Appeals judges' votes in three-judge panels with unanimous decisions, 1982–2008	59.7% on panel with two white male judges 35.9% on panel with one nontraditional judge 5.3% on panel with two nontraditional judges 34% liberal votes (N = 11,625)

TABLE A14 Rare event logit model estimates for effects of opinion author race-gender on likelihood of separate opinion by white male judges

	SEPARATE OPINION	DISSENTING OPINION
Opinion author is female and/or minority	0.110 (.101)	0.134 (.112)
Controls		
Minority party on panel	0.553** (.088)	0.607** (.095)
Majority opinion policy consistent with ideology	–0.821** (.093)	–0.935** (.104)
Constitutional challenge	0.335** (.100)	0.266** (.113)
Civil rights	0.127 (.110)	0.258 (.117)
Civil liberties	0.879** (.178)	0.830** (.200)
Prior publication	0.331** (.091)	0.244* (.102)
Reversed lower court	0.363** (.088)	0.334** (.096)
Age	0.002 (.004)	0.005 (.005)
Constant	–2.787 (.311)	–3.339 (.340)
N	11,280	11,171

Note: *p < .05; **p < .01 (one-tailed test). Standard errors in parentheses. Includes only participations by white male judges who did not author the majority opinion using the Multi-User Database, 1982–2008. Output for time and circuit variables omitted for space reasons.

TABLE A15 Rare events logit model estimates for effects of panel diversity on likelihood of separate opinion

	SEPARATE OPINION	DISSENTING OPINION
Demographically heterogeneous panel	0.115 (.122)	0.028 (.147)
Controls		
Ideologically heterogeneous panel	0.392** (.087)	0.402** (.103)
Constitutional challenge	0.298** (0.090)	0.194* (.106)
Civil rights	0.153 (.099)	0.263** (.111)
Civil liberties	0.932** (.175)	0.720** (.205)
Prior publication	0.331** (.081)	0.224** (.095)
Reversed lower court	0.311** (0.079)	0.306** (.091)
Constant	–2.190 (.147)	–2.759 (.177)
N	6,242	6,242

Note: *p < .05; **p < .01 (one-tailed test). Standard errors in parentheses. Uses three-judge panel decisions from the Multi-User Database, 1982–2008, excluding those with any non–appeals court judge sitting by designation. Output for time and circuit variables omitted for space reasons. Alternative specifications with different measures of panel diversity (for example, a dummy variable with all white male panels and racially mixed as the excluded category) did not yield substantively different results.

TABLE A16 Negative binomial regression model estimates for effects of varying levels of panel diversity on points of law

	MODEL 1	MODEL 2	MODEL 3	MODEL 4
Mixed panel	0.050 (.040)	—	—	—
Demographically heterogeneous panel	—	0.099^{+} (.062)	—	—
Token diversity	—	—	0.006 (.037)	0.038 (–.042)
Nontraditional majority	—	—	—	0.095^{++} (.058)
Controls				
Ideologically heterogeneous panel	–0.035 (.041)	–0.031 (.041)	–0.031 (.041)	–0.036 (.041)
Workload	–0.002 (.004)	–0.002 (.004)	–0.002 (.004)	–0.001 (.004)
Dissent rate	–1.057 (.902)	–1.025 (.901)	–1.032 (.902)	–1.058 (.902)
Mixed treatment	0.450 (.057)	0.451** (.057)	0.450** (.057)	0.450** (.057)
Constitutional challenge	0.263** (.054)	0.263** (.054)	0.264** (.054)	0.264** (.054)
Civil rights	0.062 (.050)	0.064 (.050)	0.062 (.050)	0.064 (.050)
Total attorneys	0.034** (.005)	0.034** (.005)	0.033** (.005)	0.034** (.005)
Prior publication	0.042 (.044)	0.042 (.043)	0.040 (.044)	0.041 (.044)
Constant	1.875 (.145)	1.890 (.142)	1.913 (.142)	1.868 (.145)
N	1,294	1,294	1,294	1,294

Note: $^{+}p < .10$ (one-tailed test); $^{++}p = .05$ (one-tailed test); $^{*}p < .05$ (one-tailed test); $^{**}p < .01$ (one-tailed test). Models significant at $p < .001$. Unanimous, signed majority opinions from Multi-User Database, 1997–2002. Output for time and circuit variables omitted for space reasons.

TABLE A17 Heteroskedastic probit model estimates for effects of panel diversity and other influences on white male judges' voting

INDEPENDENT VARIABLE	COEFFICIENT (S.E.)
Choice model	
Judicial ideology	–0.269* (.066)
Seated with DD	0.215** (.058)
Seated with RR	–0.177** (.049)
Circuit ideology	–0.126 (.114)
Criminal case	–0.761** (.095)
U.S. supports liberal position	0.784** (.102)
U.S. supports conservative position	–0.114* (.052)
Conservative lower court decision	–0.814** (.096)
Constant	0.285 (.096)
Variance model	
Sitting with one nontraditional judge	0.029 (.043)
Sitting with two nontraditional judges	0.182* (.109)
Ideologically heterogeneous panel	–0.008 (.048)
Ideological extremism	0.148 (.116)
Size of circuit	0.088** (.024)
Number of years on the bench	0.008 (.007)
Number of years on the bench, squared	–0.0001 (.0002)
N	11,625

Note: Wald test of ln $sigma^2$ is rejected at the 0.003 level; chi^2 (7) = 21.62, meaning the variance is significantly different from 1. *p < .05; **p < .01 (one-tailed test). Uses votes by white male judges in unanimously decided cases from 1982 to 2008 in the Multi-User Database. Output for time and dummy circuit variables omitted for space reasons.

Chapter 5

TABLE A18 Descriptive statistics for key variables in circuit analysis

DEPENDENT VARIABLES	
Circuit dissensus	Range: 0.005–0.063 Median = 0.025 SD = 0.014
Liberal vote	Sex discrimination cases: N = 1,727 37.9% liberal Race discrimination cases: N = 1,615 34.6% liberal
INDEPENDENT VARIABLES	
Proportion of female judges, by circuit year	Range: 0–0.333 Median = 0.15 SD = 0.074
Thresholds of female judges, by circuit year	Across circuit years (N = 231): 73.6% had at least 10% women among serving judges 52.8% had at least 15% women among serving judges 31.6% had at least 20% women among serving judges 12.6% had at 25% women among serving judges 6.5% had at least 30% women among serving judges
Number of women in circuit, by year	Across circuit years (N = 231): Token woman: 22.5% Two or more: 70.1%
Female chief judge serving in a given year, by circuit	Sex discrimination cases: N = 1,727 16.9% of observations came from a circuit that had a female chief judge serving
Minority chief judge serving in a given year, by circuit	Race discrimination cases: N = 1,615 5.3% of observations came from a circuit that had a minority chief judge serving
Nontraditional chief judge (woman and/or minority)	Sex discrimination cases: N = 1,727 22.9% of observations came from a circuit that had a chief judge who was not a white male serving Race discrimination cases: N = 1,615 20.5% of observations came from a circuit that had a chief judge who was not a white male serving

Note: Analyses utilize data collected by Epstein, Landes, and Posner (2013).

TABLE A19 GLM estimates for effects of circuit composition and other influences on dissensus

	PROPORTIONAL MODEL	TOKEN MODEL
Proportion of women	–0.668* (.384)	—
Token woman	—	0.005 (.065)
Two or more women	—	–0.150* (.080)
Controls		
Cases	–0.000 (.000)	–0.000 (.000)
Number of judgeships	0.015 (.016)	0.019 (.017)
SD, circuit ideology	–2.13** (.447)	–1.96** (.502)
Circuit ideology	0.042 (.128)	0.018 (.131)
Constant	–3.04** (.203)	–3.17 (.231)
	N = 208 AIC = 0.355210 BIC = –1013.90	N = 208 AIC = 0.355224 BIC = –1013.89

Note: *p < .05 (one-tailed test); **p < .05 (two-tailed test). Standard errors in parentheses. One- and two-year lags for the proportion of women in model 1 are not significant. In the token model, a court with no women is the excluded reference category. Data from Epstein, Landes, and Posner (2013). All models estimated using numbered circuits only. Output for time and circuit variables omitted for space reasons.

TABLE A20 GLM model results for threshold models of circuit dissensus

	MODEL 1	MODEL 2	MODEL 3	MODEL 4	MODEL 5
10% or more	–0.133* (.053)	—	—	—	—
15% or more	—	–0.103* (.045)	—	—	—
20% or more	—	—	–0.030 (.050)	—	—
25% or more	—	—	—	–0.041 (.062)	—
30% or more	—	—	—	—	0.086 (.072)
Controls					
Cases	–0.00 (.000)	–0.00 (.000)	–0.00 (.000)	–0.00 (.000)	-0.00 (.000)
Court size	.016 (.016)	.015 (.016)	.010 (.016)	.012 (.016)	.012 (.016)
SD of circuit ideology	–1.94** (.473)	–2.19** (.438)	–2.32** (.460)	–2.26** (.440)	–2.23** (.445)
Circuit ideology	.018 (.139)	–0.036 (.136)	.041 (.129)	.058 (.129)	.048 (.128)
Constant	–3.07** (.212)	–3.02** (.204)	–2.96** (.210)	–2.99** (.201)	–2.99** (.203)
	N = 208 AIC = 0.355190 BIC = –1013.90	N = 208 AIC = 0.355200 BIC = –1013.90	N = 208 AIC = 355224 BIC = –1013.89	N = 208 AIC = 0.355224 BIC = –1013.89	N = 208 AIC = 0.355224 BIC = –1013.89

Note: Controls for circuit and time periods omitted for space reasons. *p < .05 (one-tailed test); **p < .05 (two-tailed test). One and two-year lags for the proportion of women in model 1 are not significant. All models estimated using numbered circuits only. Data from Epstein, Landes, and Posner (2013).

TABLE A21 Logit estimates for effects of critical mass and other influences on likelihood of a liberal vote

	MODEL 1A: RACE DISCRIMINATION	MODEL 1B: RACE DISCRIMINATION	MODEL 2A: SEX DISCRIMINATION	MODEL 2B: SEX DISCRIMINATION
African American	.386 (.414)	–1.02* (.494)	—	—
Female	—	—	.654 (.399)	.657 (.439)
Percent minority	4.82* (2.39)	—	—	—
Percent female	—		4.95* (1.98)	—
Percent nontraditional	—	.004 (1.53)	—	4.58** (1.71)
African American × percent minority	2.57 (3.18)	—	—	—
African American × percent nontraditional	—	7.08** (1.85)	—	—
Female × percent female	—	—	–1.88 (2.28)	—
Female × percent nontraditional	—	—	—	–1.44 (1.73)
Controls				
Hispanic	–0.183 (.292)	–0.142 (.290)	—	—
Ideology	–0.254 (.171)	-0.151 (.180)	–0.618† (.153)	–0.632† (.152)
Lower court direction	1.68† (.186)	1.67† (.185)	1.13† (.128)	1.14† (.129)
Seated with RR	.023 (.151)	.091 (.157)	–0.124 (.114)	–0.136 (.114)
Seated with DD	.321 (.194)	.295 (.197)	.417† (.185)	.422† (.185)
Circuit ideology	–1.21 (.721)	–1.61† (.635)	1.41† (.677)	1.62† (.678)
Constant	–1.76† (.549)	–1.12† (.552)	–1.90 (.402)	–2.45† (.557)
N	1,556	1,499	1,658	1,658

Note: $^{+}p < .10$ (one-tailed test); $^{*}p < .05$ (one-tailed test); $^{**}p < .01$ (one-tailed test); $^{\dagger}p < .05$ (two-tailed test). Standard errors in parentheses. All models

TABLE A22 Logit estimates for effects of critical actors and other influences on likelihood of a liberal vote

	MODEL 1: RACE DISCRIMINATION CASES	MODEL 2: SEX DISCRIMINATION CASES
Female chief judge	—	.767** (.269)
Minority chief judge	1.04** (.406)	—
Controls		
African American	.698** (.208)	—
Hispanic	–0.167 (.291)	—
Female	—	.310* (.154)
Ideology	–0.218 (.173)	–0.642** (.147)
Lower court direction	1.65† (.186)	1.15† (.129)
Seated with RR	.036 (.153)	–0.169 (.114)
Seated with DD	.281 (.193)	.400† (.186)
Circuit ideology	–2.04† (.649)	1.78† (.705)
Constant	–2.04† (.511)	–1.91† (.374)
N	1,556	1,658

Note: +p < .10 (one-tailed test); *p < .05 (one-tailed test); **p < .01 (one-tailed test); †p < .05 (two-tailed test). Standard errors in parentheses. All models significant at p < .001. Data from Epstein, Landes, and Posner (2013): 1995–2008. Output for time and circuit variables omitted for space reasons.

TABLE A23 Logit estimates for critical actor interaction models, likelihood of a liberal vote (figure 11)

	MODEL 1: RACE DISCRIMINATION CASES	MODEL 2A: SEX DISCRIMINATION CASES	MODEL 2B: SEX DISCRIMINATION CASES
African American	.547** (.224)	—	—
Female	—	.202 (.183)	.194 (.181)
Female chief judge	—	.684** (.274)	—
Nontraditional chief judge	.935** (.232)	—	.539** (.206)
Female × female chief judge	—	.555* (.319)	—
Female × nontraditional chief judge	—	—	.402 (.312)
African American × nontraditional chief judge	1.20* (.547)	—	—
Controls			
Hispanic	−0.173 (.290)	—	—
Ideology	−0.221 (.171)	−0.659 (.150)	−0.664† (.148)
Lower court direction	1.68† (.190)	1.15† (.129)	1.14† (.129)
Seated with RR	.039 (.154)	−0.173 (.114)	−0.182 (.115)
Seated with DD	.274 (.196)	.393† (.187)	.390† (.186)
Circuit ideology	−1.88† (.640)	1.70† (.704)	1.58† (.691)
Constant	−1.97† (.443)	−1.90† (.373)	−2.21† (.417)
N	1,556	1,658	1,658

Note: +p < .10 (one-tailed test); *p < .05 (one-tailed test); **p < .01 (one-tailed test); †p < .05 (two-tailed test). Standard errors in parentheses. All models significant at p < .001. Data from Epstein, Landes, and Posner (2013): 1995–2008. Output for time and circuit variables omitted for space reasons. Because the variable for minority chief judge perfectly predicted success in the model, it was dropped from the estimation.

NOTES

Introduction

1. We explore this in more detail in the final chapter.
2. There continue to be robust debates in the academic literature over the usage of the terms "Hispanic" and "Latino" to describe individuals of Spanish origin or descent. Here, we follow the practices of the U.S. Census Bureau and the Pew Hispanic Center and use the terms interchangeably. These disagreements also extend to whether "ethnicity" or "race" is the appropriate label to use when describing Latino populations. For instance, the Chicano movement in the 1960s made a concerted effort to use the term "race" in order to parallel the struggle of Latinos more closely with that of African Americans, rather than with other European immigrant groups (Darder and Torres 1998, 9). Chapter 1 examines in more depth some of the challenges associated with conceiving of a collective Latino identity.
3. In our analysis of individual decision making that uses data from the Multi-User Database, we do not include district court judges who are sitting by designation or federal judges who do not sit on a circuit court (for example, International Trade). We do include information on these judges when constructing panel-level measures, including the ideological predisposition of the panel.
4. Epstein et al. make these data available at a web site associated with the publication of *The Behavior of Federal Judges:* http://epstein.wustl.edu/research/behaviorJudges/index.php.
5. Our data also include corrections to the original database and update that focused on erroneously identified judges. In our update for 2003–8, we minimized this source of error by using automated content analysis for approximately one-third of the variables and online coding (with drop-down

menus, including a list of federal judges from the Federal Judicial Center dataset from which a coder could select).

6. To promote comparability across circuits, our individual level analyses begin in 1982. As noted earlier, until 1980, the end of the Carter administration, minority and women judges on the appeals courts were virtually nonexistent. Additionally, the Fifth Circuit was split in 1981 to create the new Eleventh Circuit.
7. Following the conventions established by Songer (1997), we do not include unpublished decisions in our observation set and acknowledge the limitations of excluding them. In future research, we hope to investigate whether diversity is related to publication decisions and evaluate whether these dynamics hold in those cases where the opinion was not published. We also follow the conventions established by Songer (1997) in which votes are coded in terms of the policy content along a liberal-conservative dimension. For example, a vote supporting the position of a litigant claiming a civil rights violation is coded as "liberal" whereas a vote against that position is coded as "conservative." In criminal cases, a vote supporting the position of the defendant (or prisoner) is coded "liberal" whereas a vote against is coded "conservative." In labor-economics cases, liberal votes include those in which judges supported the positions taken by unions, the federal government in regulatory and tax cases, and individual plaintiffs in tort cases. Conservative votes include those in which judges supported the positions taken by management (against unions), opposed those taken by the federal government in regulatory and tax cases, and supported corporate defendants in tort and insurance cases filed by individuals.
8. Epstein provides updated data through 2010 at http://epstein.wustl.edu/research/JCS.html.
9. For an excellent discussion on logit models and how they may be used in studies of judicial decision making, see the appendix in Hettinger, Lindquist, and Martinek (2006).
10. Distributive politics cases were identified as appeals where individuals and businesses are pitted against one another in a private civil law case.
11. Our analysis of issue coverage in the majority opinion is limited to a shorter time period (1997–2002) due to the availability of data. Moreover, our observations are limited to majority opinions that did not include a non–appeals court judge sitting by designation because existing research finds district court judges are more susceptible to influence by their colleagues on the panel and less likely to author the majority opinion (Collins and Martinek 2011).

ONE Race, Ethnicity, and Judging

1. The source for these figures is the Pew Hispanic Center National Survey of Latinos 2008 conducted as part of Pew's Social and Demographic Trends Project's Racial Attitudes in America Survey, which sampled 3,086 adults

between September 5 and October 6, 2007. The survey data may be accessed at http://www.pewhispanic.org/. This survey is the source for figures cited here on Latino public opinion unless noted otherwise.

2. Biographical portrait, "William Hastie," Just the Beginning Foundation, www.jtbf.org.
3. Biographical portrait, "Wade McCree," Just the Beginning Foundation. In the next two paragraphs, we draw on the Federal Judicial Center's database of judicial biographies and Just the Beginning Foundation to gather biographical material on African American judges.
4. Biographical portrait, "Joseph Hatchett," Just the Beginning Foundation.
5. We discuss the efforts to diversify the Fourth Circuit in greater detail in chapter 5 and the conclusion.
6. Prior to Garza, Harold Medina, the son of a Mexican American, was appointed to the Second Circuit by Truman. However, he was not perceived to be Hispanic—and did not self identify as a Hispanic (Goldman 1997). The Federal Judicial Center biographical database does not identify Medina as being of Hispanic heritage.
7. Transcript, Reynaldo G. Garza interview, March 10–11, 1992, by Marc Knisely, p. 37, Library, U.S. Court of Appeals, Fifth Judicial Circuit, New Orleans.
8. Ibid., p. 13.
9. California Appellate Court Legacy Project, video transcript of interview with Arthur Alarcon by Judith Ashmann-Gerst, 2007, p. 1. http://www.courts.ca.gov/documents/Arthur_Alarcon_6035.pdf.
10. Ibid., p. 7.
11. Ibid., p. 11.
12. In contrast, Farhang and Wawro (2004) did not find evidence that judge race affected decision making in employment discrimination cases before federal courts of appeals.
13. When compiling voting records that measure the proportion of cases that support a liberal policy outcome, cases with mixed outcomes are included (and scored as "0.5").
14. In the introduction, we describe the coding conventions used to classify case outcomes and votes in terms of a left-right dimension (liberal or conservative).
15. We measure a judge's ideology using the Judicial Common Space scores, an indicator described in the introduction and noted in the appendix.
16. Specification for each model is not identical because it requires taking into account controls relevant to a particular issue area as well as differences in variables associated with using two databases. Additional information on estimates for models 1, 2, 3, and 4 is reported in the appendix.
17. The results do not change if the model includes all cases, rather than focusing only on contested cases.
18. In criminal cases, the difference between African American judges and white

judges just misses conventional levels of significance at p = .07; however, the difference between African Americans and Latinos is statistically significant at the .05 level. In distributive politics cases, the estimated differences between Latino judges' votes and those of African Americans and whites are in the expected direction, but significant only at the .054 level. There is no statistically significant difference between votes by African American and white judges in this issue area.

19. We estimated additional models to test whether the effect of judge race was conditioned by region or birth cohort. We did not find evidence of conditional relationships for either variable.

20. We are hesitant to generalize from this particular finding as the relationship failed to reach conventional levels of statistical significance ($p < .05$). We do note, however, that one analysis of black political behavior found that intragroup differences emerge only on issues of economic inequality, with more affluent blacks being less supportive of economic redistribution than lower-income blacks (Dawson 1994).

TWO Gender and Judging

1. Unless a source is noted, biographical information was obtained from the Federal Judicial Center, Judicial History Site, Biographical Directory of Federal Judges: www.fjc.gov.
2. Statistics on legal education and bar are from the American Bar Association: www.americanbar.org/content/dam/aba/administrative/legal_education_and_admissions_to_the_bar/statistics/jd_enrollment_1yr_total_gender_authcheckdam.pdf.
3. Diversifying the Judiciary, An Oral History of Women Federal Judges, Federal Judicial Center, transcript of oral history of Shirley Hufstedler, Sarah Wilson interviewer, March 10, 1995, p. 6.
4. Women Trailblazers in the Law Project Oral Histories, Box 9, Manuscript Division, Library of Congress, Washington, D.C., transcript of oral history of Stephanie K. Seymour, Nancy J. Siegel interviewer, dates of interviews: October 6, 2006; April 24, 2007; February 27, 2008, pp. 67–68.
5. Diversifying the Judiciary, transcript of oral history of Cynthia B. Hall, Sarah Wilson interviewer, March 10, 1995, p. 4.
6. Ibid., p. 12.
7. Women Trailblazers in the Law Project Oral Histories, Box 1, transcript of oral history of Rosemary Barkett, Pamela I. Perry interviewer, dates of interviews: November 6, 2006; October 29, 2007; October 11, 2008; November 2009, p. 28.
8. Women Trailblazers in the Law Project, transcript of oral history of Stephanie Seymour, pp. 49–51.
9. Women Trailblazers in the Law Project Oral Histories, Box 9, transcript of oral history of Mary Murphy Schroeder, Patricia Lee Refo interviewer, dates

of interviews: August 30, September 9, October 13, 2006; January 3, 2007, p. 34.

10. Women Trailblazers in the Law Project Oral Histories, Box 3, transcript of oral history of Betty Binns Fletcher, Kathleen J. Hopkins interviewer, dates of interviews: January 10, February 22, April 17, 2006, p. 6.
11. Diversifying the Judiciary, transcript of oral history of Cynthia B. Hall, p. 22.
12. Women Trailblazers in the Law Project, transcript of oral history of Mary Murphy Schroeder, pp. 55–58.
13. Women Trailblazers in the Law Project Oral Histories, Box 5, transcript of oral history of Carolyn Dineen King, Marcy Hogan Greer interviewer, dates of interviews: July 19, September 1, December 20, 2010; January 14, 2011, p. 70.
14. Women Trailblazers in the Law Project Oral Histories, Box 8, transcript of oral history of Ilana Diamond Rovner, Karen A. Clanton interviewer, dates of interviews: August 20, 28, September 28, November 8, 2007, p. 30.
15. Women Trailblazers in the Law Project Oral Histories, transcript of oral history of Mary Murphy Schroeder, p. 39.
16. Women Trailblazers in the Law Project Oral Histories, transcript of oral history of Ilana Diamond Rovner, p. 23.
17. Only three of the eleven Carter women had experience sitting on another court at the time of their selection (Martin 2009).
18. Women Trailblazers in the Law Project Oral Histories, transcript of oral history of Rosemary Barkett, p. 81.
19. Women Trailblazers in the Law Project Oral Histories, Box 10, transcript of oral history of Dolores Korman Sloviter, Amelia Helen Boss interviewer, dates of interviews: June 26, August 18, 2006; April 13, July 25, 2007, p. 101.
20. Diversifying the Judiciary, transcript of oral history of Shirley Hufstedler, p. 11.
21. Research on state supreme courts, however, suggests differences in decision making between male and female judges (Songer and Crews-Meyer 2000; McCall 2008).
22. For the voting record, we included votes that supported a "mixed" position; elsewhere, in analyses of individual votes, these are excluded from the set of observations.
23. Additional information on model estimates is reported in the appendix.
24. We selected 1945 as the cut point for multiple reasons. First, it marks the end of World War II. Second, women judges' accounts and empirical research on the gender composition of law schools indicate that the 1970s marked a significant transition period. Moreover, the number of women practicing as attorneys was negligible up until that point. In 1970, women made up 3 percent of the bar; by 1980, the presence of women in the legal profession had nearly quadrupled (11 percent).
25. All cohorts had judges appointed by presidents of both parties.

26. Diversifying the Judiciary, transcript of oral history of Shirley Hufstedler, p. 45
27. Diversifying the Judiciary, transcript of oral history of Betty Binns Fletcher, p. 7.
28. Women Trailblazers in the Law Project Oral Histories, transcript of oral history of Rosemary Barkett, p. 120.
29. The coding for the Multi-User Database instructs that mixed policy outcomes are identified as opinions that supported a position in between the "liberal" and "conservative" ends. As one illustration, the Seventh Circuit affirmed the conviction of a defendant who had argued that the trial court had erred in its instructions to the jury; however, the panel also remanded the case for resentencing after finding the sentence was excessive (*U.S. v. Roy Green,* 927 F.2d 1005). As another illustration of mixed outcomes, a business appealed the decision of the district court to dismiss. The Eighth Circuit panel affirmed the district court's dismissal of the counts alleging that defendants had violated federal antitrust laws but reversed the district court on the claim alleging a violation of a federal motor carrier law (*Double D Spotting v. Supervalu,* 136 F.3d 554.)
30. Although a majority of "mixed policy" cases are also "mixed treatment" cases, there are many that do not simultaneously fall into both categories. By combining these two dimensions, we strengthen the identification of middle-ground cases in that doing so excludes those cases where the panel has a uniform policy advocated in its opinion (that is, conservative) but affirmed in part and reversed in part consolidated appeals that had conflicting trial court outcomes (that is, reversing a liberal trial court outcome and affirming a conservative trial court outcome). It also excludes cases where the appellate panel has a mixed policy advocated in its opinion that affirms the status quo (that is, a mixed policy outcome in the trial court).

THREE Intersectionality and Judging

1. While we cannot say for certain, a limited pool of qualified minority women may have affected Carter's ability to identify such individuals for nomination.
2. The women were Janice Rogers Brown, Edith Clement, Deborah Cook, Carolyn Kuhl, Priscilla Owen, and Diane Sykes. Only Kuhl was not confirmed.
3. Scholars have argued that, because of their much higher workload compared to the Supreme Court, the federal courts of appeals see comparatively less bargaining and negotiation between the other judges and the opinion author, giving the circuit court opinion author greater latitude than a Supreme Court opinion author (Hinkle 2014).
4. See the appendix for more descriptive statistics about opinion authors.
5. Because of the small number of minority women overall, their uneven distribution across circuits, and our inability to account accurately for each judge's

workload (a central factor in determining opinion assignments), descriptive analytical approaches are more appropriate for this inquiry than multivariate modeling techniques. However, we acknowledge that the conclusions we can draw from frequency distributions are more limited in assessing causal relationships.

6. In an alternative specification, we estimated a logistic regression model predicting whether a minority woman would be the opinion author (on panels with a minority woman). The results indicate that minority women were marginally less likely to be assigned to write in important cases (at $p < .10$, two-tailed), more likely to be assigned in cases affirming the lower court, and more likely to be assigned when seated on liberal panels or cases with liberal outcomes. However, because we cannot account for workload considerations in opinion assignment, we cannot say with certainty that these results would hold if such a measure were included. Minority women were also significantly more likely to write the opinion themselves when they were the presiding judge, suggesting a proclivity for self-assignment, which is supported by the results from the logit model of self-assignment.
7. Because minority women might be relegated to write opinions more often in "easier" cases, we also examined whether they were more likely to write opinions in criminal cases, generally considered to be "easier" cases on appeal (Lindquist 2007), or in cases where the panel affirmed the lower court. However, the cross-tabulations do not reveal any statistically significant patterns that support the proposition that minority women are systematically assigned to write opinions in "easy" cases. Thus, we cannot say that opinion assignment patterns on the panel reflect clear, unambiguous evidence that minority women are marginalized.
8. It should be noted that the coding conventions for determining the ideological direction of the judge's vote differ somewhat from those used in the Multi-User Database of Decisions of the U.S. Courts of Appeals. For sex discrimination and Title VII cases, Sunstein et al. code as liberal any decision "where the plaintiff was afforded *any* relief" (2006, 159, emphasis added). In a case where a plaintiff raises multiple claims (or where there are multiple legal issues), a court that ruled for the plaintiff on some but not all issues would therefore be coded as ruling in a "liberal" direction. In comparison, the Multi-User Database would code the ideological direction of such an outcome as "mixed," allowing the researcher to exclude it from the analysis or make it the focus (Lindquist, Martinek, and Hettinger 2007).
9. Separate models for capital punishment and affirmative action did not yield any significant results for our covariates of interest. In alternative specifications for the gender salience model, abortion cases were included, but only black men were more liberal in abortion cases.
10. The confidence intervals for these predicted probabilities overlap, so we cannot say that this difference of magnitude is statistically significant. When the predicted values are calculated for a panel where the other two judges are

Republicans, the probability for black women decreases to .35 and to .29 for white women.

11. To ascertain whether these findings are a function of defining gender salience too narrowly, an alternative model broadened the sample to include both sex discrimination and sexual harassment cases. The results of this specification only muddy the waters further. The indicator for African American women is no longer statistically significant, though the coefficient for African American men is now positive and statistically significant. (The results for white women are unchanged.)
12. In the gender model, being seated with two Democratic appointees is positively related to a liberal vote, and more liberal judges (denoted by negative ideology scores) are more likely to support the position of the plaintiff. In the race model, the panel and individual ideology variables just miss significance at the .10 level, but greater circuit liberalism (again, denoted by negative scores) is related to a higher likelihood of a liberal vote. In both models, judges are less likely to cast liberal votes when the lower court decision is in the conservative direction, due to the strong tendency for panels to affirm the lower court ruling.

FOUR Diversity on the Panel

1. An exception is in those circuits and time periods where screening panels have been used to identify cases that merit oral argument. Typically, however, judges who sit on the screening panel associated with a case are not the same judges who will hear oral argument for that case. In circuits that pool the resources of their clerks to produce bench memoranda prior to oral argument, the memorandum may establish the baseline for future interchamber communication (Cohen 2002). In his assessment of interactions among chambers, Cohen (2002) noted that communications between judges on a panel were rare prior to oral argument (for those cases that are orally argued).
2. The statistical model used here is rare event logit (King and Zeng 1999), appropriate for unbalanced samples in which one outcome is rarer than the other. We were unable to estimate a model for concurring opinions because there were simply not enough participations that resulted in a concurring opinion. When a judge concurs in part and dissents in part, we count it as a dissent. The results appear in the appendix.
3. See the appendix for full results.
4. See also Wasby (2011) about the negotiations related to en banc decisions.
5. These data are adapted from the 1997–2002 update to the Multi-User Database of Decisions of the U.S. Courts of Appeals.
6. For more information, including an illustrative case, see Haire, Moyer, and Treier (2013). The authors provide several measurement validity tests, demonstrating that the indicator empirically captures the attention to issues in the majority opinion.

7. We also compared points of law for those panels with token diversity (only one nontraditional judge) against all white male panels. The mean number of points of law for panels with "token" diversity, 10.8, is identical to the average for all other panels (10.8). We estimated a statistical model that confirms a nonrelationship between token diversity and issue coverage in the majority opinion. See the appendix.
8. The complete model specification and results are reported in the appendix.

FIVE Diversity within the Circuits

1. Fifteen percent represents the lower boundary of what Kanter (1977) refers to as a "tilted" organization, in which representation reaches a level at which out-group individuals are no longer seen as mere tokens.
2. However, in the state supreme court literature, Martin and Pyle (2002) do investigate both gender and racial diversity of the justices, as well as diversity in their backgrounds.
3. It should be noted that circuit traditions also reflected homogeneity in other ways, such as religion. Judge Mary Schroeder suggests in her oral history that when she first arrived at the court, the Ninth Circuit had recast its Christmas party as a "holiday party" as a reaction to adding "quite a number of new judges, including Jewish judges" (transcript of oral history, p. 81).
4. Diversifying the Judiciary, An Oral History of Women Federal Judges, Federal Judicial Center, transcript of oral history of Shirley Hufstedler, Sarah Wilson interviewer, March 10, 1995, p. 23
5. Transcript, Reynaldo G. Garza interview, March 10–11, 1992, by Marc Knisely, p. 60, Library, U.S. Court of Appeals, Fifth Judicial Circuit, New Orleans.
6. Women Trailblazers in the Law Project Oral Histories, Box 9, transcript of oral history of Mary Murphy Schroeder, Patricia Lee Refo interviewer, dates of interviews: August 30, September 9, October 13, 2006; January 3, 2007, pp. 81–82.
7. Ibid., p. 82.
8. Interview with the author, December 27, 2007.
9. Women Trailblazers in the Law Project Oral Histories, transcript of oral history of Mary Murphy Schroeder, pp. 79–80.
10. Women Trailblazers in the Law Project Oral Histories, Box 10, transcript of oral history of Dolores Korman Sloviter, Amelia Helen Boss interviewer, dates of interviews: June 26, August 18, 2006; April 13, July 25, 2007, p. 98.
11. At a meeting of the Supreme Court Historical Society, Ruth Bader Ginsburg was asked why there appeared to be more civility on the Supreme Court now than in previous eras. Her response: "It's because we've had women" ("Celebration to Honor the Historic First Term of Justice Sandra Day O'Connor," 4–5).
12. Women Trailblazers in the Law Project Oral Histories, Box 9, Manuscript Division, Library of Congress, Washington, D.C., transcript of oral history

of Stephanie K. Seymour, Nancy J. Siegel interviewer, dates of interviews: October 6, 2006; April 24, 2007; February 27, 2008, p. 2.

13. Women Trailblazers in the Law Project Oral Histories, Box 3, transcript of oral history of Betty Binns Fletcher, Kathleen J. Hopkins interviewer, dates of interviews: January 10, February 22, April 17, 2006, p. 6.
14. Interview with the author, December 27, 2007.
15. Women Trailblazers in the Law Project Oral Histories, transcript of oral history of Betty Binns Fletcher, p. 6.
16. Law clerks are an important component of examining courts as organizations, in part because of the crucial research and writing support they provide to judges. Moreover, law clerks for the Supreme Court frequently go on to be leaders in the legal profession and have been appointed to the Supreme Court (for example, Justice Kagan).
17. According to Title 28, Section 45 of the U.S. Code, the chief judge is the judge in regular active service who is senior in commission of those judges who are under sixty-five years of age; has served for one year or more as a judge; and has not previously served as chief judge. If no circuit judge meets these criteria, the youngest circuit judge in regular active service who is sixty-five or over who meets the second and third criteria is selected. If this does not result in a chief being identified, the circuit judge in active service who is senior in commission and who has not previously served as chief judge is selected. Chiefs generally serve for a seven-year term and may serve after the expiration of this term until another judge is identified as eligible to serve. In addition to administrative responsibilities, the chief judge presides over any court session that she or he attends, including en bancs (unless the circuit justice is attending).
18. Women Trailblazers in the Law Project Oral Histories, transcript of oral history of Mary Murphy Schroeder, pp. 79–80.
19. Diversifying the Judiciary, transcript of oral history of Shirley Hufstedler, pp. 18–19.
20. Through 2008, eleven women (all of them white) served in the role of chief judge for their circuit: Florence Allen (Sixth Circuit), Alice Batchelder (Sixth Circuit), Edith Jones (Fifth Circuit), Carolyn King (Fifth Circuit), Sandra Lynch (First Circuit), Mary Schroeder (Ninth Circuit), Stephanie Seymour (Tenth Circuit), Dolores Sloviter (Third Circuit), Deanell Tacha (Tenth Circuit), Patricia Wald (D.C. Circuit), and Karen Williams (Fourth Circuit). Five African Americans and one Latino (all men) also served as chief judge up through 2008: Harry Edwards (D.C. Circuit), William Hastie (Third Circuit), Joseph Hatchett (Eleventh Circuit), A. Leon Higginbotham (Third Circuit), Spottswood Robinson III (D.C. Circuit), and Juan Torruella (First Circuit). While all the African American chief judges were appointed by Democratic presidents, Judge Torruella was a Republican appointee, as were four of the female chief judges (Batchelder, Jones, Tacha, and Williams).

21. Women Trailblazers in the Law Project Oral Histories, transcript of oral history of Dolores Korman Sloviter, p. 93.
22. Ibid., p. 94.
23. Ibid., p. 95.
24. Ibid.
25. After retiring from the bench, Judge Higginbotham wrote a law review article in which he argued in favor of judicial diversity: "When all judges come from the ranks of the ruling race, they are often viewed more as representatives or advocates for the ruling race than as judges committed to a partial rule of law" (1993, 1035, qtd. in Scherer 2005b, 74).
26. Women Trailblazers in the Law Project Oral Histories, transcript of oral history of Dolores Korman Sloviter, p. 101
27. Women Trailblazers in the Law Project Oral Histories, Box 5, transcript of oral history of Carolyn Dineen King, Marcy Hogan Greer interviewer, dates of interviews: July 19, September 1, December 20, 2010; January 14, 2011, p. 111.
28. Ibid., p. 167.
29. As we discuss in the concluding chapter, President Barack Obama has appointed a historic number of Asian Americans to the federal bench, and only one of his circuit court appointees (Jacqueline Nguyen) was appointed to the Ninth Circuit. Nguyen is the first Asian American woman to serve as a federal appellate judge.
30. In August 2007, the Ninth Circuit was featured in *The Third Branch* for having the first all-Hispanic panel in the history of the federal courts of appeals: Kim McLane Wardlaw, Arthur Alarcon, and Ferdinand Fernandez.
31. Two other Latino nominees to the Fifth Circuit (Jorge Rangel and Enrique Moreno) were blocked by Texas senators Phil Gramm and Kay Bailey Hutchinson during the Clinton administration (Steigerwalt 2010, 62).
32. See the press release "President Clinton Appoints Roger Gregory" at http://clinton4.nara.gov/WH/new/html/Fri_Dec_29_135529_2000.html.
33. There is also evidence that Helms blocked Clinton's nominees as retaliation for Clinton's failure to renominate Terrence Boyle, a former Helms aide whose earlier nomination by George H. W. Bush had not received any action in the Senate (Steigerwalt 2010, 63).
34. By the end of George H. W. Bush's presidency, women had been appointed to ten of the twelve circuits (Scherer 2005b, 81).
35. The Eleventh Circuit had two African American judges serving in 1999, but they did not overlap; Hatchett retired in May 1999, and Wilson began serving in July 1999.
36. For a full explanation, see Allen McDowell and Nicholas J. Cox, "How Do You Fit a Model When the Dependent Variable Is a Proportion?" August 2004, http://www.stata.com/support/faqs/statistics/logit-transformation/.
37. We also ran a specification that included an additional control for vacancies. While the vacancy measure was statistically significant, it did not change the

substantive results for any of the models, so we do not present the results here.

38. To ensure comparability across circuits, the D.C. Circuit was excluded from this analysis because of its distinctive caseload, particularly the dominance of administrative law issues (Lindquist 2007), as well as its reputation as a proving ground for potential Supreme Court nominees, which potentially incentivizes the writing of dissents.
39. Unfortunately, we are unable to evaluate thresholds lower than 10 percent, as those variables were dropped during estimation because of collinearity problems. Other alternative specifications indicated that there was no significant curvilinear relationship and that the percentage of women falls out of significance around 18 percent.
40. These models assume that the effect of women's presence on dissent would be swift (that is, happen in the same year). In supplemental analyses (not shown), we also tried "leading" the dependent variable by one year and two years to see whether additional time for women's influence within the court to take hold mattered. However, in these models, the variables for women's relative presence were no longer statistically significant.
41. Because the output for interaction terms in logit models is not directly interpretable, we followed Brambor, Clark, and Golder (2006), who note, "If a multiplicative interaction model is employed, it is nearly always necessary for the analyst to go beyond the traditional results table in order to convey quantities of interest" (74). Consequently, although the coefficient on the interaction term for African American judges and the proportion of a circuit that is female and/or minority is statistically significant in the Title VII model, graphing the marginal effects and standard errors reveals that there are no significant differences between black and white judges at any observed level of diversity. Moreover, the size of the error bars indicates that we cannot meaningfully distinguish the effect of circuit diversity at one level from any other level.
42. We do not evaluate distributive politics here as a substantive representation area for Hispanic judges in order to keep the focus on discrimination claims. However, in supplemental analyses, we found no interactive effect between Hispanic judges and the identity of the chief judge. There was also no interactive effect found between African American judges and the identity of the chief judge in criminal cases.
43. In the race discrimination models, a minority chief judge appeared in only 5 percent of the observations, while in the sex discrimination models, a female chief judge served in 20 percent of the observations. Additionally, as we are testing expectations drawn from the comments about and behavior of nontraditional chief judges, we focus only on substantive representation, rather than testing for the ideological influence of the chief judge within the circuit. However, we do account for circuit ideology as well as circuit fixed effects, both of which reflect the chief judge's preferences to some extent.

44. Although the variable for minority chief judges is operationalized such that it includes both African American and Latino chief judges as minorities, in practice it primarily captures the effect of black chief judges because only one Hispanic judge was a chief judge during this period.
45. These differences are statistically significant at the .05 level.
46. We were unable to test the interaction effect between African American judges and minority chief judges because the interaction term perfectly predicted success and was dropped from the model.

Conclusion

1. Taken from the American Presidency Project at the University of California, Santa Barbara, available at http://www.presidency.ucsb.edu/ws/?pid=78283#axzz2h30RT4g7.
2. Frank Green, "Fourth Circuit Shedding Conservative Reputation," *Richmond Times-Dispatch,* November 9, 2012, http://www.timesdispatch.com/news/state-regional/government-politics/th-circuit-shedding-conservative-reputation/article_bc5d4a00-3208–11e2-a877-0019bb30f31a.html.
3. "GOP Set to Question Judge's Impartiality," *New York Times,* July 13, 2009.
4. Senator Chuck Grassley, Questions for the Record, Senate Judiciary Committee, Patricia Ann Millett, Nominee U.S. Circuit Judge for the D.C. Circuit.
5. This sentiment is echoed by the Obama administration. Christopher Kang, senior counsel to the president, explained, "The president's record on diversity is something that we're incredibly proud of. . . . We're hoping we set a bar, and the fact that we are so public about what that bar is . . . that the next president, Democratic or Republican, is going to have to meet it too" (quoted in Goldman, Slotnick, and Schiavoni 2013, 18–19).

BIBLIOGRAPHY

Abrahamson, Shirley S. 1984. "The Woman Has Robes: Four Questions." *Golden Gate University Law Review* 14: 489–504.

Allen, David W., and Diane E. Wall. 1993. "Role Orientations and Women State Supreme Court Justices." *Judicature* 77: 156–65.

Antonio, Anthony Lising, Mitchell J. Chang, Kenji Hakuta, David A. Kenny, Shana Levin, and Jeffrey F. Milem. 2004. "Effects of Racial Diversity on Complex Thinking in College Students." *Psychological Science* 15(8): 507–10.

Applegate, B. K., F. T. Cullen, and B. S. Fisher. 2002. "Public Views toward Crime and Correctional Policies: Is There a Gender Gap?" *Journal of Criminal Justice* 30(2): 89–100.

Aries, Elizabeth. 1998. "Gender Differences in Interaction: A Reexamination." In *Sex Differences and Similarities in Communication,* ed. D. J. Canary and K. Dindia, 65–81. Mahwah, N.J.: Erlbaum.

Bartels, Brandon L. 2011. "Choices in Context: How Case-Level Factors Influence the Magnitude of Ideological Voting on the U.S. Supreme Court." *American Politics Research* 39(1): 142–75.

Baum, Lawrence. 1997. *The Puzzle of Judicial Behavior.* Ann Arbor: University of Michigan Press.

———. 2006. *Judges and Their Audiences: A Perspective on Judicial Behavior.* Princeton, N.J.: Princeton University Press.

Bazelon, Emily. 2009. "The Place of Women on the Court." *New York Times Sunday Magazine,* July 7. http://www.nytimes.com/2009/07/12/magazine/12ginsburg-t.html?pagewanted=all.

———. 2013. "The Making of a Justice: 'My Beloved World' by Sonia Sotomayor." *New York Times,* January 18, 2013. http://www.nytimes.com/2013/01/20/books/review/my-beloved-world-by-sonia-sotomayor.html.

Beckwith, Karen. 2007. "Numbers and Newness: The Descriptive and Substantive Representation of Women." *Canadian Journal of Political Science* 40(1): 27–49.

Bedolla, Lisa Garcia, Jessica L. Lavariega Monforti, and Adrian D. Pantoja. 2006. "A Second Look: Is There a Latina/o Gender Gap?" In *Intersectionality and Politics: Recent Research on Gender, Race, and Political Representation,* ed. Carol Hardy-Fanta, 147–71. New York: Haworth Press.

Benesh, Sara C. 2006. "The Contribution of Extra Judges." *Arizona Law Review* 48: 301–15.

Berring, Robert C. 1987. "Legal Research and Legal Concepts: Where Form Molds Substance." *California Law Review* 75: 15–27.

Best, Rachel Kahn, Linda Hamilton Krieger, Laura B. Edelman, and Scott R. Eliason. 2011. "Multiple Disadvantages: An Empirical Test of Intersectionality Theory in EEO Litigation." *Law and Society Review* 45: 991–1025.

Beutel, Ann M., and Margaret Mooney Marini. 1995. "Gender and Values." *American Sociological Review* 60: 436–48.

Biernat, Monica, and Diane Kobrynowicz. 1997. "Gender- and Race-Based Standards of Competence: Lower Minimum Standards but Higher Ability Standards for Devalued Groups." *Journal of Personality and Social Psychology* 72(3): 544–57.

Black, Earl, and Merle Black. 2002. *The Rise of the Southern Republicans.* Cambridge, Mass.: Belknap Press of Harvard University Press.

Black, Ryan C., and Ryan J. Owens. 2013. "Bargaining and Legal Development in the United States Courts of Appeals." *American Politics Research* 41(6): 1071–101.

Blume, J. 2010. "The Dance of Death, or (Almost) No One Gets Out of Here Alive." *South Carolina Law Review* 61(3): 465–534.

Bonneau, Chris W., and Heather M. Rice. 2009. "Impartial Judges? Race, Institutional Context, and U.S. State Supreme Courts." *State Politics & Policy Quarterly* 9(4): 381–403.

Boyd, Christina L., Lee Epstein, and Andrew D. Martin. 2010. "Untangling the Casual Effects of Sex on Judging." *American Journal of Political Science* 54(2): 389–411.

Brambor, Thomas, William Roberts Clark, and Matt Golder. 2006. "Understanding Interaction Models: Improving Empirical Analyses." *Political Analysis* 14(1): 63–82.

Bratton, Kathleen A. 2005. "Critical Mass Theory Revisited: The Behavior and Success of Token Women in State Legislatures." *Politics and Gender* 1(1): 97–125.

Bratton, Kathleen A., and Rorie L. Spill. 2002. "Existing Diversity and Judicial Selection: The Role of the Appointment Method in Establishing Gender Diversity in State Supreme Courts." *Social Science Quarterly* 83(3): 504–17.

Bratton, Kathleen, Kerry Haynie, and Beth Reingold. 2006. "Agenda Setting and African American Women in State Legislatures." In *Intersectionality and Politics: Recent Research on Gender, Race, and Political Representation,* ed. Carol Hardy-Fanta, 71–95. New York: Haworth Press.

Brennan, William J., Jr., Robert L. Carter, William T. Coleman Jr., and Owen Fiss. 1991. "A Tribute to Justice Thurgood Marshall." *Harvard Law Review* 105: 23–76.

Brooks, Richard R. W., and Haekyugn Jeon-Slaughter. 2001. "Race, Income, and Perceptions of the U.S. Court System." *Behavioral Sciences and the Law* 19: 249–64.

Browne, Irene, and Joya Misra. 2003. "The Intersection of Gender and Race in the Labor Market." *Annual Review of Sociology* 29: 487–513.

Cameron, Charles, David Epstein, and Sharyn O'Halloran. 1996. "Do Majority-Minority Districts Maximize Substantive Representation in Congress?" *American Political Science Review* 90(4): 794–812.

Carey, John M., Richard G. Niemi, and Lynda W. Powell. 1998. "Are Women State Legislators Different?" In *Women and Elective Office: Past, Present, and Future,* ed. Sue Thomas and Clyde Wilcox, 87–102. New York: Oxford University Press.

Carp, Robert, Ronald Stidham, and Kenneth L. Manning. 2014. *Judicial Process in America.* 9th ed. Los Angeles: Sage/CQ Press.

Carroll, Susan J., ed. 2001. *The Impact of Women in Public Office.* Bloomington: Indiana University Press.

Carter, Lief. 1979. *Reason in Law.* Boston: Little, Brown.

Casellas, Jason P. 2011. *Latino Representation in State Houses and Congress.* Cambridge: Cambridge University Press.

"A Celebration to Honor the Historic First Term of Justice Sandra Day O'Connor on the Supreme Court." 2012. *Supreme Court Historical Society* 34(2): 1–5.

Chen, Edward M. 2003. "The Judiciary, Diversity, and Justice for All." *Asian Law Journal* 10: 127–42.

Cheurprakobkit, S. 2000. "Police-Citizen Contact and Police Performance Attitudinal Differences between Hispanics and Non-Hispanics." *Journal of Criminal Justice* 28(4): 325–36.

Chew, P. K., and R. E. Kelley. 2008. "Myth of the Color-Blind Judge: An Empirical Analysis of Racial Harassment Cases." *Washington University Law Review* 86: 1117–63.

Childs, Sarah, and Mona Lena Krook. 2006. "Should Feminists Give Up on Critical Mass? A Contingent Yes." *Politics & Gender* 2(4): 522–30.

———. 2008. "Critical Mass Theory and Women's Political Representation." *Political Studies* 56: 1–12.

Choi, Stephen J., and G. Mitu Gulati. 2007. "Trading Votes for Reasoning." Southern California Law Review 81: 735–79.

Christensen, Robert K., and John Szmer. 2012. "Examining the Efficiency of the U.S. Courts of Appeals: Pathologies and Prescriptions." *International Review of Law and Economics* 32(1): 30–37.

Christensen, Robert K., John Szmer, and Justin M. Stritch. 2012. "Race and Gender Bias in Three Administrative Contexts: Impact on Work Assignments in State Supreme Courts." *Journal of Public Administration Research and Theory* 22: 625–48.

Coates, Jennifer. 1988. "Gossip Revisited: Language in All-Female Groups." In *Women in Their Speech Communities,* ed. Jennifer Coates and Deborah Cameron, 84–122. London: Longman.

Coffin, Frank M. 1994. *On Appeal: Courts, Lawyering, and Judging.* New York: W. W. Norton.

Cohen, Jonathan Matthew. 2002. *Inside the Appellate Courts: The Impact of Court Organization on Judicial Decision Making in the United States Courts of Appeals.* Ann Arbor: University of Michigan Press.

Collins, Paul M., Jr. 2008. "The Consistency of Judicial Choice." *Journal of Politics* 70(3): 861–73.

Collins, Paul M., Jr., and Wendy L. Martinek. 2011. "The Small Group Context: Designated District Court Judges in the U.S. Courts of Appeals." *Journal of Empirical Legal Studies* 8: 177–205.

Collins, Paul M., Jr., Kenneth L. Manning, and Robert A. Carp. 2010. "Gender, Critical Mass, and Judicial Decision Making." *Law & Policy* 32(2): 260–81.

Collins, Todd A., and Laura Moyer. 2008. "Gender, Race, and Intersectionality on the Federal Appellate Bench." *Political Research Quarterly* 61(2): 219–27.

Correll, Shelley J., and Cecilia L. Ridgeway. 2006. "Expectation States Theory." In *Handbook of Social Psychology,* ed. John Delamater. New York: Springer.

Cox, Adam B., and Thomas J. Miles. 2008. "Judging the Voting Rights Act." *Columbia Law Review* 108(1): 1–54.

Crenshaw, Kimberle. 1989. "Demarginalizing the Intersection of Race and Sex: A Black Feminist Critique of Antidiscrimination Doctrine, Feminist Theory and Antiracist Politics." *University of Chicago Legal Forum* 140: 139–67.

———. 1991. "Mapping the Margins: Intersectionality, Identity Politics, and Violence against Women of Color." *Stanford Law Review* 43(6): 1241–99.

———. 1998. "A Black Feminist Critique of Antidiscrimination Law and Politics." In *The Politics of Law,* ed. David Kairys. Rev. ed. New York: Basic Books. Reprinted in *The Law of Sex Discrimination,* 3rd ed., ed. J. Ralph Lindgren, Nadine Taub, Beth Anne Wolfson, and Carla M. Palumbo, 356–62. 2005. Belmont, Calif.: Thomson Wadsworth.

Cross, Frank B., and Emerson H. Tiller. 1998. "Judicial Partisanship and Obedience to Legal Doctrine: Whistleblowing on the Federal Courts of Appeals." *Yale Law Journal* 107(7): 2155–76.

Crowe, Nancy E. 1999. "The Effects of Judges' Sex and Race on Judicial Decision Making on the U.S. Courts of Appeals, 1981–1996." Ph.D. diss., University of Chicago.

Dahlerup, Drude. 1988. "From a Small to a Large Minority: Women in Scandinavian Politics." *Scandinavian Political Studies* 11(4): 275–97.

———. 2006. "The Story of the Theory of 'Critical Mass.'" *Politics and Gender* 2(4): 511–22.

Darcy, Robert, Susan Welch, and Janet Clark. 1994. *Women, Elections, and Representation in Democratic Nations.* Lincoln: University of Nebraska Press.

Darder, Antonia, and Rodolfo D. Torres. 1998. "Latinos and Society: Culture,

Politics, and Class." In *The Latino Studies Reader: Culture, Economy, & Society,* ed. Antonia Darder and Rodolfo Torres, 3–26. Blackwell: Oxford.

Darity, W. A., Jr., J. Dietrich, and D. Hamilton. 2005. "Bleach in the Rainbow: Latin Ethnicity and Preference for Whiteness." *Transforming Anthropology* 13(2) 103–9.

Davis, Sue. 1992. "Do Women Judges Speak in a Different Voice—Carol Gilligan, Feminist Legal Theory, and the Ninth Circuit." *Wisconsin Women's Law Journal* 8: 143–74.

———. 1993. "The Voice of Sandra Day O'Connor." *Judicature* 77: 134–39.

Dawson, M. C. 1994. *Behind the Mule: Race and Class in African-American Politics.* Princeton, N.J.: Princeton University Press.

Duerst-Lahti, Georgia, 2002. "Knowing Congress as a Gendered Institution: Manliness and the Implications of Women in Congress." In *Women Transforming Congress,* ed. Cindy Simon Rosenthal, 20–49. Congressional Studies Series No. 4. Norman: University of Oklahoma Press.

Duerst-Lahti, Georgia, and Rita-Mae Kelly. 1995. *Gender Power, Leadership, and Governance.* Ann Arbor: University of Michigan Press.

Eagly, Alice H., and Blair T. Johnson. 1990. "Gender and Leadership Style: A Meta-Analysis." *Psychological Bulletin* 108: 233–56.

Edwards, Harry T. 2003. "The Effects of Collegiality on Judicial Decision Making." *University of Pennsylvania Law Review* 151: 1639–90.

Eilperin, Juliet. 2013. "Senate Confirms Highest-Ranking Openly Gay Judge in the U.S. Tuesday." *Washington Post,* September 24. http://www.washington post.com/blogs/post-politics/wp/2013/09/24/senate-to-confirm-highest -ranking-gay-judge-in-the-u-s-tuesday/.

Epstein, Lee, William M. Landes, and Richard Posner. 2013. *The Behavior of Federal Judges: A Theoretical and Empirical Study of Rational Choice.* Cambridge, Mass.: Harvard University Press.

Epstein, Lee, Andrew Martin, Jeffrey Segal, and Chad Westerland. 2007. "The Judicial Common Space." *Journal of Law, Economics, and Organization* 23: 303–25.

Farhang, Sean, and Gregory Wawro. 2004. "Institutional Dynamics on the U.S. Court of Appeals: Minority Representation under Panel Decision Making." *Journal of Law, Economics & Organization* 20: 299–330.

Farhang, Sean, Jonathan P. Kastellec, and Gregory J. Wawro. Forthcoming. "Opinion Assignment and Control of the Law on the U.S. Courts of Appeals." *Journal of Legal Studies.*

Fraga, Luis Ricardo, Linda Lopez, Valerie Martinez-Ebers, and Ricardo Ramirez. 2006. "Gender and Ethnicity: Patterns of Electoral Success and Legislative Advocacy among Latina and Latino State Officials in Four States." In *Intersectionality and Politics: Recent Research on Gender, Race, and Political Representation,* ed. Carol Hardy-Fanta, 121–45. New York: Haworth Press.

Giles, Micheal W., Virginia Hettinger, and Todd Peppers. 2001. "Picking Federal Judges: A Note on Policy and Partisan Selection Agendas." *Political Research Quarterly* 54: 623–41.

Giles, Micheal W., Thomas G. Walker, and Christopher Zorn. 2006. "Setting a Judicial Agenda: The Decision to Grant En Banc Review in the U.S. Courts of Appeals." *Journal of Politics* 68(4): 852–66.

Gilligan, Carol. 1982. *In a Different Voice: Psychological Theory and Women's Development.* Cambridge, Mass.: Harvard University Press.

Ginsburg, Ruth Bader, and Laura W. Brill. 1995. "Women in the Federal Judiciary: Three Way Pavers and the Exhilarating Change President Carter Wrought." *Fordham Law Review* 64: 281–90.

Goldman, Sheldon. 1997. *Picking Federal Judges: Lower Court Selection from Roosevelt through Reagan.* New Haven, Conn.: Yale University Press.

———. 2002. "Assessing the Senate Judicial Confirmation Process: Index of Obstruction and Delay." *Judicature* 86: 251–57.

Goldman, Sheldon, and Matthew D. Saronson. 1994. "Clinton's Nontraditional Judges: Creating a More Representative Bench." *Judicature* 78: 68–73.

Goldman, Sheldon, Sara Schiavoni, and Elliot Slotnick. 2009. "W. Bush's Judicial Legacy: Mission Accomplished." *Judicature* 92: 258–88.

Goldman, Sheldon, Elliot Slotnick, and Sara Schiavoni. 2011. "Obama's Judiciary at Midterm: The Confirmation Drama Continues." *Judicature* 94: 262–303.

Goldman, Sheldon, Elliot Slotnick, Gerard Gryski, and Sara Schiavoni. 2005. "W. Bush's Judiciary: The First Term Record." *Judicature* 88: 244–75.

———. 2013. "Obama's First Term Judiciary: Picking Judges in the Minefield of Obstructionism." *Judicature* 97: 7–47.

Goldman, Sheldon, Elliot Slotnick, Gerard Gryski, and Gary Zuk. 2000–2001. "Clinton's Judges: Summing Up the Legacy." *Judicature* 84: 228–55.

———. 2003. "W. Bush Remaking the Judiciary: Like Father Like Son?" *Judicature* 86: 282–311.

Gottschall, Jon. 1983. "Carter's Judicial Appointments: The Influence of Affirmative Action and Merit Selection on Voting on the U.S. Courts of Appeals." *Judicature* 67: 165–73.

Grey, Sandra. 2002. "Does Size Matter? Critical Mass and New Zealand's Women MPs." *Parliamentary Affairs* 55(1): 19–29.

Gruenfeld, Deborah. 1995. "Status, Ideology and Integrative Complexity on the U.S. Supreme Court: Rethinking the Politics of Political Decision-Making." *Journal of Personality and Social Psychology* 68(1): 5–20.

Gruenfeld, Deborah, and Andrea B. Hollingshead. 1993. "Sociocognition in Work Groups: The Evolution of Group Integrative Complexity and Its Relation to Task Performance." *Small Group Research* 24: 383–405.

Gruenfeld, Deborah, and Jared Preston. 2000. "Upending the Status Quo: Cognitive Complexity in U.S. Supreme Court Justices Who Overturn Legal Precedent." *Personality and Social Psychology Bulletin* 26(8): 1013–22.

Gruenfeld, Deborah, M. C. Thomas-Hunt, and Peter H. Kim. 1998. "Cognitive Flexibility, Communication Strategy, and Integrative Complexity in Groups: Public versus Private Reactions to Majority and Minority Status." *Journal of Experimental Social Psychology* 34: 202–26.

Gruhl, John, Cassia Spohn, and Susan Welch. 1981. "Women as Policymakers: The Case of Trial Judges." *American Journal of Political Science* 25(2): 308–22.

Gryski, Gerald, and Gary Zuk. 2006. *Update to the Multi-User Database on the Attributes of United States Appeals Court Judges, 1801–2000.* http://artsandsciences.sc.edu/poli/juri/attributes.htm.

Guinier, L., M. Fine, J. Balin, A. Bartow, and D. L. Stachel. 1994. "Becoming Gentlemen: Women's Experiences at One Ivy League Law School." *University of Pennsylvania Law Review* 143(1): 1–110.

Guthrie, Chris, Jeffrey J. Rachlinski, and Andrew J. Wistrich. 2000. "Inside the Judicial Mind." *Cornell Law Review* 86: 777–830.

Haire, Susan B. 2006. "Judicial Selection and Decisionmaking in the Ninth Circuit." *Arizona Law Review* 48: 267–285.

Haire, Susan, Laura Moyer, and Shawn Treier. 2013. "Diversity, Deliberation, and Judicial Opinion Writing." *Journal of Law and Courts* 1(3): 303–30.

Hammonds, Evelynn. 1997. "Toward a Genealogy of Black Female Sexuality: The Problematic of Silence." In *Feminist Genealogies, Colonial Legacies, Democratic Futures,* ed. M. Jaqui Alexander and Chandra Talpade Mohanty, 170–82. New York: Routledge.

Hancock, Ange-Marie. 2007. "When Multiplication Doesn't Equal Quick Addition: Examining Intersectionality as a Research Paradigm." *Perspectives on Politics* 5(1): 63–79.

Hannagan, Rebecca J., and Christopher W. Larimer. 2010. "Does Gender Composition Affect Group Decision Outcomes? Evidence from a Laboratory Experiment." *Political Behavior* 32: 51–67.

Harris, Angela. 1990. "Race and Essentialism in Feminist Legal Theory." *Stanford Law Review* 42(3): 581–616.

Hastie, William H. 1973. "Toward an Equalitarian Legal Order." *Annals of the American Academy of Political and Social Science* 407: 18–31.

Hawkesworth, Mary. 2003. "Congressional Enactments of Race-Gender: Toward a Theory of Raced-Gendered Institutions." *American Political Science Review* 97: 529–50.

Haynie, Kerry L. 2001. *African-American Legislators in the American States.* New York: Columbia University Press.

Herrick, Rebekah. 2011. *Representation and Institutional Design.* Lanham, Md.: Lexington Books.

Hettinger, Virginia A., Stefanie A. Lindquist, and Wendy L. Martinek. 2003. "The Role and Impact of Chief Judges in the United States Courts of Appeals." *Justice System Journal* 24: 91–117.

———. 2004. "Comparing Attitudinal and Strategic Accounts of Dissenting Behavior." *American Journal of Political Science* 48: 123–37.

———. 2006. *Judging on a Collegial Court: Influences on Federal Appellate Decision Making.* Charlottesville: University of Virginia Press.

Higginbotham, A. Leon. 1993. "Seeking Pluralism in Judicial Systems: The American Experience and the South African Challenge." *Duke Law Journal* 42: 1028–68.

Hinkle, Rachel. 2014. "One of These Judges Is Not Like the Others: Authors and Panel Effects in the U.S. Courts of Appeals." Unpublished conference paper presented at the annual meeting of the Midwest Political Science Association.

Howard, J. Woodford. 1981. *Courts of Appeals in the Federal System.* Princeton, N.J.: Princeton University Press.

Huddy, L. 2001. "From Social to Political Identity: A Critical Examination of Social Identity Theory." *Political Psychology* 22(1): 127–56.

Hurwitz, Jon, and M. Peffley. 2005 "Explaining the Great Racial Divide: Perceptions of Fairness in the U.S. Criminal Justice System." *Journal of Politics* 67(3): 762–83.

Hurwitz, Mark S., and Drew Noble Lanier. 2008. "Diversity in State and Federal Appellate Courts: Change and Continuity across 20 Years." *Justice System Journal* 29(1): 47–70.

Ifill, S. A. 2000. "Racial Diversity on the Bench: Beyond Role Models and Public Confidence." *Washington & Lee Law Review* 57: 405–95.

Jaffee, S., and J. S. Hyde. 2000. "Gender Differences in Moral Orientation: A Meta-Analysis." *Psychological Bulletin* 126(5): 703–26.

Janis, Irving L. 1972. *Victims of Groupthink: A Psychological Study of Foreign-Policy Decisions and Fiascoes.* 2nd ed. Boston: Little Brown.

Jehn, Karen A., Gregory B. Northcraft, and Margaret A. Neale. 1999. "Why Differences Make a Difference: A Field Study of Diversity, Conflict and Performance in Workgroups." *Administrative Science Quarterly* 44(4): 741–63.

Jilani, Nadia A., Donald R. Songer, and Susan W. Johnson. 2010. "Gender, Consciousness Raising, and Decision Making on the Supreme Court of Canada." *Judicature* 94: 1–17.

Johnson, Kevin, and Luis Fuentes-Rohwer. 2004. "A Principled Approach to the Quest for Racial Diversity on the Judiciary." *Michigan Journal of Race & Law* 10: 5–54.

Johnson, Richard A., and Gary I. Schulman. 1989. "Gender-Role Composition and Role Entrapment in Decision-Making Groups." *Gender & Society* 3(3): 355–72.

Jost, John T., Mahzarin R. Banaji, and Brian A. Nosek. 2004. *Political Psychology* 25(6): 881–919.

Juenke, Eric Gonzales, and Robert R. Preuhs. 2012. "Irreplaceable Legislators? Rethinking Minority Representatives in the New Century." *American Journal of Political Science* 56: 705–15.

Kaheny, Erin B., Susan B. Haire, and Sara C. Benesh. 2008. "Change over Tenure: Voting, Variance, and Decision Making on the U.S. Courts of Appeals." *American Journal of Political Science* 52(3): 490–503.

Kahneman, Daniel. 2011. *Thinking, Fast and Slow.* New York: Farrar, Straus, and Giroux.

Kanter, Rosabeth Moss. 1977. *Men and Women of the Corporation.* New York: Basic Books.

Karpowitz, Christopher F., and Tali Mendelberg. 2007. "Groups and Deliberation." *Swiss Political Science Review* 13: 645–62.

Karpowitz, Christopher F., Tali Mendelberg, and Lee Shaker. 2012. "Gender Inequality in Deliberative Participation." *American Political Science Review* 106(3): 533–47.

Karst, K. L. 1984. "Woman's Constitution." *Duke Law Journal* 33(3): 447–508.

Kastellec, Jonathan P. 2007. "Panel Composition and Judicial Compliance on the U.S. Courts of Appeals." *Journal of Law, Economics, and Organization* 23(2): 421–41.

———. 2013. "Racial Diversity and Judicial Influence on Appellate Courts." *American Journal of Political Science* 57(1): 167–83.

Kathlene, Lyn. 1994. "Power and Influence in State Legislative Policymaking: The Interaction of Gender and Position in Committee Hearing Debates." *American Political Science Review* 88(3): 560–73.

Kaufmann, K. M. 2003. "Cracks in the Rainbow: Group Commonality as a Basis for Latino and African-American Political Coalitions." *Political Research Quarterly* 56(2): 199–210.

Keiser, Lael R., Vicky M. Wilkins, Kenneth J. Meier, and Catherine A. Holland. 2002. "Lipstick and Logarithms: Gender, Institutional Context, and Representative Bureaucracy." *American Political Science Review* 96: 553–64.

Kennedy, Carole. 2003. "Gender Differences in Committee Decision-Making: Process and Outputs in an Experimental Setting." *Women & Politics* 25(3): 27–45.

Kenney, Sally J. 2013. *Gender and Justice: Why Women in the Judiciary Really Matter.* New York: Routledge.

Kim, Pauline T. 2008–9. "Deliberation and Strategy on the United States Courts of Appeals: An Empirical Exploration of Panel Effects." *University of Pennsylvania Law Review* 157: 1319–81.

Kinder, Donald R., and Nicholas Winter. 2001. "Exploring the Racial Divide: Blacks, Whites, and Opinion on National Policy." *American Journal of Political Science* 45: 439–53.

King, Gary, and Langche Zeng. 1999. "Logistic Regression in Rare Events Data." Department of Government, Harvard University. http://GKing.Harvard.Edu.

Kluger, R. 1976. *Simple Justice: The History of* Brown v. Board of Education *and Black America's Struggle for Equality.* New York: Knopf.

Kritzer, H. M., and T. M. Uhlman. 1977. "Sisterhood in the Courtroom: Sex of Judge and Defendant in Criminal Case Disposition." *Social Science Journal* 14(2): 77–78.

Kuersten, Ashlyn K., and Susan Haire. 2007. "Update to Multi-User Database on the United States Courts of Appeals, 1997–2002." http://artsandsciences.sc.edu/poli/juri/appct.htm.

Leal, David. 2007. "Latino Public Opinion: Does It Exist?" In *Latino Politics: Identity, Mobilization, and Representation,* ed. Rodolfo Espino, David L. Leal, and K. J. Meier, 27–43. Charlottesville: University of Virginia Press.

Lindquist, Stefanie A. 2007. "Bureaucratization and Balkanization: The Origins and the Effects of Decision-Making Norms in the Federal Appellate Courts." *University of Richmond Law Review* 41: 659–706.

Lindquist, Stefanie A., Wendy L. Martinek, and Virginia A. Hettinger. 2007. "Splitting the Difference: Modeling Appellate Court Decisions with Mixed Outcomes." *Law & Society Review* 41(2): 429–56.

Long, J. S., and J. Freese. 2003. *Regression Models for Categorical Dependent Variables Using Stata.* Rev. ed. College Station, Tex.: Stata Press.

Lopez, D., and Y. Espiritu. 1990. "Panethnicity in the United States: A Theoretical Framework." *Ethnic & Racial Studies* 13(2): 198–224.

Lucas, J. W., and A. R. Baxter. 2012. "Power, influence, and diversity in organizations." *Annals of the American Academy of Political and Social Science* 639(1): 49–70.

Maltzman, Forrest, James F. Spriggs, and Paul J. Wahlbeck. 2000. *Crafting Law on the Supreme Court: The Collegial Game.* Cambridge: Cambridge University Press.

Mansbridge, Jane. 1999. "Should Blacks Represent Blacks and Women Represent Women? A Contingent 'Yes.'" *Journal of Politics* 61(3): 628–57.

Marini, M. M. 1990. "Sex and Gender: What Do We Know?" *Sociological Forum* 5(1): 95–120.

Martin, Elaine. 1990. "Men and Women on the Bench: Vive La Difference?" *Judicature* 73: 204–8.

———. 1999. "Women Judges: The New Generation." In *Women in Politics: Outsiders or Insiders?,* ed. Lois Duke Whitaker. Upper Saddle River, N.J.: Prentice Hall.

———. 2009. "U.S. Women Federal Court Judges Appointed by President Carter." *Feminist Legal Studies* 17: 43–59.

Martin, Elaine, and Barry Pyle. 2002. "Gender and Racial Diversification of State Supreme Courts." *Women and Politics* 24: 35–52.

———. 2005. "Women of the Courts Symposium: State High Courts and Divorce: The Impact of Judicial Gender." *University of Toledo Law Review* 36: 923–48.

Martin, Patricia Yancey, John R. Reynolds, and Shelley Keith. 2002. "Gender Bias and Feminist Consciousness among Judges and Attorneys: A Standpoint Theory Analysis." *Signs* 27: 665–701.

Martinek, Wendy L. 2010. "Judges as Members of Small Groups." In *The Psychology of Judicial Decision Making,* ed. David Klein and Gregory Mitchell, 73–84. New York: Oxford University Press.

Matthews D. R., and J. W. Prothro. 1966. *Negroes and the New Southern Politics.* New York: Harcourt, Brace & World.

McCall, Leslie. 2009. "The Complexity of Intersectionality." In *Intersectionality and Beyond: Law, Power, and the Politics of Location,* ed. Davina Cooper Graham, Jane Krishnadas, and Didi Herman, 49–76. New York: Routledge-Cavendash.

McCall, Madhavi. 2008. "Structuring Gender's Impact: Judicial Voting across Criminal Justice Cases." *American Politics Research* 36(2): 264–96.

McClain, Paula D., Jessica D. Johnson Carew, Eugene Walton Jr., and Cansis S. Watts. 2009. "Group Membership, Group Identity, and Group Consciousness: Measures of Racial Identity in American Politics?" *Annual Review of Political Science* 12: 471–85.

McClain, Paula, and Joseph Stewart. 2006. *Can We All Get Along? Racial and Ethnic Minorities in American Politics.* Boulder, Colo.: Westview.

McDowell, Allen, and Nicholas J. Cox. 2004. "How Do You Fit a Model When the Dependent Variable Is a Proportion?" http://www.stata.com/support/faqs/statistics/logit-transformation/.

McLeod, Poppy Lauretta, S. A. Lobel, and T. H. Cox. 1996. "Ethnic Diversity and Creativity in Small Groups." *Small Group Research* 27(2): 248–64.

Meier, Kenneth J., and Joseph Stewart Jr. 1992. "Active Representation in Educational Bureaucracies: Policy Impacts." *American Review of Public Administration* 22: 157–71.

Menkel-Meadow, Carrie. 1985. "Portia in a Different Voice: Speculations on a Women's Lawyering Process." *Berkeley Women's Law Journal* 1: 39–63.

Miller, A., H. P. Gurin, G. Gurin, and O. Malanchuk. 1981. "Group Consciousness and Political Participation." *American Journal of Political Science* 25: 494–511.

Milliken, Frances J., and Luis L. Martins. 1996. "Searching for Common Threads: Understanding the Multiple Effects of Diversity in Organizational Groups." *Academy of Management Review* 21(2): 402–33.

Montoya, Lisa J. 1996. "Latino Gender Differences in Public Opinion: Results from the Latino National Political Survey." *Hispanic Journal of Behavioral Sciences* 18: 255–76.

Morin, Jason L. 2014. "The Voting Behavior of Minority Judges in the U.S. Courts of Appeals: Does the Race of the Claimant Matter?" *American Politics Research* 42(1): 34–64.

Moyer, Laura P. 2008. "Organizations, Complexity, and Decision Making in the U.S. Courts of Appeals." Ph.D. diss., University of Georgia.

———. 2013. "Rethinking Critical Mass in the Federal Appellate Courts." *Journal of Women, Politics, and Policy* 34(1): 49–71.

Negowetti, Nicole. 2014. "Judicial Decisionmaking, Empathy, and the Limits of Perception." *Akron Law Review* 47: 693–751.

Nemeth, Charlan J. 1986. "Differential Contributions of Majority and Minority Influence." *Psychological Review* 93(1): 23–32.

Orey, Bryon D'Andra, Wendy Smooth, Kimberly Adams, and Kisha Harris-Clark. 2006. "Race and Gender Matter: Refining Models of Legislative Policy Making in State Legislature." In *Intersectionality and Politics: Recent Research on Gender, Race, and Political Representation,* ed. Carol Hardy-Fanta, 97–119. New York: Haworth Press.

Ostberg, C. L., and Matthew E. Wetstein. 2007. *Attitudinal Decision Making in the Supreme Court of Canada.* Vancouver: University of British Columbia Press.

Owens, Chris T. 2005. "Black Substantive Representation in State Legislatures from 1971–1994." *Social Science Quarterly* 86(4): 779–91.

Page, Scott E. 2007. "Making the Difference: Applying a Logic of Diversity." *Journal of Management Perspectives* 21(4): 6–20.

Page, Susan. 2004. "Bush Is Opening Doors with a Diverse Cabinet." *USA Today,* December 9. http://usatoday30.usatoday.com/news/washington/2004-12-09-diverse-usat_x.htm.

Papke, L. E., and J. Wooldridge. 1996. "Econometric Methods for Fractional Response Variables with an Application to 401(k) Plan Participation Rates." *Journal of Applied Econometrics* 11: 619–32.

Pelled, L., K. Eisenhardt, and K. Xin. 1999. "Exploring the Black Box: An Analysis of Workgroup Diversity, Conflict, and Performance." *Administrative Science Quarterly* 44: 1–28.

Peresie, Jennifer L. 2005. "Female Judges Matter: Gender and Collegial Decision-Making in the Federal Appellate Courts." *Yale Law Journal* 114: 1759–90.

Pitkin, Hanna. 1967. *The Concept of Representation.* Berkeley: University of California Press.

Pitts, David W. 2005. "Diversity, Representation, and Performance: Evidence about Race and Ethnicity in Public Organizations." *Journal of Public Administration Research and Theory* 4(15): 615–31.

Poggione, Sarah. 2004. "Exploring Gender Differences in State Legislators' Policy Preferences." *Political Research Quarterly* 57(2): 305–14.

Posner, Richard A. 2008. *How Judges Think.* Cambridge, Mass.: Harvard University Press.

Pugh, Meredith D., and Ralph Wahrman. 1983. "Neutralizing Sexism in Mixed-Sex Groups: Do Women Have to Be Better Than Men?" *American Journal of Sociology* 88(4): 746–62.

Reingold, Beth. 1996. "Conflict and Cooperation: Legislative Strategies and Concepts of Power among Female and Male State Legislators." *Journal of Politics* 58: 464–85.

———. 2000. *Representing Women: Sex, Gender and Legislative Behavior in Arizona and California.* Chapel Hill: University of North Carolina Press.

Reingold, Beth, and Adrienne Smith. 2012. "Welfare Policymaking and Intersections of Race, Ethnicity, and Gender in U.S. State Legislatures." *American Journal of Political Science* 56(1): 131–47.

Revesz, Richard L. 1997. "Environmental Regulation, Ideology, and the DC Circuit." *Virginia Law Review* 83: 1717–72.

Ridgeway, Cecilia. 2001. "Gender, Status, and Leadership." *Journal of Social Issues* 57(4): 637–55.

Ridgeway, Cecilia, and Lynn Smith-Lovin. 1999. "The Gender System and Interaction." *Annual Review of Sociology* 25: 191–216.

Rinehart, Sue Tolleson. 1991. "Do Women Leaders Make a Difference? Substance, Style and Perceptions." In *Gender and Policymaking: Studies of Women in Office,* ed. Debra L. Dodson, 93–102. New Brunswick, N.J.: Center for the American Woman and Politics, Eagleton Institute, Rutgers University.

Rosenthal, Cindy Simon. 1998. *When Women Lead: Integrative Leadership in State Legislatures.* New York: Oxford University Press.

Ruhe, John, and John Eatman. 1977. "Effects of Racial Composition on Small Work Groups." *Small Group Behavior* 8(4): 479–486.

Saint-Germain, Michelle. 1989. "Does Their Difference Make a Difference? The Impact of Women on Public Policy in the Arizona Legislature." *Social Science Quarterly* 70(4): 956–68.

Sanbonmatsu, Kira. 2006. *Where Women Run: Gender and Party in the American States.* Ann Arbor: University of Michigan Press.

Scherer, Nancy. 2005a. "Blacks on the Bench." *Political Science Quarterly* 119(4): 655–75.

———. 2005b. *Scoring Points: Politicians, Activists, and the Lower Federal Court Appointment Process.* Stanford, Calif: Stanford University Press.

Scherer, Nancy, and Brett Curry. 2010. "Does Descriptive Race Representation Enhance Institutional Legitimacy? The Case of U.S. Courts." *Journal of Politics* 72(1): 90–104.

Scherer, Nancy, and Banks Miller. 2009. "The Federalist Society's Influence on the Federal Judiciary." *Political Research Quarterly* 62(2): 366–78.

Schweiger, William, R. Sandberg, and Paula L. Rechner. 1989. "Experiential Effects of Dialectical Inquiry, Devil's Advocacy, and Consensus Approaches to Strategic Decision Making." *Academy of Management Journal* 32: 745–72.

Sen, Maya. 2014. "How Judicial Qualification Ratings May Disadvantage Minority and Female Candidates." *Journal of Law and Courts* 2(1): 33–65.

Shapiro, R. Y., and H. Mahajan. 1986. "Gender Differences in Policy Preferences: A Summary of Trends from the 1960s to the 1980s." *Public Opinion Quarterly* 50(1): 42–61.

Sherry, Susanna. 1986. "Civic Virtue and the Feminine Voice in Constitutional Adjudication." *Virginia Law Review* 72: 543–616.

Sigelman, L., and S. Welch. 1991. *Black Americans' View of Racial Inequality.* Cambridge: Cambridge University Press.

Simien, Evelyn M. 2007. "Doing Intesectionality Research: From Conceptual Issues to Practical Examples." *Politics & Gender* 3: 264–271.

Slotnick, Elliot E. 1982–83. "Lowering the Bench or Raising It Higher: Affirmative Action and Judicial Selection during the Carter Administration." *Yale Law and Policy Review* 1: 270–98.

———. 1983–84. "The Paths to the Federal Bench: Gender, Race, and Judicial Recruitment Variation." *Judicature* 67: 371–88.

Smith, T. W. 1984. "The Polls: Gender and Attitudes toward Violence." *Public Opinion Quarterly* 48(1): 384–96.

Smooth, Wendy. 2006. "Intersectionality in Electoral Politics: A Mess Worth Making." *Politics & Gender* 2: 400–414.

———. 2011. "Standing for Women? Which Women? The Substantive Representation of Women's Interests and the Research Imperative of Intersectionality." *Politics & Gender* 7(3): 436–41.

Solberg, Rorie Spill. 2006. "Court Size and Diversity on the Bench: The Ninth Circuit and Its Sisters." *University of Arizona Law Review* 48: 247–66.

Solimine, M. E., and S. E. Wheatley. 1994. "Rethinking Feminist Judging." *Indiana Law Journal* 70: 891–920.

Sommers, Samuel R. 2006. "On Racial Diversity and Group Decision Making:

Identifying Multiple Effects of Racial Composition on Jury Deliberations." *Journal of Personality and Social Psychology* 90: 597–612.
Sommers, Samuel R., L. S. Warp, and C. C. Mahoney. 2008. "Cognitive Effects of Racial Diversity: White Individuals' Information Processing in Heterogeneous Groups." *Journal of Experimental Social Psychology* 44: 1129–36.
Songer, Donald R. 1997. "The United States Courts of Appeals Database." Ann Arbor, Mich.: Inter-university Consortium for Political and Social Research. www.cas.sc.edu/poli/juri/appct.htm.
Songer, Donald R., and Kelly Crews-Meyer. 2000. "Does Judge Gender Matter? Decision Making in State Supreme Courts." *Social Science Quarterly* 81(3): 750–62.
Songer, Donald R., Sue Davis, and Susan B. Haire. 1994. "A Reappraisal of Diversification in the Federal Courts: Gender Effects in the Courts of Appeals." *Journal of Politics* 56: 425–39.
Songer, Donald R., Reginald S. Sheehan, and Susan B. Haire. 2000. *Continuity and Change on the United States Courts of Appeals.* Ann Arbor: University of Michigan Press.
Sotomayor, Sonia. 2002. "Raising the Bar: Latino and Latina Presence in the Judiciary and the Struggle for Representation." *La Raza Law Journal* 13: 87–94.
Spitzer, Matthew, and Eric Talley. 2013. "Left, Right and Center: Strategic Information Acquisition and Diversity in Judicial Panels." *Journal of Law, Economics, and Organization* 29: 638–80.
Stasser, Garold, and Z. Birchmeier. 2003. "Group Creativity and Collective Choice." In *Group Creativity: Innovation through Collaboration,* ed. P. B. Paulus and B. A. Nijstad, 81–93. New York: Oxford University Press.
Staudt, Nancy, Barry Friedman, and Lee Epstein. 2008. "On the Role of Ideological Homogeneity in Generating Consequential Constitutional Decisions." *University Pennsylvania Journal of Constitutional Law* 10: 361–86.
Steffensmeier, Darrell, and Chester L. Britt. 2001. "Judges' Race and Judicial Decision Making: Do Black Judges Sentence Differently?" *Social Science Quarterly* 82(4): 749–64.
Steigerwalt, Amy. 2010. *Battle Over the Bench: Senators, Interest Groups, and Lower Court Confirmations.* Charlottesville: University of Virginia Press.
Suedfeld, Peter, and Philip Tetlock. 1977. "Integrative Complexity of Communications in International Crises." *Journal of Conflict Resolution* 21(1): 169–84.
Sun, Ivan Y., and Yuning Wu. 2006. "Citizens' Perceptions of the Courts: The Impact of Race and Recent Experience." *Journal of Criminal Justice* 34: 457–67.
Sunstein, Cass. 2003. *Why Societies Need Dissent.* Cambridge, Mass.: Harvard University Press.
Sunstein, Cass, David Schkade, Lisa M. Ellman, and Andres Sawicki. 2006. *Are Judges Political? An Empirical Analysis of the Federal Judiciary.* Washington, D.C.: Brookings Institute.
The Supreme Court: Home to America's Highest Court. 2009. C-SPAN documentary.

Swain, Carol M. 1993. *Black Faces, Black Interests: The Representation of African Americans in Congress.* Cambridge, Mass.: Harvard University Press.
Swers, Michele. 2001. "Understanding the Policy Impact of Electing Women: Evidence from Research on Congress and State Legislatures." *PS: Political Science and Politics* 34(2): 217–20.
Tacha, Deanell Reece. 1995. "W Stories: Women in Leadership Positions in the Judiciary." *West Virginia Law Review* 97: 683–702.
———. 1996. "The C Word: On Collegiality." *Ohio State Law Journal* 56: 585–92.
Tetlock, Philip E., Jane Bernzweig, and Jack L. Gallant. 1985. "Supreme Court Decision Making: Cognitive Style as a Predictor of Ideological Consistency of Voting." *Journal of Personality and Social Psychology* 48(5): 1227–39.
Thomas, Sue. 1991. "The Impact of Women on State Legislative Policies." *Journal of Politics* 53(4): 958–76.
———. 1994. *How Women Legislate.* New York: Oxford University Press.
Tsui, A. S., T. D. Egan, and C. A. O'Reilly. 1992. "Being Different: Relational Demography and Organizational Attachment." *Administratively Science Quarterly* 37: 549–79.
Uhlman, Thomas M. 1978. "Black Elite Decision Making: The Case of Trial Judges." *American Journal of Political Science* 22(4): 884–95.
U.S. Census Bureau. "The Asian Population: 2010." March 2012. http://www.census.gov/prod/cen2010/briefs/c2010br-11.pdf.
Wald, P. M. 2004. "Six Not-So-Easy Pieces: One Woman Judge's Journey to the Bench and Beyond." *University of Toledo Law Review* 36: 979–94.
Walker, Thomas, and Deborah Barrow. 1985. "The Diversification of the Federal Bench: Policy and Process Ramifications." *Journal of Politics* 47(2): 596–617.
Wasby, Stephen. 1977. "Communication within the Ninth Circuit Court of Appeals: The View from the Bench." *Golden Gate University Law Review* 8: 1–26.
———. 2003. "The Work of a Circuit's Chief Judge." *Justice System Journal* 24(1): 63–90.
———. 2011. "Why Sit En Banc." *Hastings Law Journal* 63: 747–802.
Washington, L. 1994. *Black Judges on Justice: Perspectives from the Bench.* New York: New Press.
Webster, Murray, and James E. Driskell. 1978. "Status Generalization: A Review and Some New Data." *American Sociological Review* 43(2): 220–36.
Weinberg, J. D., and L. B. Nielsen. 2011. "Examining Empathy: Discrimination, Experience, and Judicial Decisionmaking." *Southern California Law Review* 85: 313–52.
Weitzer, R. 2002. "Incidents of Police Misconduct and Public Opinion." *Journal of Criminal Justice* 30(5): 397–408.
Welch, Susan, Michael Combs, and John Gruhl. 1988. "Do Black Judges Make a Difference?" *American Journal of Political Science* 32(1): 126–36.
Wermiel, Stephen J. 2003. "The Civil Rights Era: A Look Back by Those Who Lived and Litigated through It." *American University Law Review* 52(6): 1409–29.

Westergren, Sarah. 2004. "Gender Effects in the Courts of Appeals Revisited: The Data since 1994." *Georgetown Law Journal* 92: 689–708.

Wheelan, S. A., and A. F. Verdi. 1992. "Differences in Male and Female Patterns of Communication in Groups: A Methodological Artifact?" *Sex Roles* 12: 993–1007.

Wheeler, Russell. 2012. "Judicial Nominations and Confirmations in Obama's First Term." Brookings Institute. http://www.brookings.edu/~/media/research/files/papers/2012/12/13%20judicial%20nominations%20wheeler/13_obama_judicial_wheeler.

Whicker, Marcia, and Malcolm E. Jewell. 1994. "The Feminization of Leadership in State Legislatures." *PS: Political Science and Politics* 26(4): 706–12.

Williams, Helen M., and Lindsey J. Mean. 2004. "Measuring Gender Composition in Work Groups: A Comparison of Existing Methods." *Organizational Research Methods* 7: 456–74.

Williams, Margaret. 2007. "Women's Representation on State Trial and Appellate Courts." *Social Science Quarterly* 88(5): 1192–204.

Wolbrecht, Christina. 2000. *The Politics of Women's Rights: Parties, Positions, and Change.* Princeton, N.J.: Princeton University Press.

Wold, J. T. 1978. "Going through the Motions: The Monotony of Appellate Court Decisionmaking." *Judicature* 62: 58–65.

Yoder, Janice D. 1991. "Rethinking Tokenism: Looking Beyond Numbers." *Gender and Society* 5(2): 178–92.

Yoon, Albert. 2005. "As You Like It: Senior Federal Judges and the Political Economy of Judicial Tenure." *Journal of Empirical Legal Studies* 2(3): 495–549.

INDEX

The letter t *following a page number denotes a table.*

Recent Titles in the Series
Constitutionalism and Democracy

Gregg Ivers and Kevin T. McGuire, eds. / *Creating Constitutional Change: Clashes over Power and Liberty in the Supreme Court*

Stuart Streichler / *Justice Curtis in the Civil War Era: At the Crossroads of American Constitutionalism*

Virginia A. Hettinger, Stefanie A. Lindquist, and Wendy L. Martinek / *Judging on a Collegial Court: Influences on Federal Appellate Decision Making*

James R. Rogers, Roy B. Flemming, Jon R. Bond, eds. / *Institutional Games and the U.S. Supreme Court*

Vanessa A. Baird / *Answering the Call of the Court: How Justices and Litigants Set the Supreme Court Agenda*

Christine L. Nemacheck / *Strategic Selection: Presidential Nomination of Supreme Court Justices from Herbert Hoover through George W. Bush*

Barry Alan Shain, ed. / *The Nature of Rights at the American Founding and Beyond*

Mark C. Miller / *The View of the Courts from the Hill: Interactions between Congress and the Federal Judiciary*

Eileen Braman / *Law, Politics, and Perception: How Policy Preferences Influence Legal Reasoning*

Amy Steigerwalt / *Battle over the Bench: Senators, Interest Groups, and Lower Court Confirmations*

Martin J. Sweet / *Checkmate: The Persistence of Unconstitutional Laws*

Todd C. Peppers and Artemus Ward, eds. / *In Chambers: Stories of Supreme Court Law Clerks and Their Justices*

Jeffrey D. Hockett / *A Storm over This Court: Law, Politics, and Supreme Court Decision Making in Brown v. Board of Education*

Jennifer Barnes Bowie, Donald R. Songer, and John Szmer / *The View from the Bench and Chambers: Examining Judicial Process and Decision Making in the U.S. Courts of Appeals*

Susan B. Haire and Laura P. Moyer / *Diversity Matters: Judicial Policy Making in the U.S. Courts of Appeals*